Praise for "The Seven Gifts"

The life of an entrepreneur often means not having much free time, but when I do have a chance to pick up a book, it's always something that I can directly apply to my business. "The Seven Gifts" isn't about business but more so about the people we all interact with in our day-to-day lives. As a business owner, I spend most of my time communicating and working with customers and employees, so David's insights into how people function and think is invaluable for anyone who has to deal with people. "The Seven Gifts," in my opinion, should be mandatory reading for anyone in business, especially those in a management position, especially those in Human Resources. David provides a foundation to understand people's differences and ways to improve personal and professional relationships through the lens of the Seven Gifts.
—Charles Navarro, Owner, LN Engineering

David Whitacre opens up his unique and impactful perspective on what makes people tick in "The Seven Gifts." While most observe others' actions through their individual lensing/context, David's analysis and archetypes of specific behavioral traits and tendencies offers a fresh construct. The framework illustrated in "The Seven Gifts" will open readers' eyes as to why people act the way they do, and help in the understanding of motivations, impediments, and limitations in daily human interaction.
—Brian Schneider

"The Seven Gifts" thrusts our inward motivations to outward displays. We have been let in on an indispensable human cypher. Who hasn't wondered what compels people to behave the way they do? What makes us tick? How can we harness our Gifts with efficiency and purpose? Using his own Gift, David Whitacre channels his genius, identifying and elucidating each Gift with laser precision and impenetrable design. His knack for writing and telling stories will keep any reader turning the pages...but this is not some kind of theatrical yet vacuous flight of fancy. The ideas presented in this book will linger and persist long after the book is done. Once you recognize and understand the Gifts, you will see them everywhere.
—Tara Moore

David B. Whitacre's book is a page-turning delight that satisfies one of life's burning desires: to better understand oneself and fellow humankind. Whitacre describes a life experience of thought-provoking complexities, contradictions, and keen observations...before outlining his unique perspective of the Seven Gifts. The Gifts brilliantly portray each chassis for seven personality profiles that seemingly encompass all of us. What make "The Seven Gifts" stand out among the plethora of personality predictors are its lucidity and its practicality. The Gifts are each presented in a positive light that we can all easily identify, then appreciate in ourselves and others. "The Seven Gifts" puts a spiritually soft brush on Enneagram types, while also bringing a more practical interpretation to Zodiac signs. A fascinating yet easy read that truly enlightens the mind.
        —Bucky Brooks, Principal, Copekan Brooks

Whitacre's writing is like a series of pictures pinned to a clothesline. The wind wafts each one in turn, highlighting each gently, then moves on to the next story. I love his insight into the repetitiveness of human behavior. I knew this was within people, but couldn't formulate it like his book has.
        —Steven Nicol, MD

Volume One is a timely and heartfelt story of a young man's awakening as he toggles between the racial and socioeconomic divisions of Kansas City's disparate classes. It is both an endearing and evocative tale, and helps to inform us of the author's perspective on humanity in engaging and personal ways. Volume Two is a whole other experience. Part spiritual. Part practical. Wholly original. It manages to categorize people and personalities without judgment, which is no easy task. And it displays a sensitivity to human nature that is a gift unto itself in the world we live in today. Along the way, Whitacre converts his life's triumphs and tragedies into thoughtful and meaningful experiences for others, a how-to guide for redemption. Be it for business or for personal growth, "The Seven Gifts" is a true gift for all of us, indeed.
        —Grant Pace, Owner, CTP Advertising

THE SEVEN GIFTS

THE SEVEN GIFTS

Ancient Wisdom Reveals the
Deep Mystery of Who We Really Are

DAVID B WHITACRE

Henschel
HAUS
www.henschelHAUSbooks.com

Milwaukee, Wisconsin

Published by
HenschelHAUS Publishing, Inc.
www.henschelHAUSbooks.com
Milwaukee, Wisconsin

ISBN (hardcover): 978159598-805-8
ISBN (paperback): 978159598-806-5
E-ISBN: 978159598-807-2
Audio: 978159598-847-8 (Forthcoming)
LCCN: 2021930845

Illustrations: Syed Muhammad Waqas, Instagram: @cashie_art
Cover design and graphics: Michelle Lawrence
ML Creative Design & Marketing, m7awrence@icloud.com

Printed in the United States of America

FOR LIZA

GIFT MAP

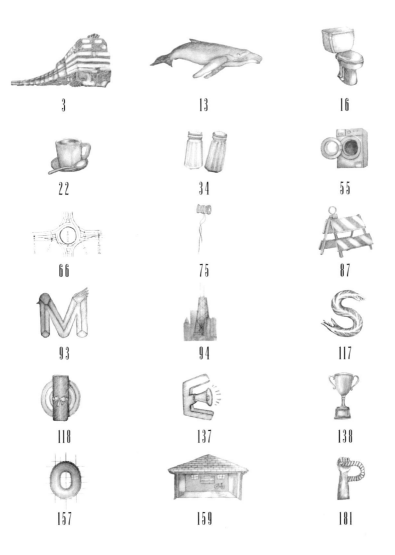

GIFT MAP

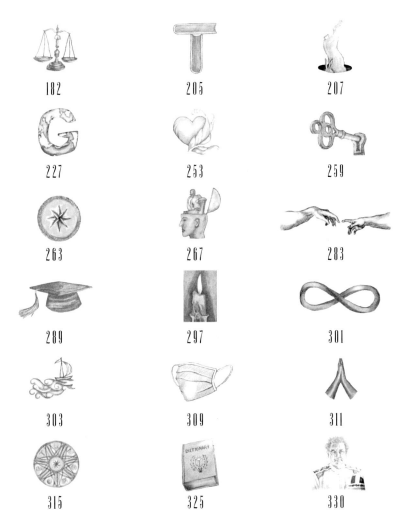

182

205

207

227

253

259

263

267

283

289

297

301

303

309

311

315

325

330

FOREWORD

I AM HONORED TO INTRODUCE YOUR AUTHOR and this book to you. I met David over twenty-five years ago when my late wife Lita introduced me to him. Lita died recently when cancer tragically and unexpectedly took her from me and our three boys. In truth, I didn't care for David when I met him back then as I thought he was brash, arrogant, and forceful. Looking back, I also have to admit some of that probably came from the fact that Lita insisted that he act as my best man at our wedding, a guy I did not even know that well at the time.

David was Lita's professional mentor and one of her dearest friends in life. He was heartbroken as well when she passed away. I think he taught her above all other things to be fearless and to never take any bull from anyone. Lita had a lot of energy and could wear people out sometimes, including me, but she never seemed to wear out David. I think he probably wore her out from time to time though.

Life has a way of changing people. David and I have evolved and grown a lot together over the years. We shoved our swords in the fire and watched them melt and be formed into something new and hopefully better. I now count him as one of my closest friends in life. He is the only person who calls me Big John; I always smile because I think it shows I am big in his heart.

I don't want to sound preachy but the subject of this book, *The Seven Gifts,* can change your entire outlook on people forever. And it has the power to change your life. Did you ever wonder why a relationship did not work well, or was the source of frustration? Or maybe why another did work well? Or why someone did not seem to understand what you were trying to say? Why the person could not hear you?

Lita, David, and I talked about these things together and shared the topics of this book for almost twenty years, and it helped to transform us and to know answers. In the process of making the Gifts come alive, David also tells his American story, and an amazing story it is. I think you will really have fun learning and listening to his tales. George W. Bush once said: "One of the great things about books is sometimes there are some fantastic pictures." You will probably enjoy that part too.

Lita, I know you are reading this too. I miss you. I kiss you.

(Big) John McCollum

Author's Note

SOME READERS, ESPECIALLY SOME WHO possess certain Gifts, may enjoy reading Volume I before Volume II. If someone went to an observatory to look through a big telescope up into the sky, he or she may want to first hear about the telescope itself before looking through it…to find out how and when it was built, what kind of lenses it uses, the orientation or perspective it employs, etc. But another might just want to look into the sky and let the telescope speak for itself, seeing these inquiries as distractions.

My Gift and I both prefer the former approach; that's why I wrote this book in the manner that I did. If you read it this way, I hope you find it more illuminating and entertaining. It may even help someone to parse the information in a more meaningful way.

I know well that we are all individuals and that you may not share my Gift. You decide. Or your Gift may even guide your path.

At the end of the day, as your author and tour guide to the Seven Gifts, I can only tell you the story that only I know.

David B Whitacre

VOLUME ONE

DIARIES

I WAS ON THE TRAIN COMING HOME FROM work the other day when I felt it floating to a slower speed. I noticed we were not near a scheduled stop. I looked around the car. No one else had looked up. All were trapped in the prism, the prison, of screens mostly. A few were napping.

No one seems to notice things anymore in the outer world. I can't remember the last time I saw a teenager just looking out the window, studying things. I remember when I was a boy and my dad was "letting the clutch out" down a Missouri farm road, which meant he was laying on the accelerator for all the car was worth.

We flew right past a farmer standing in his driveway and I snapped my head around to watch him through the rear windshield after we soared by, trying to see through the tunnel of dust following us. It was easy to move around in the car because no one wore seat belts back then. I had become an imaginary criminal and was hoping the farmer would at least react to us, shake his fist or maybe even flip us off if I was lucky. But he just nodded his head and started slowly walking across the dirt road towards his mailbox.

I snapped my head back again, now imagining the police were chasing after us, and since we were coming up on the next farm fast, I saw that the mailbox was now on the same side as the driveway was. Now what was that about? Why did Farmer Joe have to walk across the road to get his mail while Farmer Bob did not?

I considered asking my dad, but why risk slowing the car down? As I thought about it, I realized that the grand designers of the American countryside, whoever they were, lined up all the mailboxes on one side so that the mail trucks did not have to go both ways, back and forth. There were not enough farms and farmers to justify that, unlike my own neighborhood.

I felt good about myself, that I had figured that out, and had not had to ask a grown-up. Back then, grown-ups would sometimes say stop bugging me kid. Give it a break. You're dumb. Or something like that.

I don't know if people these days would notice something like those mailboxes. I don't know if most kids even know what a clutch is, let alone what it does. Everyone seems trapped by screens. These are the times we live in. But I have digressed from my story already. I would apologize to be courteous, but the apology would be fake. I'm not really sorry. I digress a lot.

Back on the train, people did look up from their glows when the tin voice of the conductor came through the speaker. I heard the murmurs of it through my ear buds. I dislike many forms of technology. But not all. I like music. He said there was a mechanical issue that we needed to stop for, and that it would only be a few minutes. All train conductors are liars. Practiced liars. Convincing liars.

I noticed my typewriter, I mean my laptop, was getting low on gas, so I stopped writing and closed up shop. I call it a typewriter whenever possible, and never hook it up to the Internet as a small protest. I decided I would protest even harder and did not pull out my smartphone to read the news.

As we sat on the tracks, the train powered down now, I saw the need to entertain myself. My head was in the ether of *The Seven Gifts* from writing, so I looked at the two ladies sitting across from me and said to the one on my right: "I'll bet I can guess what your Gift is." I used the declarative, not the interrogative, and said it with a tone that suggested I was just continuing a discussion that was already in progress.

I had noticed that she was a little overweight and did not take really good care of herself. She was dressed a bit chaotically in her nursing clothes, unlike her friend who was manicured and more fashionable, and she had a purse that was way too big with way too much stuff in it, a display of preparation for events that were not statistically likely. I promise I am not saying this to be rude or disrespectful. My mom might have

4

given me a ten-dollar butt tanning for that. But you could say that she perhaps radiated messiness. Disorder. The entropy of the universe.

I knew exactly who she was. I would have bet the farm on it.

She and her friend displayed eyes that wondered whether I was a creep, a smart-ass, or a jerk. Or perhaps all three. After a pause, she said "Sure. Why not?" Now the thing about Chicago folks is that they all usually have some game in them. If you show them you have some vinegar, they will want to show you that they have some too.

To my two newly made acquaintances, my afternoon entertainments, I inquired if it was okay if I asked my subject two questions first. Her friend, deciding to join in, said "Go for it." The two of them were obviously bored too and needed a distraction as much as I did. They had deferred any questions about what I meant by Gift. That word gets thrown around sometimes, and I guess they figured it would come out in the wash. For all I knew, she thought I was going to tell her what jewelry she was wearing that I thought had been given to her as a present. But it was too late for her to ask now, wasn't it?

The truth was I did not have to ask her any questions. I already knew what her Gift was. I could have asked her what her favorite planet or birth month was, which may have been fun because it would have thrown them both off scent. But I decided to take a different path.

The first question was how long had she known her friend here, and the second was whether she was married, and had kids. Neither noticed that was technically three questions. I learned they had known one another for almost twenty years, having gone to high school together in Lake Zurich, and yes she was married with three kids.

I'm from there too. Lake Zurich was the place Sandra Bullock told George Clooney she was from when the two of them were floating in space together in the movie *Gravity*. I don't care for George very much, but I know a lot of women do. I decided to stay focused and did not mention George to them. Why help him?

I told her the name of her Gift. Then I started to explain what I believed her central motivation in life was. As I slowly spoke, I saw the recognition penetrate across the pools of her eyes. Then I leaned forward and dropped my voice to a little lower volume to deliver the next part, the deeper part. I did this for dramatic effect.

I suspect it won't come as a revelation here when I say that women are generally a lot more emotionally intelligent than men are, so they can tune in to this stuff a hell of a lot faster. I also don't care much if it's culturally incorrect to say that these days. I'll call it like I see it. And I don't mind when others do too.

At this point in the same discussion, a man would be thinking what kind of cheese he was going to lay on his burger off the grill when he got home from work, cheddar or Swiss, and then concluding he might as well just do both, deserving both in his mind after a hard day's work.

I explained how she felt about what she did for her husband and kids, and also her work as a nurse. I gently shared what likely made her happier than anything else in life, and also what likely made her saddest. Her eyes welled up, wet now, and she raised her forearm to her face and looked away, out the window she was next to. It had hit her dead center. She was feeling a lot and trying to hide it.

Her friend intuitively put her arm around her and said "Oh honey, you never told me…" I pushed back on my cushioned train bench, a symbolic exiting, and watched the tenderness pass between them, with the deepest brand of reverence in my heart.

With a similar reverence, when I am by the ocean, I like to watch the sun dent the early morning sky, rising to vaporize any remaining fragments of darkness with a burn that is as intense as it is silent, signaling the beginning of another of life's cycles. And when I learn that the moon is full, I like to look up and watch the liquid orange circle pour colors into the clouds beneath it, clouds like sponges full of a pageant of pastel paints, forming a gentle sofa of color for the moon to sit on, to sit and watch over humanity at night, signaling the same cycle is over.

I had seen the same reverence in the face of a man a few weeks back, the morning after a night full of Illinois snow. I was sitting in my car at a stoplight. He was driving a utility truck from the 70s. It was not any factory color, having been painted over a few times, rusting, with mismatched tires and wheels, no badging or signage of any kind. The man behind the smudged window was a bit unkempt and wore an ancient hooded sweatshirt like you would see in an old boxing gym.

Just like you know when the surface of water starts thrashing around something is underneath it, I knew he was one of two Gifts based on what I saw. Either, or. He was a likely an independent HVAC man, a plumber, an electrician, or more likely a handyman, a jack-of-all-trades, like a one-man band I sometimes saw in my youth. He needed to charge more for his work.

We were the only two in our little theatre of the intersection. He got the light and gently rolled the van into the turn towards my direction, massaging it with care. I got the impression first that his truck was wounded, like a bird with a broken wing, an old part worn or blown somewhere, and that he was being ginger to avoid creating more damage. I was wrong. I watched as he turned into a wide arc, and then lined up the truck almost like he was pulling into a parking spot. He was angling for something. And then he lifted his gaze, put his thumb under his chin, resting his head as his soulful eyes now found their planned target.

The sun hit his face, our sun of billions of years of compressed gasses and intense fire, as he let his eyes now trace the tops of the trees slowly, then the field, the baseball diamond, the school yard, pensively studying the world blanketed and sealed in the purity and goodness of white. I watched him watching, and as he passed, I could see the stubble on his face, the marriage of joy and sadness in the caverns of his eyes. He had recited a concise morning poem during a few fragile, frozen moments at a suburban intersection, said a prayer in the grandest cathedral of all. Reverence.

The fact of it is that it is not unusual for me to hear people say, people I don't know that well, "How could you possibly know all of those things about me? I've never even met you before." And then I tell them about the Seven Gifts.

Unexpectedly, the conductor's credibility spiked, just like a sizzling stock or a Bitcoin surge. The train began moving. People actually looked up this time, wondering whether the momentum would continue. The conductor seized the opportunity to lock in profits, his aluminum announcement beginning with: "Like I said, ladies and gentlemen…"

Damned conductors are good liars. I wondered if they got professional lying lessons in Conductor School. By locking in the price, selling on the spike, the conductor planned to claim that a new and separate event had occurred if the train stopped again. Memories aside, all I have shared here took place in the span of about ten to fifteen minutes on my train ride home.

I think a reasonable person would observe that people are complex creatures, each like a Rubik's cube, a seemingly impossible and complicated puzzle. People are intricate and mysterious, more than we can possibly know. Yet it is also true that there are some people who have figured out how to solve a Rubik's cube in just a few moves.

I'm not saying I am special or anything like that. This is not an original thought. I think Mark Twain wrote about this, in a parallel manner, the idea that you could learn to see the essence of people, to distill them down to their crystal center. It's how Tom Sawyer got his fence painted and made a few bucks, without ever so much as lifting a brush, by understanding the center of the neighborhood boys.

And when I was a kid, instead of playing games on little screens, you could go to the local carnival and a man there would try and guess your weight within three pounds if you were willing to risk a dollar for a prize if he was wrong. But that was actually not within three pounds, if you think about it. It took me losing some money I had earned raking leaves to see that three on either side is technically within six. But I don't think many people would notice that these days. Especially young people, who may not even notice the carnival game, or maybe even the carnival itself.

People are fascinating creatures, more interesting than pretty much anything else in this world. All it takes is noticing. And practice. Practicing noticing.

TO KNOW THYSELF IS THE
BEGINNING OF WISDOM.

Socrates, Philosopher

CALL ME DAVID.

I've had lots of nicknames in the past, but it's better to use my government name. Because if you want to know about the Seven Gifts, you should know my name, and maybe even a little of who I am. You may have to decide first if you can trust me or not. After all, I am claiming that there might be an easier way to understand every single person in the whole world, in all of human history. That's a pretty big one.

So, why did the great American writer, Herman Melville, begin his iconic tale with a similar, famous line?

I think because gaining a true understanding of any narrative, any history, and arguably any information at all begins with knowing the perspective of the voice, the speaker, the storyteller. Melville's start immediately sets the stage for what we will hear…a tale from Ishmael's perspective. *Moby Dick* would likely be very different if told by someone else in the book, through a different lens.

I recently saw a compelling documentary on Netflix that pointed out that the American Cancer Society, the American Heart Association, and the American Diabetes Association are all primarily funded by the American beef, dairy, and processed food industries, revealing a convincing fault line of conflicts of interests. Adding this dimension of information might make you at least think twice about accepting dietary counsel from those folks. Knowing their perspective helps us to see how they might color or warp things.

And when people hide their true perspective with ill intention, old Western movies gave a name for it. They called it "holding cards under the table." And of course, folks got shot up for doing that. That's why cowboys always played with guns on the game table.

So let me put my cards on the table before I explain the Seven Gifts, so that you might be able to understand a bit of my warp, and be able to know why I have come to see the Gifts the way I do. Watching a baseball game from behind home plate is a very different experience than watching it from the top of the bleachers. How I have come to see and experience the Seven Gifts has quite a bit to do with the seat I have held during the baseball game of life.

None of us truly reside in the moment. We see it through the soup of our history, experience, and feelings.

When I first heard of the Gifts, I did not believe a word of it. So, if you are skeptical already, join the club. How could there be any credible shortcuts, any *Cliff Notes* to understanding the complexity of our humanity? How could any single system explain so much about who we are, what we do, and why we do what we do? And do it with alarmingly penetrating detail and predictability.

Ironically, I now understand years later that some of the Gifts are specifically designed to not accept the Gifts, or paradigms like it, at face value. So now, I feel like I comprehend better some of the initial skepticism some folks may experience. But consider yourself informed and even warned now, at the outset, because I can promise you this:

Once you go forward with the Gifts, you can *never* go back. How you see and understand people may change *forever*. Like seeing images through the Hubble Space Telescope for the first time, you can peer into aspects of our humanity you may have never seen before. *And once you see them, you can't un-see them.*

As these new images appear, you could immediately recognize friends, coworkers, children, celebrities, husbands, wives, parents, teachers, world leaders, even those you may have lost to the sands of time. You could end up seeing everyone in new and completely different ways. In the best of circumstances, you could become able to now see someone's behavior that has been an aggravation in the past as a blessing, because you can know where it emanates from, deep in the human universe from light years ago. It's also true that learning about your own Gift is very much like discovering a unique set of abilities and skills, like a superpower.

Every word in this book is true and mainly verifiable. Some names have been changed to protect the innocent, the foolish, the ill-intended, the weary, the beloved, and the pedestrian.

IN THE UPSTAIRS BATHROOM OF OUR rented home in Kansas City, I found myself standing barefoot on cold tile, holding a bucket with a cleaning brush in it that was intended for the toilet. I remember wanting to go outside to play. My mother was standing in the doorway glaring at me. She was mad, and I was trapped.

"David... Stop wasting time! Toilet water is the *cleanest* water in the world!"

Her voice was charged, her double-barreled eyes intense. She was not in the mood for any challenges from me, a dumb little nine-year-old boy. It was 1971, and I was not looking forward to putting my hands in the toilet, especially since we could not afford the luxury of rubber or plastic cleaning gloves. It was all hands-on, or hands-in. I suddenly remembered the gravelly hand cleaner my dad kept in his art studio.

For survival, I had begun to learn the value of finding "inside lanes," a term I had just recently learned from the neighborhood boys, wherever I could find them in life. I started feeling clever that I had remembered that Gojo hand cleaner could probably kill any of the angry bacteria and germs off my hands if I was forced into toilet submission.

My mom would tell me that germs and bacteria were bad soldiers. That was how she got me to eat broccoli. She would tell me I had to feed my good soldiers and keep them prepared for battle. I didn't like broccoli, but I ate it to help the right soldiers. My inside lane would be the Gojo instead.

My parents were both artists, quintessential children of the 60s. My dad taught at the local art institute, sculpted, and could coax new shapes out of wood, glass, and steel with subtlety and nuance. He could construct a bedroom set out of scrap wood, and then refine it by muting the flaws in the materials through sealing it all in high-gloss white enamel paint. Seeing it in its finished form, you felt like it belonged in the Guggenheim museum. My mother was a seamstress, photographer, designer, and practical-life-engineer. She could make exactly anything out of exactly nothing.

Even though we were nearly dirt poor at times as many artists are, and our refrigerator only meagerly stocked with cheap foods, my mother would make me and my buddy Mitch Butterworth afternoon lunches, and when we looked down at our plates, we saw intricate clown faces staring back at us.

She fashioned eyelashes out of carrots, sculpted eyes out of olives, finessed lips out of pickles, and beckoned tongues out of inexpensive Braunschweiger (which some folks call liverwurst). Mitch and I shamelessly ate the clowns like we were leading men in a horror movie. And then we impetuously demanded ketchup next time, to simulate bleeding. We cared little that ketchup would taste horrendous slopped on noses made of cauliflower chunks.

Mitch's refrigerator was better stocked, but he insisted we eat at my house. I noticed the irony in all of this, and began to understand that wealth and treasure were not necessarily related to money. In Mitch's eyes, I was a rich man, as I was the one who lived full-time in the house with the clowns. And my mother, our personal lunch sous chef, was my birthright, so I became an aristocrat in his mind. Mitch's teenage brother got drafted to go to Vietnam and never came back. I guess I was luckier than Mitch in more ways than one.

My parents, especially my mother, had me working early in life, sometimes hard. Saturday afternoons were for housecleaning. This was not considered a game. The house, and the dirt in it, were very real. Thus, my mother was not pleased with my stalling, especially after I had been granted my once-a-week television pass on Saturday morning to watch cartoons like *Rocky and Bullwinkle*. Mom didn't like rewards to be given ahead of being earned in general though. She liked incentives.

Television was black-and-white back then. If I was lucky, I could catch Tarzan and maybe a John Wayne western movie during my Saturday morning reprieve. I studied John Wayne on the screen and tried to imitate him. He was a man's man, I thought. Most boys my age learned a lot about manhood from John Wayne and Tarzan.

I noticed that Mr. Wayne would waggle his hips a little bit when he walked, or maybe it is more accurate to say he sauntered and waggled. Papa, my dad's dad, would waggle his hips when he bowled at the local alley up on High Street as he was setting up for his shot. "Just like glass Davey" he would say to me, and then turn around and let the ball glide. Then he would reiterate the point to make sure I understood. "Just like glass." He moved just like John Wayne did. Usually there were no pins left standing from the glass and glide.

After my Saturday morning movie, I would waggle and saunter into the kitchen, no bowling ball in hand, to find my mom. "Good morning, little lady…" I would begin, tipping my invisible cowboy hat. "This ole poke has been out on the prairie too long and I'm mighty hungry. How's about you whipping up some eggs Tijuana for me?" No matter how many times I said the same thing, she would laugh at my impression of the Duke until her tummy hurt. I did not know what Tijuana meant, and certainly would not eat anything called that in real life, but I liked saying *Teee-aaawaaannnnaaa…*

While the part about the clean toilet water initially sounded suspect to me, I observed my mother seemed pretty resolved in her proclamation. And, at nine years old, I had an ever expanding awareness that there was a chance that I could be wrong or unaware at least with respect to some of the facts of life. The more I thought about it, a theory supporting her position began to form in my mind. A credible syllogism. I reasoned accordingly, in my young mind: It would make sense that the omniscient designers of our world would insist that immaculately clean water be placed in toilets to counteract all the dirt and sewage that was placed in it. Like a balance. An equilibrium.

I maintained my sacred faith in the Gojo hand cleaner that I now remembered was to be used on dry hands only, and bravely stuck them in the toilet to clean. After several minutes of toilet scrubbing, where I also got to practice not gagging, I heard my mom giggling downstairs.

I set the bucket down and quietly sneaked to lean over the hardwood stair rail on the upstairs landing of the old house, to see if I could eavesdrop on my mother and her younger sister, my Aunt Dolly. "I told David that toilet water was the cleanest water in the world to get him to clean it…." Mom was still giggling. Dolly chose not to comment. I don't ever remember considering Aunt Dolly an enemy.

I yelled. I figured that was the right response. Sort of like my job at that point. But alas the toilet had already been cleaned. My mother made a speech about how it was for my own good, that I hadn't been listening to her or minding her, blah, blah, blah…

But I did learn something important that day. Yes, I learned that toilet water was not the cleanest in the world. I also learned parents tell fibs. But there was something bigger that my mother may not have specifically intended. I learned an important lesson about being a critical thinker. Don't trust anything you hear. Test it yourself. Become a primary observer. Don't let anyone else filter. Don't let other people do your thinking for you.

To reclaim my developing sense of masculinity and to restore my self-esteem, I snuck into my dad's studio and smeared Gojo on my hands, scrubbing away the germs and the memory of my being hoodwinked. I was reading Alexandre Dumas's *Three Musketeers* under my sheets at night using my flashlight, and remembered that I fancied myself as D'Artagnan, the Fourth Musketeer who was added later. And D'Artagnan always lived to fight again. I vengefully snuck a dollop of my dad's Brylcreem and smoothed my hair back.

PAPA REINFORCED AND EXTENDED MOM'S LESSON. My grandfather Charlie grew up in poverty with his brother Louis in Ohio farm country at the turn of the century. Their dad abandoned the family, then the mom escaped as well, and the young boys defaulted to being raised by a variety of aunts. Times were tough. With their agrarian upbringing, they started a flower shop when they eventually struck out in the world together, Whitacre Flowers, on Columbus's South End.

The plan worked well until the Great Depression hit and it became evident that the flower shop could not support two families. Family mythology offered that Charlie (Papa) was the fitter of the two brothers, and so he took on the charge of foraging out in the world for financial survival. He became, against odds, the manager of all the newspaper boy circulation routes for the *Columbus Dispatch* newspaper.

For my dad and his brother Dave, it was Little League heaven. In the darkness of early morning and the thickness of hanging dew, they developed their precision throwing arms landing papers on porches with satisfying thuds, felt the quarters become heavy in their pockets, and acted like royalty among the other boys since, after all, Papa was King of the Paper Boys in Paper Boy Land.

I was born in German Village in Columbus, down the street from Plank's Beer Garden, and can remember from an early age Papa bringing us groceries for our threadbare refrigerator. The neighborhood was filled with Germans who had avoided the Nazis. The large family behind us kept a small fenced-in backyard full of turtles that they summarily used for soup as the budget required.

I watched the turtles pensively from where I sat on top of the kitchen counter next to my mother as she washed dishes. Mom would take the opportunity to remind me it was important to be a good boy, implying that I may end up with the turtles if I was not.

Papa had a legendary sense of humor, seemed more at ease in the world than anyone I ever knew, and could communicate with a child of any age just as if he were a close friend and could clearly see things just as the child did. And he absolutely loved the opposite sex.

While my parents were busy being artists, Papa would steer me out on the front stoop of his small house covered with white metal siding. Sitting on his wicker-chair-porch throne smoking Camel cigarettes, he would intentionally shut the front door so the other adults could not hear us. He lifted me up, as I was somewhere between four and five years old at the time, and set me on the table next to his ashtray.

With his signature conspiratorial smile, he proceeded to teach me every conceivable swear word there was without any editing or exceptions. Like his filterless cigarette, he had me inhale each word, slowly and intentionally work on pronunciation, savoring each syllable. I could not wait to share what I had learned with Mitch, in whispers, over courses of clowns.

When my mom smelled a rat, she sent Sally, my step-grandmother, to spy on us. Papa and I watched the front door slowly open. "What are you doing with the boy, Charles?"

"Ohhhh…nothing, Sarah. Honey bun. Sugar loaves. Sweet tea. I was just telling Davey about the new neighbors." Papa could lie with a smoothness and credibility that could vie with the skills of any Academy Award actor.

Everything…his body language, his eyebrows, his carefully crafted voice tones, even how he flicked his Camel with a dismissive, carefree gesture and picked the tobacco pieces off his tongue. Davey and I are just floating down a river on a raft. No big deal. No need for any drama. Boys will be boys. All is good sticky buns. No worries. "Sugar toes. Come over here and give me a smooch, honey." I watched him try and lure her.

"CHARLES! That's enough! What things do you want the boy to hear?" Sally was not an educated woman. Papa told me once he had saved her from working in a factory somewhere. And then, her angry face would crack and she would start to smile ever so slightly. And Papa would make a smooching gesture more quietly, even a little seductively. It was working on her. I could hardly believe it.

At the age of four or five, it was a lot to take in. In a moment, I experienced what felt like a totality of vying concepts including betrayal, humor, deception, partitioning, mischief, loyalty, fun, illusion, tension, and anxiety. Different forms of ethics within ethics within ethics. An echo chamber of adult realities. I froze. And watched. And then did what any good male heir would do. I lied as well.

Yes, Papa was explaining about the neighbors to me, I said to her. I even made a little, baby Papa effort to provide some details that had one foot in the truth and one foot out. Sally quietly closed the door while looking into my eyes, still scanning my little spirit for lying anomalies, and then Papa and I promptly returned to our respective swear word so I could understand how to properly intonate.

But Papa's best ongoing teaching tool was the coffee spoon. In his small, working-class home, he spent many of his retired hours from the *Dispatch* sitting with me at a small, white round Formica kitchen table. I remember the smooth 1950s edges and feel of that table, like something out of *The Jetsons* cartoon, the only evidence of modern style in his abode, perhaps by my parents' encouragement. He sat at the table with me like a friendly lion preening his whiskers, sipping coffee that slowly percolated all day on the little gas stove steps away, filling the small house with natural gas and coffee smells.

I remember that the coffee can on the counter was always a version of Folgers red, but that it was never actually Folgers red, because Papa only adjudicated what was on sale at the Hen House grocery store on High Street. Folgers was, simply, an unnecessary luxury. Any knockoffs were just fine Davey. I remember that my father once told me that, from a dietary perspective, he was raised exclusively on what happened to be on sale each week. Instead of the South Shore Diet, he was on the Hen House Sale Diet. Papa was a graduate student of The Great Depression, with an undergrad degree in childhood poverty.

The cigarette smoke would curl and float up under the kitchen table light, suspended until he gestured again, while Papa animated the whole world around us. I revered him. I idolized him with every bone in my body. Coffee was an all-day affair. He would take me down a road, a story, a drama, a quandary and, as soon as I was fully lost in it and therefore distracted, I would feel the burning hot coffee spoon starting to sear my skin. The lesson.

When the spoon dropped, Papa's eyes would dance, and his laugh went from a cold start to a wheezing loss of breath in a split second. He couldn't speak or breathe he was so caught up in laughter. Of course, I always jerked my hand away before any real burning damage could set in. And then my memory would register that he had just stirred the coffee and gently tapped the side of the porcelain cup as he was rounding a corner in his story before he laid the hot spoon on my hand without me noticing. The unconscious sound of the spoon clinking gently on the side of the porcelain. He was like a magician.

It took years before I had calculated his magic trick. I learned to sit a longer distance away from him, watch when he stirred, and paid close attention that he did not cause me to lose track of where I was in physical time and space when he spun his mesmerizing yarns. It took discipline to not be hypnotized, to not fall under his spell. To not be completely lost in his words.

Years later, I drove across America's landscape repeatedly between Kansas City and Providence, Rhode Island, in my Midwestern hot rod that Papa had paid for from his savings wrought from his working-class salary, traversing back and forth to my distant university on the east coast. Papa's kitchen table became my halfway lighthouse in the wide expanse of the ocean called America. Since he had let me drive his Ford Fairlane around the neighborhood when I was a young boy, I felt confident driving and traveling anywhere as a young man. The whole country was no big deal. His neighborhood had felt bigger to me when I was driving around it, at the ripe unlicensed age of twelve, than any national interstate highway system felt in my late teens.

As I studied literature, philosophy, and psychology at one of the world's great schools, I began to understand Papa, my parents, even people like the butcher Papa always spoke to at the Hen House, differently. I began to see, for example, that my Papa was every bit the philosopher that the great Existentialists were...Kierkegaard, Camus, and Nietzsche. He also had a very specific and complex ethical system...like Kant, Aquinas, Hume, and Hobbes. As I learned more intellectually, he became an even greater embodiment of many things in my mind: the Great Depression, World War II, the Greatest Generation. He was at once an iconic peasant farmer, a mythic pool hustler like Minnesota Fats, and a scratch golfer.

I remember sitting one night at my checkpoint on the long journey back home across the country, under the cone of incandescent yellowish light at the white table, noticing Papa becoming older, his eyes red-rimmed, his coughing verging on hacking now, his skin becoming more pickled, his silver smooth hair thinning...mesmerized by the smoke of the Camel cigarette frozen in the air between us...suspended like time itself.

Papa knew instinctively my growing romanticism for him and his history. He could see I was becoming more sophisticated, more cultured, and more educated, but he also saw my obvious weaknesses for loyalty and nostalgia. He gestured with his hand through the smoke and began explaining how his little world on Front Street was changing. He was like Brando or De Niro as he spoke.

The two little kids who lived next door, children he had regularly held court with from his wicker-chair-porch throne, were now gone... moved on and out while becoming victims of divorce. The Rohr family a couple of doors down was never seen much anymore because the two boys my age had left the nest, becoming firefighters or policemen he thought. The smoke moved above us, resonating with the changes, like fluctuations in space-time.

And then there was old man Ricketts across the street, who always seemed to be a parallel to Papa generationally. Ricketts was a hard man who drove an older pickup truck and always carried grease under his fingernails. For some reason, Papa explained, there seemed to be a change underway because a young girl had moved in their home recently, about my age, who seemed to be different than the rest of them. Even exotic you might say.

"What do you mean exotic, Papa?" I had not remembered him ever using that word before. That was a new one in my Papa studies. Papa smoothed his silver hair back, readying himself to explain. I studied his razor stubble. I could smell the cheap hand soap he shaved with. I waited and I coveted the moment. It was like watching a great movie. I craved theatre popcorn.

Her skin was sort of a brownish hue, he explained, like she wasn't a natural part of the family. Maybe adopted? But she is stunning, Davey. Wooaahh, boy. His eyes bulged theatrically. She's so pretty she's hard to look at. He shielded his eyes to illustrate how hard she was to look at. Then Papa wanted to move on it seemed. I could tell he was tired of talking. He was getting older. I could see it. His smell had been changing over the years. The smell of aging. He slowly got up and shuffled to the small galley kitchen. I wondered how many bundles of heavy papers he had picked up and carried over decades at three and four in the morning without complaints.

He took a knife out of the drawer, a knife I knew that was not properly washed, as he preferred to just rinse things off after use and put them back in the drawers still wet. He started stripping the peel off a raw turnip. He cut it up in chunks on a plate, snowed salt on all of it, and shuffled slowly back to the table. He offered me a piece by floating the plate under my nose like a flying saucer. I chomped.

He glopped some more coffee in our cups and asked me if I was ready for my usual hundred bucks to make it back home. Gas and food, and a little extra walking around money. Usually all in crisp twenties he had picked up at the bank while flirting with the young teller woman I had seen him talking to there. As I was answering in the affirmative, his lightly bloodshot, aging eyes somewhat sadly lingered out the window. He noticed something, gently perked up, and said quietly and uneventfully he thought the brown-skinned girl across the street was walking up.

Just like our Labrador back home in Kansas City would register a squirrel, I jumped up and looked out the window. But my eyes weren't yet registering what Papa was seeing. I saw Ricketts crappy old truck, but nothing else. The sound of spoon clinking porcelain never registered, like it never did.

I heard Papa's wheezing laugh the same moment I felt the heat burning my skin. I jerked my head around. He had transformed and now looked like a madman, like a crazy scientist, eyes ablaze and bulging, his skin stretched tight and contorted against his aging face, pulled by the oblong shape his mouth had formed, his wispy hair standing straight up, seemingly full of static electricity from some unknown source.

Space-time slowed perceptibly, as if the white Formica table had opened up a wormhole. We froze for a second or two, unable to breathe…Papa because he was laughing so hard inside he could no longer move, and I because of my growing realization I had been had. The old man had got me, one last time. In an instant, I realized that there was no Rickett family mystery, no surrogate daughter, and most of all no exotic. It had taken a half hour or more of trickery but, once again, he proved who the Jedi Master was.

Papa always reminded me, as we made our way around Columbus… the Hen House, Plank's Beer Garden, the golf driving range down the street from his house, the family flower shop of dirt floors and innumerable unnamed cousins who ran past me shrieking and barefoot when I showed up… that I was the last surviving male in our Whitacre line, like

The Last of the Mohicans. I knew who the Mohicans were because John Wayne shot at them or befriended them, depending on the situation. When Pop said that, about me being the last male heir, I wasn't sure if that meant he expected me to become the pope or rob a big bank.

When the old man passed away, a part of me died also. My innocence. My lost innocence. My youth. My sense of place in the world. My compass point. I was, and am, aware that so much was lost not just in his passing as an individual, but also in the passing of his generation. His personal life story invoked scenes in my imagination parallel to those rendered by the great Russian writers I was now studying…Tolstoy, Dostoyevsky, and Chekhov. His life in rural Ohio, growing up abandoned by parents, poor, hungry, and without formal education.

I was reminded at his funeral service of the last movie scene of Pasternak's *Doctor Zhivago*, a commonplace man whose life story had a grandeur and scale seemingly unparalleled, all of which was nearly invisible to the eyes of the world, hidden amongst the pedestrian. Invisible and epic simultaneously. As the casket closed and was taken behind the final curtain, as the mass of people shuffled out, his wife Sally with tears in her eyes, holding Kleenex that had likely been on sale these last few weeks, looked at him one last time longingly and then walked out.

Sally, who had worked in the factory. Sally, who had endured his infidelities perhaps so she could become wealthy among factory society and shop the flea markets and Schottensteins and Lazarus relentlessly day in and day out, with her $147 per month Social Security check, being driven around like aristocracy by retired ladies of the factory who were inclined to take in their retirements in similar, albeit not as wealthy fashions as she was now able to. Sally, Columbus factory worker royalty.

Sally, who shopped five days a week year-round in anticipation of Christmas, slowly and methodically filling the attic, the attic of thin, squeaky wooden stairs of danger, with gifts that gathered dust so that when you opened them eventually you wondered if they were historical items with aged price tags on them. Sally, who taught me not to judge the quality of people's hearts by their education level, who accepted me as her own even though she had probably never seen a university, and who made me think ahead and tell her I was actually a half size bigger when she asked me in the earlier months of the year for that information, as I came to know I would be by the time I opened the box.

Sally, who was picked up and driven by Louise and Grace and Martha and Shirley and Denice and Barbara and Pearl and all the other women's names of that generation. Sally, who always introduced them to me and then offered me up for a kiss or a hug as a royal sacrifice, smudging my face and cheeks and lips with cherry-red lipstick, filling my shirt with the smell of cheap perfume and hairspray as they rubbed breasts against me and winked, their hugs getting longer as I grew older. I loved to hate it and I hated to love it.

And Papa, who would wave goodbye to the departing Plymouth Fury full of shoppers and purses and hairspray, smile at me, and say that Claire the driver wants to…with me, and then make a gesture I can't gesticulate on a page, comprised of a pointing finger on one hand and a circle on the other. "PAPA!" I yelled.

Just as the entire family, and the crowd, and Sally, and then I had emptied the funeral home, I looked back and then ran in. I dove behind the curtain and claimed him as mine. I insisted that death back up for that moment. I ripped him up from the casket and squeezed him hard, telling him I loved him as life itself. He felt like the paper maché mountain my mom built with me when I was little. Paper maché Papa.

I can't claim to be a wise man. But I can claim to be a skeptical man. Papa taught me, in his own way, to be an independent thinker. A Primary Thinker. And to never accept things just because people said them. And so did my parents, especially my mother. So I share this part of my story to say that I am not accustomed to believing things simply because people say them. I did not believe the Seven Gifts when I first heard about them.

I was looking for the hot spoon. I was not accepting the toilet water was clean. I would have to test this body of knowledge myself, in my own way, in my own time, and in the real world with real people.

32

THERE IS ANOTHER ASPECT OF MY LENS, my warp, my bend that I am compelled to share that may be important, as I make my way towards revealing the Gifts to you. I would rather you hear the story in 3-D instead of in 2-D.

I guess it's like sharing a diary with you, my Gift Diary. All of these things are pieced together in me, like a scrapbook where I cut out things from life and glue them on pages in my heart. Maybe that is how all of us get through this crazy movie of existence, and try to make meanings in it, to create sense of it all. We make a collage of feelings and memories inside, a craft book, like craft beer made from local ingredients, and then look through it when we need to, and then make collages and scrapbooks of ourselves looking through our collages and scrapbooks. Prayers to somewhere. Hopes that our lives would have meaning and significance. Like the *Golden Record* traveling out of our galaxy right now.

The *Voyager One* interstellar planetary probe was launched on my fifteenth birthday in 1977. What occurred to us to say to the universe on behalf of the entire totality of our existence? A collage. Carl Sagan, the famous astronomer and storyteller, was commissioned by NASA to figure out what to send from our species across interstellar space, through forward time. Originally, the thought was to bolt on a couple of infinity plaques, but Sagan threw down a space poem by mixing an album instead. The *Golden Record* contained images, sounds from earth, and music. Bach, Louis Armstrong, Stravinsky, and Chuck Berry were included to try and say something to whom and to what is out there, about who and what we are or were.

If I think about this deepest primal yearning, this deepest instinct of our race, I imagine *Voyager* hurtling each second by second now into new distances never before attained by man, a *Golden Record* huddled close to a phonograph in the cosmos, in a vehicle that has an illustration on it, an instructional manual of sorts, a picture showing mystery beings how to play the record. Making collages and collages of making collages. See me. Hear me. Look at my little scrapbook of meanings. It's all I have. All I am. *Johnny B. Goode* playing in the black void of space, as we hope someone can hear it.

How could poor artists become any poorer? Why, get divorced of course. At age eleven, my parents fell apart, and I went into the future under my mother's roof. She had no visible means of supporting us, and child support of less than two hundred bucks a month would certainly not swing it. In short order, she began what she called the "BBS" campaign, announcing to me what premise we would be living under from now on: Beg, Borrow, and Steal. Or else, simply, we were not going to make it.

She laughed when she said it, but I suspected there was some seriousness in there somewhere. I also saw a moral paradox because my mother would have fed me to the turtles if I ever stole anything. As time passed, I saw the "S" really stood for Salvage and that I was to keep my eyes out for things other people no longer wanted which might be useful to the cause.

One of my first lessons in BBS School was that all ketchup, mustard, salt, pepper, and napkins came at no cost in America. They were free of charge everywhere. We would never have to worry about those things, she explained. And sometimes, toilet paper and paper towels were free also, depending on where you were…a hotel, a theatre, a school, etc.

Mom started her own sewing business, cocktail-waitressed until late in the night (something that never settled with me), and dove into the dumpsters at the City Market to retrieve unwanted vegetables from local farms for the Crock Pot at our dinner table. Mom did not have time to cook, so she relied on the Crock Pot heavily. I joked and told her the food tasted like garbage. "Garbage Stew," we called it. I became the man of the house, took care of my only sibling, my little sister Eva, fixed meals, cleaned and maintained all manner of things (and toilets), and got myself to and from school.

My mother was unstoppable. A force of nature. She was not scared of anything, and would walk in anywhere and begin negotiating any matter. And she was really beautiful to boot. She worked fourteen hours a day. Eva and I did not see her very much unless we went to her work-place. Yet she was laser-focused on my education and my developing mind. Just as I was traversing the halfway mark of fourth grade in the public school system, as if our lives were not already complicated enough, she dragged me into the most exclusive private boys' preparatory school in Kansas City and begged them to test me.

Once they had evidently agreed to do so behind closed doors, she re-emerged, looked at me urgently and said: "Do your best Shoe Shine." That was my new nickname, as I regularly made some extra minibike money at the barber shop situated next to her sewing business shining shoes. I remember learning to snap my polishing rag with dramatic flair, luring the dollars out of Morton Sosland's (of Sosland Envelope) pockets. I resolved to become a snake charmer, like I had read about in *The Jungle Book*.

After the test was done, they said she was right I should be in a school like theirs, a place that would challenge me and keep up with me and pass me up if needed. Yes, tuition would be free, but she had to pay for my lunches. A check would be needed. I watched her close the administrator's door gently again, signaling that I was not to listen, but the warm lights were quiet and did not hum much in places with expensive carpets, and I was good at overhearing things by that point.

"Here. Here. This is my checkbook that shows everything I own." She continued in a plain and clear and calm, yet dramatic voice: "I will give you all of it. Everything. Every penny. All the money I have in the world." I got a glimpse of her tearing a check out of her checkbook and scribbling. Then the administrator came out. C.B. Lueck was his name. I recall he looked defeated, exasperated, like he now understood that his rules and guidelines and definitions and agendas held no meaning in my mother's world and likely never would. "Welcome, David," he said.

We walked out to the parking lot where our 1960s black Volkswagen sat, the half-moon shaped object that had over a billion miles on it. I was convinced that was why the Nazis almost took over the world—because they could build a billion-mile car. It used to be Aunt Dolly's altogether, but now she shared it with us.

Aunt Dolly was younger than my mom. She was wild, very pretty in a hippie-style way, and went through men like Kleenex. What made our VW even more distinct in the preparatory school parking lot was the fact that Aunt Dolly had hand-painted a black-and-white likeness of Jean Harlow on the rear lid. Aunt Dolly was a bartender, not a barmaid according to her, at Harlow's Bar down in the market district, within the industrial bottoms of the city. She lived in our little basement and came home really late at night from work, sometimes so late at night that it was sunny outside.

As Aunt Dolly explained with ashes emanating from her glowing European-style Dunhill cigarette, ashes that then flew around the interior of the VW as she ground through the gears, her eyes squinting from the smoke, all above the whining of the strained engine, Jean Harlow was a "lady of the night," a sex symbol from the 1930s. And she was born right here in good old Kansas City.

She would wink at me, in a very Jean Harlow kind of way, the Coors cans clinking underfoot as they rolled back and forth as the car sped along, the moving road visible beneath us through a rusted hole in the floor, and invite me to sing with her:

Well, I don't care if it rains or freezes,
Long as I have my plastic Jesus
Riding on the dashboard of my car.

There was no plastic Jesus in the Volks, but Aunt Dolly loved the song anyway. It was from the movie *Cool Hand Luke*. Paul Newman sang it. He was a really cool, man's man actor like John Wayne. Paul Newman even raced big go-karts called Porsches in real life. Like Cool Hand Luke's song, and Cool Hand himself, all the adults in my family seemed to have an underlying rebellion, a sense of conspiracy.

It would be hard for me to ever not remember my Aunt Dolly, for all of these reasons and others. How could I forget that she left the door wide open in our only bathroom after showering while she was fixing up her hair and makeup in all of her lovely glory?

I guess I can freely confess now, forty-five years later, that I would try to make up reasons to converse with her while she was in that state. This would not be a surprise to Aunt Dolly I suspect. In the middle of our conversation, as I tried not to stammer, she would say: "You getting an eyeful, Shoe Shine?" I would scamper away, red-faced, and retreat to the garage and my separate world of go-karts and minibikes and lawnmower engines. Yes, Aunt Dolly, I got an eyeful. Sometimes my childhood seemed a lot to take in.

I overheard once, lying on the waterbed in my room next to that faithful, blessed bathroom, my mother telling her to shut the door since I should not be seeing her that way. Aunt Dolly replied in a gamely tone: "Well, Diane, the boy needs to learn about feminine anatomy some-how…" I thought *Yes, that is probably exactly what Jean Harlow would say as well.* I hoped that my anatomy lessons would continue, as fruitful as I felt they were. I saw no harm in them, unlike my mother.

It would probably not surprise anyone, based on appearances alone, that our black Volkswagen Beetle could only survive trips, as opposed to take them. Each time we went anywhere it was like reaching Mount Everest, or surviving a tsunami, or living to tell a tale. My mom said good job on the test Shoe Shine, as she stripped the gears in the Volks, and then explained that she hoped Mr. Lueck would not try to cash the check she had provided, the check for $34.57, because she had not yet recorded a $20 check for groceries before she showed him the ledger.

I know it might sound crazy, but I have thought about that moment quite a bit since then, because I couldn't fit the pieces together in my head at the time. I eventually concluded that my mother had not wanted to show C.B. Lueck just how poor we really were. In other words, she was okay with him seeing we were poor, but not that poor.

Life is all in the proportion of things. What feels like a pittance to one is an absolute fortune to another. What is a crime punishable by prison in one neighborhood is called something else and accepted, maybe even praised, in another. Thanks largely to my mom, and perhaps to BBS, I still feel like I have hit the jackpot if I have a crisp twenty in my pocket, just like Papa used to hand me, regardless of where I live and what model car I drive, all these years later.

In short order, I was attending the prep school with the sons of some of the wealthiest and most powerful families the city proffered, my long hair that was common at the local art institute my dad taught at, and all. The Hall family, the same one of Hallmark Cards (for example) became part of my new crowd. I was brutalized initially by the boys, in short order, since I was from essentially a completely different planet and radical differences did not readily fit in that environment. This was not, after all, a greenhouse with many different types of plants, only carnations, perhaps of marginally different colors, all neatly aligned.

And then one day, a flood hit us. A flood of biblical proportions. I have never seen anything like it, before or since. The Plaza Flood of 1977.

Kansas City is home to the world's first outdoor, planned shopping center of sorts, the J.C. Nichols Country Club Plaza. Back in those days Brush Creek was snuggled up next to it, unprotected and a little bit wild. On a September day, all hell broke loose and a rain poured that just would not stop, and it revealed that the Army Corps of Engineers had neither anticipated nor tested matters properly.

Brush Creek turned into a version of a raging Missouri River, tossed cars and trucks around like they were pieces of idle trash, and transformed the Plaza into a bathtub with the drain clogged, drowning all the stores in eight-to-ten feet of creek water, some up to their ceilings. The damage was unimaginable to all the neighborly Kansas City folks. There was not a dry basement within miles.

My mom had her sewing shop in the lower level of one of the stores. We drove there and unlocked the door to see what cards we had been dealt. The very first step leading down to her shop was underwater. I pictured Singer and Husqvarna sewing machines floating in dark water, suspended around balls of yarn, dress patterns, and mannequins that could not swim.

Insurance was for the middle classes and above. When you have the choice between food and premiums, you become what some people call self-insured by default. But Mom was not going to be outdone by a flood; she had kids to school and feed. She got on the phone and implemented whatever BBS back-up plan she had conjured on the spot out of both sheer desperation and necessity.

The very next morning, she drove me down to the Plaza in our old van, a freshly-minted cardboard box from the city's industrial clothing district sitting in back. I remember the box was the result of her doing something on credit. I had turned fourteen one week earlier. She pulled the van up to the central intersection of the Plaza, opened the back, and told me to unload the box and the picnic table she had jammed in amidst sewing equipment. I opened the box and my mom pulled out a new tee shirt that had a lithographed image on it of the tallest structure on the Plaza, the J.C. Nichols clock tower, tilting in waves of water. Underneath the image, it said: "Plaza Beach."

She said we were out of money, out of luck, almost out of gas, and she was relying on me to sell these tee shirts to all potential customers for eight dollars each. She handed me a five and a few singles to get me started with some change, and jumped back in the van hollering that we needed food money, that she would be back by 4:00 PM, and she had recovery work to do at the sewing shop. I pictured scuba-diving in my mind.

The morning only offered dark cloudy skies and the smell of dank sewer water and rotting brush. I thought this was another one of my mom's crazy ideas that had no relation to the normal world most people lived in. I figured out fast that I had to engage people to explain I had shirts to peddle. Otherwise, they just assumed I was saving something from the flooded buildings and shops. Most just blankly nodded and walked right by. They had places to go and things to scoop up and bury.

One woman walked up with her husband and seemed objectively interested and asked questions, but things soon got ugly. "You have some nerve! Lives have been destroyed and here you are trying to make some money off of people's pain and tragedy! You should be ashamed of yourself!" She yelled loud enough for other people to hear, and they all started giving me bad looks too. It felt like a dogpile, when everyone just started piling on top and you couldn't get out from under it. And then she stormed away. I just froze. I was trapped. I wasn't carrying that heavy box all the way home anytime soon. Then, as if she had not already given me enough of a shellacking, she walked all the way back and yelled again: "You ought not to think of just yourself! If you were trying to help victims of the flood that would be different! Why don't you try to think about the victims?"

As I watched her husband try to calm her as she walked away, I thought *wait a second, I am helping the victims, dammit. The shop is underwater.* I waited until the square cleared out and the potential customer base had turned over. Then I went about changing my pitch. In a clear and confident voice, I proclaimed that buying the Plaza Beach tee shirts would help flood victims. A small line formed and then started growing. The box slowly started emptying. Was I accepting donations, someone asked? I sensed that there was a natural line there I should not cross, and said "we" were not able to take charitable donations, implying I was part of a formal organization. A family is a formal organization is it not?

An older Black woman wandered by after I had handled a buying surge and looked fondly at the shirts I now had on full display in different positions, up on trees, over bushes, on the table, and on my chest. She said her son would love one of those, that they made her smile. Sure, I said, buy him one, what size is he, he can get a nice memento and help flood victims along the way. She said no…no…and started to lumber away. I called after her and asked why she wouldn't buy one for him, and she said over her shoulder they didn't have that kind of money. *Wait a minute,* I thought. *What am I doing here?*

I called to her again and asked her if she was a victim of the flood. She turned and said of course she was, weren't we all? I said that she and her son qualified for assistance, that I was authorized by the organization to issue up to two shirts per family in need, and I just needed to know her son's size since I could see she was a small. Now I knew for sure I was part of a formal organization.

And so that's how it rolled the rest of the day. I sold low to people who could not afford more, and sold high to those who wore jewelry and expensive watches. I know the study of economics is a formal matter conducted at great universities like Harvard, and behavioral studies take place as well in labs at places like MIT, but you sure can learn a hell of a lot about those subjects by selling tee shirts after a major disaster. Also, the tuition is a lot less.

I looked up at the clock tower when the last tee shirt sold; it read a little past 2:30 PM. Truth be told, I could have sold a thousand more of them. I was on fire by that point. I could have started an evangelical church down the street from Billy Graham and given him a run for it. Lots of folks, flood victims, got free shirts that day. And many paid a lot more than eight bucks, especially when the box got light towards the end.

The husband of the woman who got pissed off at the beginning of my Plaza Flood tee-shirt-selling-lesson-day snuck back at the very end, without her, and bought three extra-larges. I charged him $36. When he looked at me, I looked right back at him with corporate, neutral eyes and told him he had saved $4, 10%, because the organization allowed discounts on purchases of three or more.

I walked around and looked at the shell of House of Toy restaurant, the high-water mark outside of the empty Jack Henry men's clothing store, and the now filthy Roman-looking fountain with horses that looked like they had flown off the reins of chariot riders. At around 4:00 PM, I heard the tattered and bruised mufflers of my mother's old work van in the distance.

"How did you do Shoe Shine?" she asked me through the passenger window as she turned down John Denver's *Rocky Mountain High.* I handed her $427 and went to get the picnic table I had stuffed behind the bushes.

"How did you end up with that amount?" I could see that it was more than she expected, that she was even a little surprised, and I felt good. It is always a nice feeling when your mom is proud of you.

I started to try and explain and she said forget it, I had done great. She said that $400 was going straight into the BBS fund, and that I got $27 for my go-kart fund, like a tip you would get if you did a good job shining shoes.

"Mom, are we victims of the flood?" I asked. She puffed on her Dunhill, having adopted Dolly's point of view on them. I could not understand at the time how it made any sense that my mom was salvaging for food for us, while smoking seven-dollar-a-pack European cigarettes. That was a small fortune in the 70s. Decades later, I watched folks pay $7 for a fancy cup of coffee smack in the middle of a major financial crisis. Then I understood why.

All of us need a luxury, even homeless people and poor families living in garbage dumps. If anyone deserved the Dunhill, my mom did. She puffed and thought, and then said "You're not a victim Shoe Shine, and you never will be." Puff. "You can always do something to make your situation better."

Well, I sure had that day. And I knew exactly where $25 of that was going. The next day, I made my way over to the Murowski household.

Frank Murowski was my age and my buddy, and he had a harelip. I think he had about sixteen or seventeen brothers and sisters. A lot of the working-class families bred kids like rabbits. They did not use condoms or "The Pill." That was sacrilegious in many homes in the neighborhood.

Frank's dad was a union tradesman, and his mom worked part-time at Visitation Parish, the Catholic Church where all the Catholics went, which was mostly everyone. Technically, their household made a lot more money than our "organization" did, but the fact that they had about forty-eight mouths to feed between all the Murowskis cancelled all of that out, making us even. I know that world thinkers like Karl Marx wrote about social classes and caste systems, but you can learn a lot also just by growing up in Visitation Parish.

Frank's older brother Pete was who I was there to see that day though. Pete was known as "Skeet" in the neighborhood, and he pretty much ran the tables up and down the block. I thought of Skeet immediately when I saw *The Godfather* movie later in life. He was the godfather of the neighborhood. Skeet had taken complete dominion over his parents' garage and filled it with lawnmowers, tractors, riding mowers, chainsaws, minibike parts, chunks of go-karts, welding equipment, and a stereo that could light the whole place up. He always kept the door shut, so you had to bang real hard so he could hear you over Lynyrd Skynyrd, Peter Frampton, Elton John, or The Who to get access. Even Mr. Murowski knocked to get permission to enter. I couldn't believe it.

The thing that worried me about the Murowskis was that all of their teeth were buck. In other words, most all the neighborhood kids had buck teeth, meaning their two front teeth looked stupid. No one could afford braces. Only prep school kids wore those. But all of the Murowskis' teeth were buck, so all the teeth looked like little ski slopes coming out at angles, like a cartoon or something.

When families were as poor as we were, people started improvising for food, and that was what worried me about this. Once Skeet told me to come over to the corner of the garage so he could show me something.

He opened up an old freezer that was filled with chunks of dark, gray-looking stuff wrapped in Saran Wrap.

"What's that?" I asked.

"Squirrel" he said. "Want some?"

As I was shaking my head no, he explained that squirrel was really good, you could make squirrel stew, you could barbecue squirrel, you could make squirrel jerky strips, etc. I immediately thought of the turtles in the backyard of the house behind us in German Village.

"What else is in there? Are there any birds in there?" I asked.

You see, a lot of the neighborhood boys carried light rifles, twenty-twos, around the local parks, usually around dusk so that the cops couldn't tell if they were BB guns or not. If the Murowskis were shooting squirrels, it was logical to me that they might be eating sparrows or ravens or other local fare because those creatures were good target practice. "Are you crazy?" he asked me.

Skeet was a really good judge of people, and he sure got my number fast. I walked into his garage with Frank one day, after knocking, and Skeet said that he had a Tecumseh chainsaw motor that he could help put on my go-kart so I could outrun the cops every time. The cost was a mere $25. I had dreamt about that Tecumseh for weeks after that, before any flood came.

We lived behind the park next to the Murowskis, a place everyone called Suicide Hill. Missouri is basically completely flat, so a park that is mostly one large hill is considered like Mount Kilimanjaro. The reason why everyone called it Suicide Hill was that there were train tracks going along the bottom of the hill closer to the street, and people said that when folks wanted to commit suicide, they would just sled down when they heard a train coming. The rumor was that a lot of people died that way.

But no trains rolled down those tracks anymore, and every winter the whole neighborhood came to Suicide Hill and became daredevils riding down in every possible thing you could imagine. I just jumped over the fence in my backyard and stood at the top of the hill to see the show.

People drank way too much beer and wine and whiskey and rode down on upside-down car hoods, laying in bathtubs, jammed in kitchen pots, pancaked on kitchen pans, and encased in barrels. Some rolled down wedged in the middle of big truck tires. It was crazy. Everyone tried to do an Evel Knievel imitation. People broke bones from noon to midnight when the drinking was full throttle. Some broke bones, drank more, and kept sledding. You saw blood in the snow sometimes.

One enterprising guy even went down sitting on a toilet throne. He had wrapped metal straps around a toilet and welded the attachments to two old metal sleds. He wore a royal purple cape, a Halloween crown, and wielded a plunger as a substitute scepter. Some of his buddies, all drinking from a keg they were sliding around on a flying saucer, played along as his subjects. The King of Suicide Hill made it down about halfway, and then shattered the whole shooting match. Toilets just seem to be everywhere.

A lot of the working-class dads drank too much pretty regularly. Some of them beat their sons when they got home from work, many of them Irish…no disrespect. The daughters were exempted. My parents explained that those dads probably got the same from their dads, so they didn't know any different. I learned early you don't tangle with those boys. The first time I got into it with one of them, who was also unfortunately bigger than me, he almost killed me and probably would have finished the job if other boys from the neighborhood hadn't pulled him off.

He hit me so hard in the stomach I could feel his fist smashing up against my spine, and he hit me there a few times like that. I coughed up blood and realized that I would never again mix it up with one of those guys. They had so much anger and violence in them that it just wasn't worth trying to even out an insult. That same boy ended up getting all mobbed up, and eventually spent over twenty years in the Missouri State Penitentiary in Jefferson City. I can't imagine what he did to any of the inmates who tried to mess with him.

In the summer months, I blasted my go-kart out of my driveway and went straight to the baseball diamond at the bottom of Suicide Hill for the specific purpose of spinning it around in doughnuts to create a storm of dust that would then move over the houses in whatever direction the wind was blowing. I could make a dust storm on windy days that could almost make a whole neighborhood disappear. Why you ask? That's what the rock band ZZ Top called "hell-raising" back then.

Eventually, a few of the neighborhood women would come out, yell at me, shake their fists, and then call the police. I didn't care. As soon as the police cruiser came around the corner, I lit out for the railroad tracks since there was a flat area next to the tracks all the way down the line. All I had to do was make it to the edge of the park and I was gone because the tracks went into woods and the neighborhood streets all crisscrossed at odd angles. There was no way they could ever catch me if I made it to the edge, even if they used a chopper.

I was not worth any police choppers though, and not even once did they ever hit their lights or sirens. As soon as they saw me take off, they would stomp the accelerator to the floor and see what their Dodge hemi engine could do. On more than one occasion, their engines just choked out completely and coughed for a few valuable seconds before it spooled up. Too late. That was all I needed. I'll bet those guys spooled up the police mechanic when they got back to the station for the faulty carburetor adjustment.

The fuzz were just playing go-karts too. That's why they did not use their lights or sirens. They wanted to have some fun. When their hemi did light up, it sounded unbelievable, full of lethal power, and created a drama that suggested they were after some nationally-wanted serial killer. If they had a hot cruiser that day and got the jump on me, I would have to spin the cart around at the last minute and take off back in the other direction. If the streets were clear, they could slide their cruiser around and try and cut me off. But they never did get me. I thought I was doing a public service, helping the cops keep their hemis ready for real crime.

As soon as I made it to the woods, I could dive the go-kart somewhere behind bushes and just wait. They coasted back and forth slowly, peering into the trees, but we all knew they were going to get a real call and have go out to try and fight real crime. Time was on my side, not theirs. If I had to wait longer than usual, I would take a pee on one of the trees. As I was rinsing it, I would peek my eyes around the side to see if I could spot the cruiser. It made me feel like more of an outlaw. To this day, if I rinse the side of a tree at a golf course or something, I always peek around the tree to see if there are any cruisers. Force of habit I guess.

So I headed off to Skeet's with my $25 to get my Tecumseh chainsaw motor, all because Skeet had sold me on the idea. Part of the deal was that he would have to warranty all future tune-ups, since chainsaw motors were not my specialty. Lawnmower engines were.

"How is it being a Daisy?" Skeet asked me as he was getting the Tecumseh down. You see the prep school I went to was called Pembroke Country Day School for Boys, and all the Visitation guys who went to Rockhurst, the all-boys Catholic school, called us that. I told Skeet he had pissed me off and if he ever called me a Daisy again I would scramble his eggs, or die trying. I didn't care if he was bigger than I was. And just for that, I was dropping the price to $20 for the Tecumseh.

"Whitacre Sauce," he said while laughing, "I won't ever call you that again. I promise." Whitacre Sauce was my nickname in the neighborhood. A Jewish kid who I hung out with a lot named Jon (which is not the right way to spell John, by the way) said that my name reminded him of Worcestershire sauce. That's where all of that started. "$23," Skeet said.

"Deal," I said back.

The engine worked great and was a lot louder than my previous one, which I liked a lot. One day I rode the go-kart all the way down the train track line and made my way to the Visitation Parish parking lot and spun it around for half the day. I always brought a gas can with me on those excursions.

A police cruiser pulled in the lot, but I knew they couldn't touch me. I was on private property, the church was empty, and the walls around the lot shielded the houses around there from most of the noise. The two pulled up right next to me, they in their go-kart and I in mine, and we stared at each other.

"How did you get here?" one of them finally said.

"Officer?" I said back.

"How did you get your go-kart here? It doesn't have a license plate on it, son."

Now, if he had called me "boy," that would have been a sign of disrespect, but he called me "son" and I felt that was more of a term of endearment. So I thought a little mutual go-kart respect was in order.

"Trailer, sir. A trailer, of course."

"Where is the trailer? I don't see it."

I said, "It will be here again when it is time to go."

We stared at one another for a long time in silence. Time was on my side. They knew it and I knew it. Eventually, they got a real crime call and had to go after real criminals. The nice trooper tipped his hat to me, just like John Wayne used to in the movies. I tipped my imaginary hat right back. See you at our next chainsaw motor, hemi-testing event.

A few years later, I played basketball at my prep school. We played Rockhurst once a year. They had about 1,000 people in their class, and we had about 50, so they always rattled our cages. I knew most of them. Technically, I was one of their tribe and my buddies from the neighborhoods all knew that. My prep school friends did not.

I found myself on the free-throw line in the middle of a tough, close game against them my last year of high school. They had taken over our gym, filled it up before our parents and fans made it to the game. The refs had to clear a section of seats so that at least some of our people could sit down. I was in the midst of hundreds of them, and they all started chanting: "DAISY! DAISY! DAISY!" I backed up from the line and put the ball under one arm. I turned and faced their crowd. And then I flipped off all of them. No one was going to call me that and get away with it. Well, a riot almost broke out and luckily some of the police were there to squelch it. Thank goodness for police troopers.

I had some colleges that offered me scholarships to come play for them. I was what was called a playmaker back then, a point guard, and could shoot from far outside. One game, my dad was sitting with his buddy Mr. Koehler and I drained one at the buzzer from about forty feet right in front of where the two of them were sitting.

"That's 'Hollywood,'" he said to my dad. That was my all-time favorite nickname, the one Mr. Koehler gave me, and he always called me that after that shot. Unfortunately, only one person called me that.

Now I did not accept any college scholarships to play ball, even though showing off in coliseums and hooking up with pretty cheerleaders was awfully enticing. I came from poorer beginnings and I knew better. I knew I had to work hard at it to get anywhere, to take advantage of my best opportunities in life. Basketball was not one of them. The fact that I was going steady with the prettiest girl at the all-girls Catholic school helped me to not focus on the possible college cheerleaders. Some of the Rockhurst guys did not like it that she was on my arm and not theirs, especially Ted Handow. And Ted, if you are reading this, well, congratulations on learning how to read. I didn't think you would make it to the world of the literate.

St. Theresa's was run by nuns, some of whom were known to possess a penchant for cruelty towards the girls. My lady friend and I drove around in my old midnight-blue convertible Fiat Spider, a working man's Italian sports car, wearing silly-looking sunglasses on summer days, laughing when our hats blew off on the road behind us, never to be retrieved. We liked to listen to songs that had the word "You" in it, so we could mouth the words, and point at each other when the word "You" arrived. *You're So Vain* and *(You're) Still the One* were our favorites. In our high school minds and hearts, we were certain that we would never be separated, certain that no tragedy could befall us, certain that we would live forever.

By the way, it really frosted me when the basketball gods implement-ed the three-point line the exact year that my basketball career ended, the season of 1979-1980. All of my shots were either under the basket or out at that range. My specialty was shooting over all the downtown traffic and raining death from above. I could have had 30% to 40% more lifetime points.

Some days in life are tough and no matter how hard you try to do something, it just gets all messed up. But the game against Rockhurst did not take place on one of those days. The ref warned me not to flip off crowds and start riots. I humbly apologized and agreed to never do that again. Then I walked back up to that line for the first of two shots.

These next two free throws turned out to be the most important of my career. I bounced my usual five bounces and listened to the rise of the shouts of the Rockhurst boys as they made my eardrums warble. I looked over at their crowd and looked back at the rim. And then I drained it. I swear I knew there was no possible way I could miss.

The shouting then rose in volume, against all laws of physics and sound waves, and I thought the roof was going to get lifted off the building from the symphonic blast of male testosterone. I stepped up, looked at the crowd again, and then sank the shot with the ease of Papa's bowling glide. As I turned to run back up the court, my back to the referees and my face to my Rockhurst comrades, I flipped them all off again for good measure. They all started yelling at the ref to crucify me, but the ref just shrugged. What did the crowd expect? They all had to be more realistic in my opinion. The refs had not seen anything.

My prep school headmaster was not too happy with my expression, but some of the dads came up after the game and smiled at me and patted my back. Mr. Koehler laughed and called me "Hollywood" again. I liked Mr. Koehler. He did not care about refs or headmasters either. And my prep school buddies just loved it. They still talk about it at our reunions and offer to buy me a drink in honor of that night.

America is a lot smaller than everyone thinks it is. You know who was in the Rockhurst crowd that night? Tim Kaine, the guy that ran to take over the White House on the ticket with Hillary Clinton. Tim went to

Rockhurst. He's about my age. And Tim, if you are willing to apologize for calling me a daisy, I am willing to apologize for giving you the bird. That's only fair. You have to go first though. I didn't start it.

After I walked out of the gym that night, Frank Murowski was hanging out with a few of the remaining Rockhurst guys, harelip and all. He smiled at me and shook his head side to side. "Whitacre Sauce…"

But the chaos of my mother's world tore at me, and I became tired of being the only male permanently living in our house, a house that regularly jumped in and out of foreclosure, so I tried to run away from home, only to end up with my father.

MY DAD HAD TRIED TO REIMAGINE HIS LIFE as well after the divorce. He purchased a Laundromat for $11,000 in one of the toughest Black neighborhoods in Kansas City, in the vicinity of the art school. In my Goodwill clothes, I worked alongside him emptying the building of worn and rusting washers and dryers, turning the place into an urban living experiment, a combination studio and living space.

We were the only White faces for blocks. I felt a little bit of what Blacks and other minorities feel in this country and in the world, to know what it is like to always be different, the odd man out. Crime was rampant. I could sit in my window at night from the second floor overlooking the street and watch the car crashes, police chases, fights, drug negotiations, dancing, and seductions deep into the night.

My dad concluded I had been through a lot of turbulence after my parents' divorce, so he went down to the Teacher's Credit Union and pulled out some money and threw down for me, as they say. We were working one day and he told me to go grab some tools out of a storage room. When I opened the door, there was a brand-new Scat Cat minibike sitting there with plastic and price tags on it to evidence this was not the usual hand-me-down.

Now anyone who knows anything about minibikes in the 1970s knows that having a Scat Cat was pretty much like owning a Ferrari. I cried like a baby and felt pain and turbulence leave my body and psyche. There was even a brand-new fire engine red gas can to match, full of gas so I could fire the rocket up right away. I knew that my dad could not afford this, which made me feel even more special.

The week I got the Scat Cat it was colder outside, but Dad knew I just had to be on it, so he gave me permission to ride it in circles on the first floor of the Laundromat, which we had cleared out to the bone to make way for new art projects, photography settings, and steel and wood expressions of prose. I fired it up and slid all over the old floors, filling the laundromat with minibike smoke. Dad and I didn't care. I went to sleep that night with the smell of Scat Cat hanging in the air and a big smile on my face.

When the warmer weather came, I roared the Scat Cat up the sidewalks doing free-form wheelies. This neighborhood was different. The residents found me a curiosity, my minibike an entertainment, so I ramped up my tricks and enjoyed my showman role. Crime was so common there that they already had enough trouble getting police to respond to serious situations, so not a one of them was going to waste any of their valuable police coupons on some smart-ass White kid on a minibike.

In the morning on winter weekdays, many of the local kids would gather on the doorstep of the Laundromat, as it provided needed shelter from the cold winds until their old school bus arrived. Dad opened up the doors, wiped off runny noses and crusty eyes with warm, wet carpenter's rags, and had me serve cheap cinnamon rolls, the ones that were on sale at McGonigal's grocery down the street. From the McGonigal's Sale Diet.

One day, a long Cadillac that had been lowered and frenched pulled up slowly in front of the Laundromat. "Frenched" means all the chrome emblems and accessories had been removed and smoothed over. I recognized the car, because my dad had arranged for a job for me at Wild Child's custom car shop around the corner where I had seen it before. Wild Child looked like the offspring of one of the monsters from *Where the Wild Things Are* and a Hell's Angel. His girth suggested a tugboat and his hair flowed like an uncapped oil geyser. I never saw him without a chewed cigar and assumed he slept with one in his mouth every night.

When we were emptying and building out the Laundromat, we had used my dad's 1969 El Camino as a construction tool, basically. When we ripped out rusty and moldy and wet industrial washers and dryers that were ages old and filled with strange colored socks and stained underwear,

I smelled the same decay that I did in the dentist's office, and wondered what memories the clothes contained. We slammed all the wreckage in the back of the El Camino to be driven to the dump.

Dad and I opened the windows of the second floor and threw heavy things out of there as well, careful not to smash the glass of the car-truck below. But we ended up seriously bashing it all up in the genesis of the building, cleaning out the old to make way for the new. My dad's El Camino was a symbol of strength, prowess, power, and masculinity to me. He drove it with ease and grace and smoothness and glide, just like Papa bowled. He could almost make gestures with the car, like a gunslinger can with his weapons. Dad noticed my noticing.

When the building was done, he offered the El Camino to me if I was willing to work over my summers at Wild Child's. I would sand cars and do clean-up, which to me said I would also be cleaning toilets, while Wild Child would help me bring the car back to life. For two summers I sanded cars there, doing circles with my hands while I studied radical, streamlined, metal-flaked chariots made with Harley Davidson motorcycles as horses. There were no such things as "gloves" or "safety masks" in that world, at that time. You coughed up the day at the end of it, and hoped any chemicals you had touched would come off with Gojo hand cleaner.

My dad saw Wild Child as a street artist, and conjugated his craft to mix with the art institute crowd. Wild Child had studied with the legendary car customizer George Barris, builder of the Batmobile, in California. So I had seen that gold Cadillac before, the one that featured machined, aluminum, sculpted metal pipes streaming from the engine compartment, like an old Duisenberg. Strictly speaking, it was a knock off from the 1971 Clint Eastwood movie *Magnum Force*.

That was the movie where Clint says, "*I know what you're thinking. 'Did he fire six shots or only five?' Well, to tell you the truth in all this excitement I kinda lost track myself. But being this is a .44 Magnum, the most powerful handgun in the world and would blow your head clean off, you've gotta ask yourself one question: Do I feel lucky?*"

If you were a serious pimp in the early 1970s, you owned a car exactly like the pimp did in that movie. Otherwise, you were not a serious pimp. Wild Child had a severe ethical struggle working on those pimpmobiles. He hated what the clientele represented but considered the money a necessary evil to keep his business afloat. To mediate the matters in question, he relentlessly overcharged every single one of them. I wondered to myself about safety issues surrounding overcharging pimps. I remembered Wild Child's dilemma when I later studied ethics and morals at my Ivy League university. I wanted to pose a question to my philosophy professor in class, the learned gentleman who looked just like the old man in the Pixar movie *Up*.

He taught us about the nature of identity through the myth of Theseus's Ship when, for example, he erased the mast and sail of the ship on the chalkboard, turned back around to face us at an agonizingly slow rate of speed, and then said we would be spending the semester trying to know if it was still the same ship as it was before he swiped. But my question was: "Was it reasonable or moral for Wild Child to cater to the pimp in order that he might fund his aspirational sculpture, his only shot at the betterment of humanity towards an immortal, timeless discussion of art?" I decided to keep that one to my Kansas City self, and did not raise my hand in class.

To make the whole gold Cadillac situation even worse, I had known that Wild Child had charged the owner $10,400 for the transformation, a ridiculous sum of money in 1977.

"How did you come up with that amount?" I remembered asking Wild Child, not being able to imagine how many minibikes and go-karts that equated to.

He bit his cigar, wiped his long hair aside, and laughed. "I just made it up!"

Great, I thought. I was going to be the object of revenge here. The pimp was still probably pissed off at Wild Child, and could be thinking that I was part of the billing conspiracy. He slowly got out of his carriage and walked towards our door with the certainty of unimaginable violence.

The pimp looked like the car, frenched and lowered. He was short in stature, long on attitude, and covered head to toe in a fur coat that must have cost $10,000 or more. I knew because one of the kids at the all-girls prep school in my alternate dimension, Missy Wang, was from a family who owned a series of fur stores. "Furriers" they were called. He wore dark glasses and his hair looked just like the flowing hair of James Brown, the singer, only longer and somehow more feminine. I concluded this feminine-styled hair only made him more lethal. If he did not care what other gangsters thought of his feminine hair, he certainly would not care what the statutes said about preserving my life and my dad's either.

He came up to the doorstep slowly, with minimal gestures, like a hammerhead shark. Dad moved to open the door. I lost all ability to breathe. We were dead. The neighborhood truce was over. Our artist exemptions had expired. We were now just dumb, vulnerable White people in the wrong place. My father was unusually calm and asked him to enter. I visualized the long weapon he was holding under the fur coat. We were going to get smoked, just like the pimp bought it in *Magnum Force* when Dirty Harry took him out. This morning's pimp was going to even out a lot of scores at one time.

He rolled his head a little bit like Stevie Wonder usually did. He seemed to be casually calculating, looking out the front window of the building, casing for KCMO police cruisers perhaps. Without removing his dark glasses, he eventually managed to say in a very raspy, almost damaged voice, similar to how Miles Davis sounds, that he heard his young son came into this building while waiting for the school bus.

Darius. Yes, Darius came here often, my dad said. And he looked the pimp right in the glasses when he said this. My dad's voice was steady, confident, even vaguely gentle and neighborly. I held my breath, prayed to a God I had not met yet, and jealously wondered if my sister Eva was going to get my prized forest green Schwinn ten-speed bike after I was gone from this earth. After a frighteningly long pause, the pimp smiled and revealed a mouth full of flawless, shining, gold-capped teeth. I understood in that instant that the car was meant to match.

And with the fur, he had an ensemble. I knew what an ensemble was, because my mom was a seamstress and had explained it to me. So I immediately knew I was looking at a version of a pimp fashion ensemble of gold teeth, a gold Cadillac, and gold and honey-colored fur. I'll bet you he had a gun to match. Thank God I never saw it. Dad suggested that I might offer cinnamon rolls to our guest, but our guest demurred.

D'Artagnan, the Fourth Musketeer, would live to fight yet again. After the pimp went back to his natural habitat…the car, the streets, the neighborhood…I trembled, heart racing, while eating my McGonigal's 99-cent cinnamon rolls and readied myself to go to my private, all-boys prep school on the other side of the galaxy.

Within the hour, I was studying writing, history, and advanced calculus. And at the end of my prep school day, I went to tennis team practice. Growing up, I had taught myself tennis, after having been given an old racket with a broken string, thumping flattened balls against neighborhood church walls and cost-free backboards in public parks. Some neighborhood adult got sick of my thumping and explained I could go out on the court to play now. I became a tennis player, could find my way around the baseline with my Jimmy Connors imitation two-handed backhand, and could subsequently move with ease on the country club tennis scene, competing in wealthier crowds.

I eventually fought my way to acceptance in my new social environ and my friends there learned to appreciate my dad's black 1950 Ford pick-up truck with painted images of an Apache Indian chief on either side, as well as its sturdy railroad-tie rear bumper. Dad's truck was not hard to find in the children's pick-up circle among the Porsches, Mercedes, and Cadillacs, just like Jean Harlow's face on the back of the Volks, whenever Mom or Aunt Dolly came.

When I went to my new friends' houses, I saw Black butlers, maids, and what they called gardeners at the time. When I looked in their eyes, and they in mine, we all knew I was not part of the country club crowd, just as they weren't either. They looked at me as if I was a little Indian boy who had mistakenly wandered onto the wrong reservation. Maybe they recognized my Goodwill fashion label that my new friends did not notice. I intuited there was a sadness, a knowing, an acceptance in the hollows of their souls. My buddies did not see it, and I did not feel compelled to try to explain it. I just made sure that I treated the butlers, gardeners, and maids like royalty. Please. Thank you. Yes sir. No sir. Yes ma'am. No ma'am. That was the only response I could think of. I did not know what else to do. I was embarrassed for the entire White race. The butlers, maids, and gardeners saw my embarrassment, knew it was deserved, as did I.

In my new country club world of money, higher education, and power, I felt sometimes like I could sit in my metaphorical bedroom window and watch similar neighborhood car crashes, substance abuse struggles called Scotch and Vodka, more subtle yet just as real confrontations, power struggles, and seductions. I caddied at the country clubs and watched wealthy men drain iceless cups of liquor in the mornings, laughing knowingly from time to time. The neighborhoods were very different, but the themes and patterns similar.

I hoped they did not drink at the place my mom worked as a cocktail waitress. I stopped questioning that eventually, since I reasoned they probably did not go out of their habitat much, and went back to snake charming tip money out of their pockets as I cleaned their golf balls with the skills of a shoe shiner.

The industries of the banker, the pimp, the maid, the car customizer, and the tennis pro all varied, but were all of the same America. I was starting to understand that America was mine to play in and explore. I also saw clearly more aspirational, lofty natures in both groups of people. My Black neighbors were largely very gracious and patient with me and my dad and the art students that came and went, as they noticed we were the only Whites on their Black island. The maids, butlers, and gardeners in the split world never made me feel ashamed for having evidently defected. The upper-class Whites I grew up among also had obvious moments of ethics, loyalty, and desire for excellence.

When my oldest daughter Liza, a student at Loyola University in Chicago, tragically died in a bicycling accident a few years ago, every one of my close prep school friends seamlessly flew in to stand with me in honoring my daughter's shortened life.

I can't put words to the tenderness they brought with them.

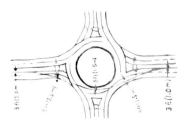

UP IN WISCONSIN THESE DAYS, THEY are building a lot of things called roundabouts so that people don't have to stop at intersections and so maybe they won't slam into one another as much. Less T-boning. I think I already knew what turnabouts were, since in my childhood I had to learn how to turn more gracefully, and sometimes quickly, from one direction to another, from one world to the next. I think learning more about the Seven Gifts has helped me do that, since it is helpful to be better able to read and comprehend people, no matter where they are from.

The trajectory of my life has emanated from the disparate worlds I have inhabited: one lower middle-class world of necessity, creativity, and plurality versus another upper-class world of higher education, privilege, and mobility. They are equally messy, but I consider them both *my own mess,* as the singer Billy Joel once said of his beloved Shea Stadium, a mess compared to Yankee Stadium but his *beloved mess* nonetheless. I have grown to love both of these worlds with all of my heart. And while the globe has always felt large and vast, America has always felt small to me, like a playground, like the scale of the streets around Papa's neighborhood.

I have painted Missouri barns high up on three-story wooden ladders in strong winds, dined at the Vice President's dinner table, bartered yard work for food with my second family of Antiguan immigrants so I could survive at college, and attended John Kennedy, Jr.'s private twenty-first birthday party at Jackie Onassis's Manhattan penthouse.

I remember that party clearly in my mind, watching Black waiters in tuxedos pour $100 bottles of *Châteauneuf-du-Pape,* the liquid of choice in the early 80s, laying white linen napkins down over the tops of their left arms, using them as fulcrums as they gently laid the tips of the bottles on them, elegantly pouring with their right. Under hushed Manhattan lights, in a room suspended with cigarette and expensive cigar smoke, I watched Jackie Onassis animate her small crowd in the background as I sipped.

When I had endorsed enough of the champagne, John Jr. pointed me towards the hallway. I walked very slowly down it, looking at hundreds of framed photos of their family, frozen images of their American history. I turned as instructed into Caroline's room. She was sitting alone on her bed, her window bare to all of New York, the lights from the metropolis refracting and spangling in the thick glass, then floating in moving patterns on her walls like a smashed and flattened swirling kaleidoscope.

I explained the instructions I had received, as well as my purpose. She smiled, patted the top of the bed next to her, and asked me to sit down and tell her about myself. Like her brother, she was kind, surprisingly simple, and fully authentic. There was not one ounce of pretense in either of them. They were fine people to the core…more evidence that both good and evil, light and dark, can come from any neighborhood.

I shared I was from Kansas Shitty and she giggled. Funny thing was that Caroline actually knew that a real Kansas City existed. Most people on the East Coast looked at me with blank stares, as if they did not know what to say when I shared my Origin Story. They could see there was a country on maps west of their region, but I think to them it was imaginary. They had the impression that beef just showed up on their plates somehow.

I told her I was not really close with her brother, a good friend of a good friend, but that we did share a deep appreciation for throwing Frisbee bombs at one another across long spaces like College Green and Sheep's Meadow in Central Park. In those moments, he was no longer a Kennedy and I was no longer whoever I was. We were just two guys trying to best the other, to feel the sun on our faces, the fire in the strength of our arms, and the sweat on our bodies.

Caroline seemed satisfied with that, so I was excused to find myself standing alone in front of the toilet, the ubiquitous toilet, the Toilet Eternal, the toilet that always seemed to follow me. I looked at the toilet water for a long moment, perhaps remembering my mom, before I expelled some of my excess *Châteauneuf-du-Pape*. The water looked pretty damn clean to me. Even if toilet water in general had turned out not to be the cleanest in the world, I thought that the Kennedys may well have had the cleanest toilet water in the world.

The next evening, my college buddies made a project of pooling their money, cajoling a doorman who one of them knew, and sent the Midwesterner into Studio 54. I spent the whole night there watching people, trapped inside this magical funhouse of celebrity and whimsy and illegality. I saw things I dare not repeat here. Eventually I gave up and just did a swan dive into the middle of it. Michael Jackson's *Thriller* had just hit the turntables and the bass throbbed with a force that threatened to bring down the building, the lights around me shattering into new colors at each thump.

Toto and I were no longer in Kansas. I ended up dancing with women, men, transvestites, transsexuals, heterosexuals, homosexuals, and all kinds of combinations of these. And I kissed some pretty women that night. I sure hope they were women anyway.

My gang left me with just enough for the cab ride to my friend's flat in the Upper East Side above his family's restaurant which sat below street level, the Harry'n Me Café. When I arrived, my buddy opened the restaurant kitchen for us as the hot sun was rising and starting to burn the wetness off sidewalks and streets, conjuring a morning steam curling up from the night surfaces, an urban version of morning paperboy dew.

The restaurant had angels hand-painted on the ceiling, and I asked my friend Nick why one of them had a basketball. He said that was supposed to be him, and shared that his mom and Harry cavorted with a lot of artists over the years, even the writer Jack Kerouac. My host made me breakfast with Italian sausage and spicy potatoes and faithfully listened to the tales of my night with knowing eyes, eyes of the best New York City tour guide a Kansas Shitty boy could ever have hoped for.

Miles south of there, in Quantico, Virginia, I fought through Officer's Candidate School with the United States Marines Corps, and got to find out what was inside people, including myself, when all were stripped down to bare studs. Later in life, I navigated the non-profit world on the South Side of Chicago, with folks like the Nation of Islam, as (once again) the only White face in sight.

I also handled a business transaction for John and Lorena Bobbitt a few months before their fateful night in 1993.* I feel I can share this now that all privacy considerations are out the window, just like other things related to their tale. So when I first saw the movie *Forrest Gump*, I felt like I could identify with him quite a bit.

I have shared these tales and personal details to try and convince you of two basic things about my perspective and, therefore, my voice. First, I do not accept information easily without testing it myself. And second, I have some experience with studying the nature and essence of people beyond their appearances, beyond society's definitions, and beyond race and class and education. My story, my American story, has taught me that people are many different things beyond their outward appearances.

I don't care much who society says you are, where you are from, and what your socioeconomic status is. I'll like you or not based on who you are. I am not concerned with what anyone else in the world says about you. I'll judge for myself. And I don't particularly care what people think

---

*John Wayne Bobbitt and Lorena Bobbitt were an American couple whose relationship made world-wide headlines in 1993 when Lorena cut off her husband's penis with a knife while he was asleep in bed. The incident occurred on June 23, 1993, in Manassas, Virginia, and the legal case surrounding the incident subsequently took place during 1993 and 1994. Lorena stated in a court hearing that, after coming home at night on June 23, 1993, her husband raped her. After her husband had gone to sleep, Lorena grabbed a knife from the kitchen, entered their bedroom, and removed her husband's penis at its base. After this, Lorena left the apartment with the severed appendage and drove away in her car. After a while, she threw it into a field. She eventually stopped and called 9-1-1. John's penis was found after an exhaustive search, and it was reattached in the hospital where he was treated. The operation took nine and a half hours.

of me either. I am going to be myself regardless. You can accept me or not, like me or not. It's all good with me.

I think it is important to take in data, especially data about people, with equanimity and an open mind and to remember that the janitor who doesn't speak English well is frequently just as compelling a figure as a CEO. The Seven Gifts put all of us squarely on the same level playing field, which is one reason I enjoy the Gifts so much.

Learning about, experiencing, and practicing knowledge of the Seven Gifts has changed my entire perspective on humanity. I feel like I have learned a critically important set of basic facts, a knowledge that helps me see more clearly who we really are as people, involving matters that lie somewhere between our collective consciousness and unconsciousness… something like a *spiritual form of biology*.

Astronauts who have traveled beyond our atmosphere have described an experience that has been called the "Overview Effect," a fundamental cognitive shift when comprehending our world. Looking back at our Earth from and in the black womb of space, they describe the epiphany of how fragile and lovely our home is, as well as a recognition that, despite how fragmented and divided we seem to be as peoples, we are in actuality astonishingly unified and alike and bound together. Seeing and comprehending the Seven Gifts provide a parallel Overview Effect. As a Gift Astronaut, it becomes possible *to see who we all really are more clearly and completely* in a deeply profound way.

The Gifts animate the tapestry of our race and the elegant pattern of our respective specialties and purposes and functions, allowing us to see how truly wonderfully made we are.

Volume Two
The Seven Gifts

Everything is human behavior.
Human behavior is extremely patterned.

Bill Binney, NSA Cryptologist

THERE IS NO RAPID WAY TO EXPLAIN the Gifts to a newcomer.

People initially tend to so vastly underestimate the sheer power, relevance, and accuracy of this information, it is hard to put words to. Language fails. I have found that, in those types of circumstances, the best hope is to latch on to a metaphor. In this case, a metaphor that hopefully illustrates when some seemingly impossible task becomes realistic to solve.

ThinThread* might be able to cross this big, mighty river. In the documentary *A Good American*, filmmaker Oliver Stone traces the story of Bill Binney, a top National Security Agency mathematician who authored a massive "puzzle-solving" system that was designed to process endless chunks of metadata containing billions of pieces of information being collected by the nation's surveillance efforts.

After the tragedy of 9/11, some NSA specialists (including Binney) argued that ThinThread would have easily prevented the terrorist attacks, because Binney and his team had come up with an entirely different way of looking at data, data that other analysts were literally drowning in, as most were unable to process the sheer magnitude of it all.

If you think about it, how could it be possible to somehow keep track of and monitor billions of bits of electronic information every minute…texts, e-mails, phone calls, etc., all around the world simultaneously? The National Security Agency (NSA) had endeavored to keep track of "key words" or "search words" like terrorist, bomb, etc. As a result of

---

ThinThread is the name of a project that the United States National Security Agency (NSA) pursued during the 1990s, according to a May 17, 2006 article in the *Baltimore Sun*. The program involved wiretapping and sophisticated analysis of the resulting data, but according to the article, the program was discontinued three weeks before the September 11, 2001 attacks due to the changes in priorities and the consolidation of U.S. intelligence authority.

this approach, gigs of metadata remained fatally stacked in endless piles in virtual memory warehouses untouched, just like a Los Angeles traffic jam.

Binney was a master cryptographer, a man whose intellect naturally visualized patterns and shapes that most of us would never see. He could see beyond *The Matrix* (the movie). In fact, his eventual thesis sought *more* information to be fed into the system, not *less*. Simply, he began with an entirely different premise to make sense of this fire hose of metadata. He looked at *how* the information passed between people, as opposed to *what* information was being passed. By looking at these behavioral patterns, the analysts could readily identify networks of bad guys and focus their efforts in the centers of those circles, in favor of recycling useless and corrupt information that led nowhere. In Binney's words:

> *"Everything is human behavior. Human behavior is extremely patterned. How do people operate? How do they interact? And how does this manifest or appear in this abstract set of communications you are looking at?"*

> *"It's a matter of getting to the point where you can understand the patterns and interpret them properly."*

> *"When you sit there and look at a problem like that and then you see… can see the problem and the break. That's exhilarating when you do."*

> *"It really is."*

I could never explain the Gifts better than these words do. Many may think of Binney as a pure mathematician pursuing the unlocking of complex algorithms, puzzles, and codes…but in truth, he is a "Primary Thinker."

I invented the term "Primary Thinker" to describe when one is using direct powers of observation, instinct, intuition, and personal intelligence to approach matters, unfiltered by other people's opinions and perceptions, and without society's bias.

I think Binney is starting from the simple observation that people, ultimately, are the ones using the math. Therefore, he reasons, if I study the people, I can unlock the math. I think it looks something like that.

Let me lay out my argument as clearly as words will allow: There is no other way to penetrate someone's inner self as quickly and deeply as understanding the Seven Gifts. You can know things about someone from the person's language, country of origin, gender, generation, sexuality, religion, etc., but there is no faster way to dive into that individual's true interior.

I heard someone say once that the biggest lies are often the easiest ones to conceal. Economic and political systems can embody fundamental oppressiveness, for example, disguised as something else. A corollary to this axiom about lies might be: *The most basic truths are often the hardest to see.* I believe this body of Gift knowledge is such an example. I also believe that, if anyone would "get" what the Seven Gifts really represent, Binney would.

In my intellectual travels, I have studied many different personality typing systems, some in the world of psychology and others in the world of literature. Carl Jung's elaboration on the presence of human archetypes fascinated. Charles Darwin's work in the area of evolution suggested personality and functional patterns as well. William Shakespeare's writings also provided a structure for repetitive personalities in humanity. And I eventually encountered Myers-Briggs typology testing when I entered the professional world.

Yet all of these approaches still suggest to me attempts to process an unaccountable, unimaginable amount of behavior…metadata being looked at with search words. I find these accounts imprecise in the sense that they try to sort and package conduct or actions. That is too much data to make meaningful sense of, in my view.

Understanding how the Seven Gifts unlocks all human behavior is nearly an exact, parallel exercise as ThinThread, because the system begins with a dramatically different premise than all of the others I have seen.

The key to the success of the Seven Gifts is this: the Seven Gifts look at *motivation*, not conduct or actions. Within the Seven Gifts, *why someone does something and what core motivation drives it is more critical than what one does.*

Is one's core motivation to provide a *service?* Is it to stand for what is *right?* To approach things in the most *efficient* manner? To create a positive *emotional effect* in others? To provide the best information qualified by proper *research?* To cause another to be *inspired to soar?* Or perhaps the motivation is to pursue a *larger cause* for the betterment of humanity?

I wonder if you could begin to catch a glimpse of yourself in any of the mirrors I just held up for you? Remember, the Seven Gifts are about emotional/spiritual motivation, not thoughts or actions. They are intuitive, not rational.

I want to clarify my use of the word "spirit" here as well, because this is an important word in understanding the Gifts. Notice that I do not use the capitalized version "Spirit." That is because I am not using this term in any religious context, not the Holy Spirit, for example. When I say "spirit" in this book, I am referring to what we might call someone's soul, one's (emotional) heart, or one's inner being. If it is important or meaningful for you to bring a capital into play here, and bring your God into the picture, go for it. In my way of thinking, all of this information is only as valuable as it is applied. So, if it helps you to visualize and apply it better any other way, I strongly encourage you to have at it. I have had an indescribable amount of fun playing with Gift Knowledge over the last decade, and encourage you to create and play as well.

A close friend who has shared Gift experiences with me over the years, and who also has experimented with the information quite a bit like I have, told me once: "It is totally unfair that you understand so much about other people through understanding their Gifts. You have a *completely* unfair advantage." And we laughed and laughed.

If you understand the Gifts and can discern what someone's Gift is, you may know more about that person than that person is aware of on some levels, and sometimes more about an individual than the people who are closest to the individual…even more in some respects than people who have known the person for a lifetime.

A person's Gift is like a computer operating system, like a natural *motivational* software. The Gift is installed at the factory; it is always running in the background; it never turns off. The Gift gives overall purpose, direction, and momentum to a person's life. One's formative years and significant experiences may add subroutines. Even then, the Gift influences the incorporation of new subroutines.

Knowledge of the Gifts can provide a new and healthy emotional and spiritual "technology" that brings language, shape, and form to things that may have been noticed or seen, but haven't been truly known or understood, and virtually never openly discussed. We assume we are hidden to others, that we are a mystery or a puzzle that can never be solved, that we are alone in the world, but understanding your own Gift, and other people's Gifts, shatters those implicit assumptions.

We *can* know who we are, and we *can* know who others are. And we can talk about that. We can share it. And we can experience great fun, understanding, and love along the way. It is wonderful to be known for who you are, for what makes your clock tick. And it is equally as wonderful to know another, and to cause that person to feel truly known. We all want to see and to be seen, and the Seven Gifts provide a unique opportunity for all of this to happen, to become possible. Knowing a person's Gift can allow for subconscious knowledge to rise to the surface of consciousness. People can literally glow when they confidently step into discussions about their Gift and other people's Gifts.

I wonder how a better understanding of a person would occur in, for example, Jung's system of archetypes? Or with Shakespeare? I don't want to be disrespectful to thinkers who are a lot brighter than I am, but I conclude many other personality typing systems can be forms of Tarot Cards. As such, they are not as meaningful or actionable in my eyes. These other systems may help us to categorize people based on their surface actions and conduct, but to really understand human beings more reliably,

I am convinced you have to see their very core, their essence...*why they do what they do.*

One way to discover your own Gift is to begin to notice what you have *endless* energy for, where no batteries are ever needed, where you feel a tremendous stamina. And to determine another person's Gift by becoming aware of when all whistles and bells are going off. A person's Gift Engine, so to speak, never runs out of gas.

Divining your own Gift, and the Gifts of others, where the Gift is not immediately obvious, can be like drilling for wells, like the wells I saw on Kansas farms. But when you eventually hit water, you'll know it. I don't think you can Know Thyself unless you Know Thy Gift. Claim your Gift when you discover it. You belong to it, and it belongs to you.

When I was going through an awakening in earlier years (Sometimes folks call this a midlife crisis!), I had to study labels of emotions and their corresponding definitions to try to become more operative and fluid in the emotional/spiritual world. I eventually became a Giftologist, a title of my own making, a practitioner in the art of the Seven Gifts, because of Liza and Lauren. My daughters were around eight and seven years old, respectively, at the genesis of my new role and readily saw their father's excitement about this new body of information. As I first learned of the Gifts, I noticed that Liza and Lauren each seemed to obviously and clearly fit into one of the seven (which does not always happen by the way).

*Identifying someone's Gift does not "pigeonhole," constrict, or define someone throughout...*it only provides a window into who the person really is, to promote better understanding. Like any power, the power of knowing someone's Gift can be used for good or nefarious purposes. Think of the Gifts as "food groups" that people can readily be identified as being from or part of, some more obviously than others. Learned behavior, parenting, and birth order can make it more difficult to quickly identify someone's Gift. Understanding someone's Gift, and becoming more familiar with your own, can be very liberating and freeing, not limiting.

By a complete and providential coincidence, I was trying to get both Liza and Lauren admitted to private schools at the time, navigating an admission process that required extensive IQ testing. When their test results came back, I was floored. Stunned. I saw the Gifts in black and white in the scores within various categories.

Liza had powerful logic, reasoning skills, and math abilities; she was a natural competitor in the academic world, her long-term memory credible. Lauren, conversely, had strong short-term memory and a high degree of visual literacy; her social/emotional intelligence was so far off the charts it could not be measured fully by the test. The IQ testing matched the Gift characteristics almost verbatim. I could not have asked for any clearer validation of the power and accuracy of this knowledge at the early stages of my interest.

A clear understanding of the Seven Gifts is essential in child-rearing. I am convinced a child cannot be understood, nurtured, and led nearly as lovingly and effectively without understanding who the child is in light of the child's Gift. Knowing a child's Gift informs more effective language to use with that child, and guides better approaches that a child can be freer to understand, relate to, and follow. The test results and my growing knowledge of the Gifts caused me to understand, when parenting or fathering, I would have to try and address the *exact same* topic with each of my daughters *completely differently.*

Liza was more likely respond to interrogatives, more intense discussions about right and wrong, and what she wanted to stand for in her life. Lauren was more likely to respond to an emotional, empathetic encounter…more "touchy-feely," you might say. Liza would watch live surgeries on cable television while eating nachos, while Lauren would run away from the same images on television as if she was imagining she was next up on the surgery table. And I could see that, with my own Gift, Liza would be easier for me and Lauren would be more challenging. I would be wise to "rehearse" with a similarly Gifted person as Lauren before making my attempt with her, Gift Consulting, you might call it. So my two lovely girls learned alongside me and we had tremendous fun.

There is nothing quite like good Gift Humor. Poking fun at other people's Gifts and allowing others to poke at yours illustrate love, care, understanding, context, and perspective. Gift Humor possesses a powerful undercurrent that allows you and others to feel *truly known and understood*, which one may say is the very essence of love. Gift Humor also helps everyone not take themselves and others too seriously.

Liza and Lauren would move the salt and pepper shakers out of their places slightly before dinner, knowing that it would grate at my Gift, and watch my reaction with delight as I eventually could not help but notice that the world was not quite right. The three of us intuitively knew that a Gift can never be shut off. You can fake that it is off, but that's about it. I could discipline myself to appear not to notice the lack of order at the table, and sometimes it is a good thing to tell your Gift to step aside, or take a seat, but we knew the Gift never left. The lack of order on the table was always looking me right in the eyes.

But mostly I became a Giftologist because Liza and Lauren started bringing their little friends over to our house so that I could sit next to them at the dinner table. On Sundays, when I was barbecuing my Kansas City ribs, I would overhear them excitedly convincing their play guest for the day to sit next to their dad at dinner because he will tell you *who you are.*

The Gift Game.

No pressure, Dad. In our little minds, we only imagine that it would be no problem for you to conjugate some of the meanings of a person's very existence here on earth in a matter of moments and be able to penetrate some of the deepest parts of another person's psyche, soul, spirit, heart, and inner world. Sure, Dad, you will have at least a few minutes to meet them so you can figure it out. We are really excited and so is our friend.

I also imagined the disaster of this poor kid trying to explain to her parents that she is going over to Liza and Lauren's house and there Mr. Whitacre is going to tell me who I am. If I were the kid's father, I would assume we have a cult going on here, maybe a hypnosis session, or possibly a fortune-teller. So it was all quite a bit to try to live up to. But as any father who has daughters knows, you would sooner die an unreasonable death than let your girls down. All the chips in the world ride on your daughters' hearts. So I had all the motivation I could possibly embrace to try to figure out this Gift thing, and fast.

The first couple of friends were relatively easy, because I had seen them in action over time. Katie, the babysitter, always put aside *anything* she had planned to help babysit for the girls, eagerly sought needed tasks to perform in our absence at our house, all while not paying a lot of attention to herself and her own needs. I made her Gift quickly, like a detective makes a perpetrator, but not without having some fun first.

I distracted them all, Papa hot-spoon style (see Volume I), by asking completely tangential, unrelated, and irrelevant questions starting with what flavor ice cream she liked, then what her favorite Disney movie was, then her favorite color, knowing where I was going to land all along. I even threw in if she thought little Tommy down the street was creepy. When I eventually began asking her if she could identify with a whole list of characteristics that I knew about her motivational Gift, she became almost alarmed because no one had ever known, seen, and conveyed some of the things I was sharing with her about her. She knew what I was sharing was true, but could not understand how I knew it because she had never shared it with anyone. She was shocked. Exposed. Vulnerable. Liza and Lauren laughed and giggled. Told you, Katie. Told you that he would tell you who you are. Ha-ha.

The next ones were harder though, because I had to operate with a lot less information. My exposure to them in physical time was much more limited, so it became a game of *Name That Tune* in one or two notes, *Name That Gift* in one or two questions or observations. I began to develop "splitter questions" meaning that if I felt I had it down to a couple of Gifts, I could fashion a question that could distinguish between two Gifts and potentially reveal which one of the two I had in front of me, similar to the game *Twenty Questions*. One of my favorite Gift-splitter questions involves asking someone to imagine being called on unexpectedly in class and asked to stand up and speak publicly on some matter. Hearing how a person would respond emotionally will typically eliminate half of the Gifts as possibilities.

There are similarities or overlapping qualities, sister or brother Gifts so to speak, so you have to find what separates and distinguishes the Gifts to get to the bottom of who someone is. It is easy to misidentify someone if you are not aware of more exact similarities and differences between the Gifts.

I also noticed, as I played the Gift Game with Liza and Lauren, that I was making some progress gaining credibility in their little hearts. I began to see that they were starting to see me as more of an authority, and that maybe someday I could use that credibility for good purpose in their lives. Maybe they would believe me more when I explained things about boys, for example. Maybe they would listen. Knowing the Gifts cannot only help build insight into one's own spirit and the spirits of others, it can also help establish you as a more credible figure to people you love and care for, especially in the case of children. Credibility with kids is critical.

I remember tender times when Liza and Lauren would bring home the travails of childhood and share with me how a particular teacher might be an ongoing irritation. "What do you think Mr. Lash's Gift is, Liza?" I might ask. "I don't know, Dad. I didn't think of that." And an entirely different discussion would ensue. We would run Gift Tests together in our minds, and try to figure out where Lash might be operating from. We might eventually figure out, through Gift Deduction, that Lash was probably the same Gift as Liza was, a likely reason that there could be some grating going on, a typical feature of Liza's specific Gift.

And then we could all laugh, seeing Lash differently now, in a more understanding way, having deflated some of the stress and tension. By going through the process of making observations about Lash from a Gift perspective, it ultimately became more and more difficult to demonize him and helped to humanize him, to cause him to be seen and experienced as just a normal, flawed person. Flawed like me and you. Understanding the Gifts involves admitting we are all flawed. If I understand that I am flawed, it becomes easier to accept flaws in others. The act of considering the Gifts calms me when I am angry or frustrated by others.

Perhaps most importantly, by spending some time with my children on these Gift questions, I could help them develop strategies to approach situations in life. For example, I might rehearse with Liza and explain that she might do well with a different starting point with Lash, now that we had potentially blown his Gift cover.

Liza…when he comes after you like that, and you start feeling like you want to throw your pencil at him, try saying: "Mr. Lash…I will answer your question but I hope it's okay if I share something with you first, because when I left class yesterday, I noticed something. I realized how intensely passionate and focused you are about science, and how resolved you are to make sure that we students can understand the awesome truth of it. I thought the other day that is probably how rockets ended up on the moon. And I just wanted to say, I see that and thank you so much for your commitment."

When she came home the next day, we could sit down together and unpack what happened. The dynamic with Lash completely changed because Liza had not spoken to Lash this time around but had talked directly to his Gift. And then we would laugh and giggle because Liza would describe the expression on Lash's face when she delivered her lines. His expression basically said: "Why, of course, what other reason or purpose could there be…?"

And that is what is so fun and entertaining about the Gifts. They are so *ridiculously* reliable. People operate out of their Gifts potentially without understanding what is actually happening because no one has taught them about the Gifts. Lash may not realize that in fact there are other motivations that could lead one to behave as he does. He is motivated to *inform others of the truth* with his motivational Gift, but the other six Gifts could be motivated to spread the truth of science for *totally different reasons.*

One might say that I had taught my daughters, in Lash's case, to be manipulative. I don't think so. Rehearsing and then speaking Lash's natural language was an act of sheer understanding. It helped Liza and Lauren to learn to ask themselves, in any situation, what a person's Gift might be…a husband's, a father's, a mother's, a boyfriend's, a girlfriend's, a teacher's, a child's, a boss's, a friend's. And it also pointed a light towards greater unity, not towards discord.

Asking myself how someone's Gift might be operating in any given situation will give me insight into how to communicate, interpret, and proceed. Even the act of asking myself this question helps to direct me towards understanding and unity. Playing around with the Gifts on a regular basis, just as part of every normal day, also invites new language, like Gift Game, Gift Questions, whether something makes Gift Sense or not, and so on. New vocabulary, by definition, invites new thinking, which in turn informs new behavior.

WHAT DO YOU SAY? ARE YOU READY to get your snorkel on and go scuba diving together now, to go down and see the Gifts? Hold your breath. Remember that the Seven Gifts are like food groups; the Gifts are generalities, and meant to identify larger tendencies. You may see that you have some characteristics of Gifts outside of your own, but if you look at the larger pattern, you will see that these traits are more pronounced in other Gifts.

After considering this body of information carefully over the last decade, experimenting with it in real life and testing every aspect of it that I can think of to date, I am convinced that these patterns are present in nature as part of our natural evolution. I think Darwin, for example, may have been interested in the Gifts, and been able to come up with far better ways than I have to prove their absolute existence.

I have no psychological, psychiatric, let alone scientific, testing to validate my observations. But that doesn't make any of what I am sharing less true. Someone had to postulate that the world was round and not flat before it could be proven scientifically later. The natural world is a great lab to experiment in. Watching what is around us carefully can sometimes tell us a lot more than academics, or even science can. *Slumdog Millionaire**, for example, won the most difficult game show quiz based on what he himself saw and heard.

**Slumdog Millionaire* is a 2008 drama film directed by Danny Boyle, written by Simon Beaufoy, and produced by Christian Colson. Set and filmed in India, it is a loose adaptation of the novel *Q & A* (2005) by Indian author and diplomat Vikas Swarup, telling the story of Jamal Malik, age 18, from the Juhu slums of Mumbai. As a contestant on the Indian version of *Who Wants to Be a Millionaire?,* he is able to answer every question correctly. Accused of cheating, Jamal recounts his story, illustrating how he is able to answer each question.

There is a difference between science and applied science, between studying in the lab and applying in the real world. I remember my neighbor Jack, who lived behind me years ago in Phoenix, told me the best story I ever heard about the difference between the two. Jack was an engineer who was really smart, and he had just started a new job in recent months helping to create highways for Maricopa County. One day, he decided to leave his engineering office of calculations and blueprints and venture out to the site where they were building one of his mammoth on-ramps. After all, he said, a good highway engineer should maybe have some sense of what goes on in the field.

When he gets there, he meanders over to a half-finished base, a gargantuan concrete foundation, a structure made of *thousands* of tons of concrete stretching into the sky, meant to hold up some ribbon of highway eventually. Jack also sees dozens of concrete trucks lined up way above him on a slash of highway that abruptly ends in space, right over the structure, where truckload after truckload of concrete continuously pours into the remaining molds that have provided form for this massive object.

Man…he thinks to himself. This is unbelievable. It is so big. Like one of the Great Pyramids in Egypt. Since he had a drink or two when he told me the story, he also confessed he fancied himself a master engineer, and a clever one too that would think to visit the site and collaborate with the construction elements. Then, after looking up at the form in the sky, he looked down. He realized that a little, red-painted wood stake was right at the corner of the form defining this shape, this shape that was now the size of a small skyscraper. Jack stared at me, filled his glass with Crown Royal, then stared at me again. "I give," I said.

Jack explained that even every junior engineer knows that the red stake is a survey device that marks the spot exactly four feet away from where something goes. Jack said he looked back up and saw all the diesel smoke pouring from the cement trucks over the shape, worsening the situation each passing moment. Seeing a chance to use his walkie-talkie, he radioed the construction chief. I wondered in my mind how cool using the walkie-talkie probably would have been and felt a little jealous. So the construction chief, responding, lumbers over whereupon Jack says: "I think we have a big problem."

After listening and looking up and down, the chief takes off his sunglasses and looks at Jack. I am imagining he is like The Duke. He says, "Jack…Jack…Jack…Let's just slow down a little bit here. This is your first day on the job. You don't understand how things work yet. *We* don't have any problems at all." He reached over, pulled the stake out, carefully walked off four back-to-back steps with his foot-long construction boots and drove the stake down into the Arizona hardpan once again, exactly four feet from the corner.

Then he put his glasses back on, looked up at the trucks pouring away, and said to Jack: "Let's try the taco truck. The food is really good. This is a survey issue. The surveyors have a problem." Then, the chief offered to buy the tacos that were made by real Mexicans. And Jack said the chief was right, the tacos were to die for, so good he wanted to find the food truck again. Even tacos can smell of conspiracy. So I think Jack figured out that day there can be a long distance between the classroom and the real world, between theory and application. I freshened up his drink and learned alongside him.

For over a decade, I have stayed on my own construction site with the Gifts. I have tried to look at both the science of what has been passed on to me, and then perhaps more importantly the applied science of it. I have found basic truths, falsehoods, and inevitable ambiguities. Hopefully, I can try to bring to light some of what I have seen. I have also tried to animate what proportions in the population as a whole I have seen as the Gifts manifest themselves. There seem to be more of certain types of Gifts than others. I can't help but see a reasonable natural order to this as well. Almost like the order that bees have, bees that are able to build and sustain hives for their preservation. About half of what I have come to know about the application of Gift knowledge is self-taught. As you learn, I hope you make many new discoveries that have escaped me.

Each of the Seven Gifts performs a specific purpose and has a particular important role to play in the larger scope of our humanity. Each Gift is enhanced by the others, and would not do well on its own, so to speak, or with other like Gifts typically. The presence of the Gifts in human spiritual nature illustrates the absolute need for diversity and differentiation. It occurs to me that the Gifts have an order to them and that some overlap, while others represent polar opposites. I am going to try and lay them out for you to see in an order that shows the one that might be closest to the next, so that you might be able to parse differences more clearly.

The Seven Gifts are: Mercy, Server, Exhorter, Organizer, Prophet, Teacher, and Giver. You might think of them as points of a compass, spokes on a wheel, or tick marks on the face of a clock.

Each Gift has a "light" side and a "dark" side, like The Force does in *Star Wars*. There are positive and negative aspects of each: Special abilities to try and lean in to, continue enhancing and cultivating, and troublesome areas that one would be wise to develop self-awareness in, and get a better handle on.

Each of us has a *primary* Gift. In other words, underneath all of one's personal history, childhood, gender, learned and parented behavior, education, sexuality, social upbringing, and economic class there is one core, central motivation, much like a center of gravity. The Gift is easier to discern in some, and more difficult in others, largely because of the complexity and layering of our human experience. And just like planets and asteroids come in and out of one another's fields of gravity, it is clear that we all can have strong Gift influences from others that resonate within us outside of our lead or primary Gift. And this is how it should be.

It makes common sense, emotional sense, and spiritual sense that we would want to develop our wisdom about the other Gifts that we are not, and strive to become more like the Gifts that we are not. In this manner, we can become more rounded, more whole, more balanced, and can enjoy life more richly and freely knowing better who we really are and who others really are.

I remember recently speaking to another close friend who knows these Gifts as I do, and I was sharing with him that I had lost a lot of weight as I was learning to eat healthy foods now. It only took me fifty years to listen to my mother and eat healthy vegetables. I told him I was enjoying wearing new and different clothes, some that you might say even reflected fashion.

Now my Gift buddy knows that Organizers like me are almost never concerned with fashion, because fashion is not typically a consideration for efficiency. If you see a professional who wears the exact same outfit day after day, having a closet filled with the exact same dress, even though a job may not require it, you have just been able to name an Organizer in one note. I took another step and shared with him that I was noticing that my fashion changes were having slight emotional effects on people I was encountering. He started laughing. "You're playing with the Gifts, aren't you, David?"

Exactly.

MERCY

EMOTIONAL EXPERT

OF ALL THE GIFTS, THE MERCY STANDS ABOVE in emotional intelligence and, therefore, relational competence. Mercys can pick up emotions in the air like a Geiger counter detects faint traces of radiation. They know what you will feel usually way before you do because of their ability to emotionally sense, comprehend, and visualize in the feeling world. You could also call a Mercy an "empath."

Take a Mercy away from being able to spend time with other people and you may come to realize that you are watching a plant being deprived of sunlight and water. Mercys are responders, and they need other people around them at all times so they have feelings to respond to.

To the rest of us, the Mercy tends to appear to overreact at times, "freaking out" over things that the rest of us may see as normal or pedestrian.

Mercys seem to be the most plentiful of the Gifts. I am guessing about 25% of the population. Maybe that is because the rest of us need emotional "hot spots," like Wi-Fi. Gift Detectives take note: One in four makes this Gift the highest probability.

I HOPE IT WILL HELP TO SHARE A SHORT Gift Story as you meet each of the Gifts.

My second daughter, Lauren, is a Mercy. When she was about six years old, she rode down Michigan Avenue during one of our first outings here in Chicago, strapped in a booster chair in the back of our minivan. Having come from a more modest Kansas City, the grand city was a lot to take in.

She sat next to her sister Liza, who is at the exact opposite end of the Gift spectrum. I was just starting to learn about the Gifts and beginning to field test this new information. Lauren looked up out her window at the tall buildings and summarily started emotionally wobbling, as I would later learn many Mercys do frequently.

"Dad, something is going to fall on us. We need to get away from these tall buildings!" In the rearview mirror, I could see her neck bent way down so she could see all the way up to the top of the John Hancock Tower. Being the insightful, emotionally literate dad I am, I immediately invalidated her feelings, thinking I could fix her.

Understanding the Gifts will help you parent your children, because it allows you to see when their natural software is operating. Speaking to your children from a perspective of understanding what their Gift may be doing at any given moment will allow you to enter their world more readily and create confidence in them, confidence that you might be able to see what they see. I did not do any of that during our van ride that day.

"Honey," I explained, "There is no reason to fear anything. These buildings are anchored almost as deeply as they are tall. Try to think about the positive things you see, like how majestic, beautiful, and proud the mighty skyscrapers are. Not like anything in Kansas City, right?" Despite assurances, she continued with her struggles. I pointed out that she was ruining the fun for the rest of the minivan riders. I instructed her to shield her eyes and stop complaining.

As fate would have it, I saw a few days later on the evening news that a tragic accident had occurred at almost the exact same spot Lauren had overheated. Some may call it a freak accident. I called it a message from the universe to me personally about the Gifts, like seeing my daughters' school admission test results, when I saw what I believe was specific scientific validation of the existence of the Gifts.

The news described that it was, in fact, one of the windiest days in the Windy City on record in recent years. Powerful gales came in off Lake Michigan at almost 70 miles per hour, with no evident storm to have agitated things. High up on the side of the Hancock Tower, a scaffold for glass cleaning had been caught in the throes of the blasts that had snuck up out of nowhere and prevented workers from retrieving it off the side of the building.

I watched footage of the scaffold banging glass windows as it squirmed about. Then one of the cables snapped, whereupon the apparatus started crashing violently into the building high up in the sky. Eventually, the final cables let go and the scaffolding launched out into the air, like a giant whale harpoon diving straight towards Michigan Avenue. Several people driving their cars along under the tower where Lauren had become frightened were killed. Some were impaled right through their car roofs.

Never underestimate the power of someone's Gift, as well as the insight, knowledge, and perspective the Gift provides, *especially* a child's Gift. A Gift knows no age. A Gift is not ever young or old…it simply is. Every Gift serves a specific and important purpose, and should be recognized as a specialty. It is wise to think in terms of what a Gift's special skill set represents and to see that other Gifts have value.

So as fate had arranged for me, I got the chance to get out the mustard, salt, and pepper, and eat some crow in front of my daughter. I had to humble my ego and admit that I was dead wrong to respond to her in the van the way I had. I admitted I had been insensitive and dumb, shared that I had learned my lesson the hard way, and potentially at great expense to others. When I explained what happened to the other Michigan Avenue drivers and riders, I saw the same grimace come over her face that I had seen in the rearview mirror. I realized in her Mercy mind she had visualized a similar tragic event in the back of the van, and also that she was seeing the actual event in her mind and feeling it in her heart as I was describing it.

Mercys see that stuff in their heads and feel those kinds of things deep within. To them, it is not irrational or freaking out, it is real. By the way, one way to recognize Mercys is to watch their faces when they are hearing stuff. If they animate their expressions a lot, especially when hearing about something stressful, painful, dangerous, or medical they may have just blown their Gift cover.

And Mercys like to hide.

LIGHT MERCY

I MENTIONED BEFORE THAT EACH GIFT has areas that would be wise to enhance and also areas that would be helpful to get a better handle on and squelch. When I use the words "light" and "dark" here, I do so only for simplicity's sake. I do not mean to imply things like good or evil. I only want to spell it out, chalk some lines on the ballfield, and then let you do with it what you will.

More than any other Gift, a Mercy is supremely capable of being considerate of other people's feelings. I learned earlier when raising a Mercy daughter that IQ tests and other evaluative tests that schools and employers typically use will likely never be able to measure the height of a Mercy's true emotional and social intelligence.

Mercys will typically be constantly studying you, both consciously and unconsciously, to try and pick up your emotional signals. They are capable of detecting the smallest of micro-expressions, and can even sometimes know what you are feeling in the moment before you do, or what you will be feeling in the future as a result of something. William Dafoe, the great actor, once said: "The body does not lie." And the Mercy is an expert at interpreting what your body is saying from an emotional perspective.

Many times this level of empathy and otherness is associated with femininity. Male Mercys especially sometimes want to disassociate with the Gift, because they are concerned others may not feel it is manly. I would suggest that the Mercy Gift is not female in nature, and that men with this Gift were not designed in error. I am constantly astounded at the emotional insight and sensitivity that Mercys can abound with. I have learned through studying the Seven Gifts that I would be wise to learn how to become more emotionally and relationally functional like they are.

Because a Mercy is an expert at visualizing causes and effects in other people's emotions, one would be wise to consult Mercys when giving (physical) gifts. When you ask them to give their input, make sure that you explain to them first that it would have a positive emotional impact on you if they gave an honest opinion. Otherwise, they may be emotionally trapped, because they could feel they would have to temper their opinion about the present you propose to give with not wanting to hurt your feelings with the truth. They wouldn't want to make you feel bad or stupid for not seeing what is to them, emotionally obvious. That is how sensitive, how emotionally aware they are.

A Mercy would also be one to consult when you want to make sure a piece of correspondence has the right tone, or whether bringing up a sensitive subject with someone is a good or bad idea. Like a tuning fork used when tuning a piano, a Mercy will be able to pinpoint emotional aspects that generally don't occur to most of the other Gifts, certainly not mine.

It is best not to ask a Mercy open-ended questions in these situations, as in "What would you do?" or "What would you say?" That could cause an overload, because the Mercy would not only be visualizing a potentially infinite number of approaches and emotional consequences to the matter at hand, but also would be seeing the same infinity with regards to the emotional effects on you if their counsel proved to be wrong. Just like the spinning circle you see on your computer when the software is overloaded. It is best to propose a specific approach and let them work with that. To a Mercy, existence is an all-consuming world of emotional cause and effect.

A Mercy possesses a superior ability to remember special dates and occasions in other people's lives, as well as their preferences. This is one area where the long-term memory of a Mercy really excels. Mercys can become so horrified if they forget your birthday, for fear of making you feel bad that they forgot you, which they generally never will. Or they may even make up a special date for you, and present you with a special token on the day you move into a new house or something like that. And a Mercy can remember things like this, things that are social or relational in nature, for a very long time, precisely because these issues are related to feelings and people, not facts per se.

A Mercy is capable of remaining in the background in silence. Mercys will generally be the ones laying back in the group, waiting and watching to see what is going to happen first, before deciding how to proceed into a situation. They shun the spotlight and don't want to ruffle feathers. They will first gather enough information, so that when they enter into the conversation they can do so in a way that is relationally agreeable, emotionally appealing, and unifying.

A Mercy wants to blend in and avoid confrontations at all costs. Mercys want to be a part of things and bask in the interplay between people, even if they are not the ones speaking up.

Mercys remain alert to areas of injustice, and will come out of their shells to stand up for the underdog. The exception to Mercys hanging back is when they are speaking for, representing, or standing up for a person or group that they see being oppressed or mistreated. If they are protecting others, watch out because they will look like some of the more outgoing or declarative Gifts. Mercys will not hesitate to get in your face in these situations, but will almost never do this on their own behalf.

A Mercy has strong short-term memory and an ability to recall facts and numbers over a shorter time frame. Typically a Mercy does a good job learning and absorbing information, things like concepts or numbers, in the moment. For example, if you called someone to get a phone number you needed but you had nothing to write it down with, if you said it out loud a Mercy could remember it, even if it was a long number; a Mercy can retain it very well over a shorter period of time, maybe for the whole day. When Mercys learn something new in school, they typically are able to retain that information in the short term, over a period of a few days.

I have seen over time that a lot of what Mercys will absorb that will stick really well in the longer term has to do with interaction with other people. In other words, they don't do as well with self-study. If they have social interaction during the learning process, they do much better. Mercys will download stuff a lot better with a study partner, because the Mercy can remember the interactions with the other person more lucidly, and therefore be able to recall the facts or details because they become linked to feelings and interactions.

A Mercy is attracted to misfits…characters who are out of the ordinary or broken. The Mercy cannot stand it when others are not included, such as the outcasts of society. If I were a homeless beggar, I would try to become proficient at identifying Mercys. This characteristic of a Mercy is, in some respects, a corollary to the Mercy's ability to stand up, perhaps aggressively, on behalf of the oppressed or downtrodden.

As a result, your Mercy daughter or son is going to be bringing some diverse and interesting people home; hopefully, they will be positively-charged characters. If there is a kid in your child's class who is wrestling with gender identity or just plain fitting in socially, you can bet your Mercy child has noticed that and tried to smooth things out somehow. If a friend of a Mercy is going through some tremendous drama in life, a Mercy will strap in and go along for the entire ride. After all, drama is a way to have a feeling party and that's what Mercys live for.

A Mercy possesses a subtle palate and has the ability to detect precise tastes and smells. If you have ever seen the children's animated film *Ratatouille* then you have a picture of the typical Mercy gastronomical skill of being able to distinguish tastes of foods, ingredients, spices, flavors, even the degree of freshness of something at a higher level than most of us. If a Mercy tells you that water doesn't taste right, you would be wise not to drink it. If you try a new dish at an eclectic restaurant and wonder what it is that you are tasting, let a Mercy try a bite. You might hear that there is a touch of honey that has been laid on top of mint, mixed with a dash of ginger. As such, Mercys make great chefs.

There is a restaurant here in Chicago called *Alinea* that has been named the best in the entire world a few times. I'll bet you a nickel the renowned chef artist Grant Achatz who commandeers it is a Mercy. He almost lost his tongue to cancer. But even if he had, I'll venture his nose and heightened sense of smell may have found him a path through it. Maybe Mr. Achatz would agree to let me see if I could guess his Gift in exchange for dinner for me and my wife if I got it right. I can't afford to eat there a second time, so this could work out very well for me and also for Mr. Achatz.

A Mercy is skilled in visual and musical matters. Matters involving colors, mood, fashion, and sound are the natural domain of a Mercy. Mercys make great graphic designers, stylists, and musicians. If you think about it that makes common sense because these are realms of emotional affectation. This color produces this feeling. These colors mixed produces that feeling. This sound transitioned into this sound creates this emotion, and so on.

Mercys can excel at playing parts and roles in public settings provided that they are playing a character and not themselves. Mercys can be great actors and will have little problem performing in front of large audiences as long as they project themselves out of their own persona into some fictitious or invented character. This is really interesting because if you ask Mercys how they would feel about being called on unexpectedly in class and asked to speak extemporaneously on a subject, they will likely say that it would make them want to hide under the desk and throw up.

Yet the same Mercy, if asked to stand up and recite some lines from a play would have little if any difficulty. Again, the concept here is I think related to the Mercy's ability to move fluently and comfortably in the world of emotional affectation, causes which produce effects on feelings. When Mercys are in character, they don't have the distortion of higher levels of self-doubt.

In earlier years, I watched my young Mercy daughter bring the house down while singing and playing the piano in an auditorium filled with a thousand people, channeling the emotions she could pick out of the air in the space, lifting and gently dropping all in attendance with her nuanced inflections, her brittle tones, even the way she let her lovely hair hang over her eyes, a gesture which conveyed dreaminess. Yet after the show at the ice cream shop, she would shyly hesitate to get out front to order her favorite flavor.

DARK MERCY

As in all of the Gifts, we see that strengths can also be weaknesses. Yin and Yang. Double-edged swords. If by chance you are a reader that is identifying yourself as a Mercy at this point, please allow me to encourage you as you read this next section. Just because some of these darker elements exist does not mean you have to be owned by them. I believe it is our purpose to try and become aware of our lower selves, our darker natures, our potential lack of emotional or spiritual health, so that we can progress and grow and blossom. Our race, after all, is here to evolve. And so are we as individuals.

As you read some of these darker elements, if you find you don't identify with them strongly, I hope you can take that as a sign of personal maturity and psychological health. Somewhere along life's way, you learned a better way from someone close to you, or you were keen enough to see something in the mirror you didn't care for and decided to do something about it. Give yourself a pat on the back if you feel like you are not mired in some of these traits. And make it a nice loving and encouraging big pat, also because it is both hard and good for Mercys to give themselves credit for anything.

Mercys generally have poor self-images and can have terrible struggles with self-esteem. A Mercy tends to over-focus on little flaws within and may constantly feel undeserving of anything, not able to measure up, not worthy, and not good enough. As a result, Mercys can appear to be meek and vulnerable, and many times they are.

Mercys, feeling low self-esteem, can place themselves in a role of the victim. In this mode it will be very difficult for them to take personal responsibility and act in any given set of circumstances. Pity parties aren't good for anyone.

The Mercy generally assumes the worst about almost everything initially and, as such, consistently projects irrational fears. A friend of mine once said to me, in reference to his Mercy Gift: "You don't want to see what's behind the curtain David." I think he was referring to the idea that Mercys walk around imagining a lot of potentially terrible things and have to constantly expend energy to hide that fact from others. Mercys are generally stuck in a negative first gear; in other words, they almost always, without fail, come out of the gate with a negative or suspicious view.

If you see someone who does not want to get on a plane for fear of flying, you most probably are looking at a Mercy. If you see Mercys acting like cats about to be dropped into a tub of water, the best thing to do is try and talk to them about what they are concerned with and validate their feelings, but not necessarily the facts.

Try real hard to control your facial expressions and eyes in the process because a Mercy will be studying you to see if you are for real, or whether it is just what the Mercy mind concludes, an opportunity for you to mock or make the Mercy feel stupid. Remember, for Mercys it is always all about feelings. If you can help them along by empathizing, encouraging, complimenting, validating, it can be a beautiful thing.

Mercys generally believe that people are out to get them, and usually assume negative motives in others as a result. If you ask a Mercy if help is needed with something, don't be surprised if the first facial expression you see is one of blanket mistrust and suspicion. You may see that Mercys look at you as if your question was just the beginning of a grand scheme against them, an evil plot that you were trying to lure them into. Mercys can believe everyone is part of a conspiracy against them. Best thing to do is try and be patient. Don't get distracted by it. Explain why you were thinking that, tell them why you were motivated to try to be kind, that they had always been helpful to you as well, etc. Give them more and more emotional information to soothe them.

If you can ever get far enough into this subject with a Mercy, you can also ever so gently share that it hurts your heart that the Mercy would believe your intentions were not the best. That it makes you feel mistrusted, misunderstood, and unappreciated. If you say it gently enough so the Mercy can know you are truly sharing your heart, you may be able to help with making progress. After all, Mercys don't like to cause negative emotions in others. They know all too well what those negative feelings are like and certainly don't want to cause them in well-meaning people. As odd as this may sound, and this is an example of it here, it is possible to use the light side of a Gift against the dark side of the same Gift, essentially to trick the Gift into doing some self-repair. I try to animate this idea a little later when I go into Gift Unicorns.

The Mercy can be controlled by fear of rejection, and can violate personal convictions as a result. A Mercy wants to blend in and get along with people, which is helpful to an extent, but too much of that instinct can create unhealthy levels of compromise. Mercys could be listening to someone talk about something they completely disagree with, but could be nodding their head slowly in agreement because they don't want to get caught up in confrontation.

Mercys may allow themselves to be treated poorly by someone, favoring avoiding further escalating conflicts. I have always wondered what percentage of wives abused in marriages, for example, are Mercy women? And for that matter, what percentage are men when the wife is the abuser?

Mercys can close their spirits down and seal them off to those they feel are insensitive. It takes them a while to get there, but when a Mercy concludes that someone is emotionally insensitive to others, the Mercy can shut down and disqualify the person. Some of the Gifts are not built to be naturally emotionally sensitive. I know, because I am one of them. It's hard for Mercys to imagine other people could not understand how insensitive they can be, unlike themselves.

The Mercy can calculate and exact emotional vengeance when they are wounded. After the World Trade Centers came down, we started calling the site Ground Zero. When a Mercy eventually blows emotionally, think of Ground Zero. A Mercy will set feelings aside, set feelings aside, set feelings aside, pressure building, and building, and building…until it blows with a vengeance that is hard to even calibrate. I say that because if a Mercy reaches that point where you are concerned, it may be a good idea to get out of the state for a few months. The simple reason is that Mercys understand more about your emotions than you do and, as such, can wreak havoc on you in ways you may not even be able to understand. I speak from experience. They know what will hurt you.

I remember hearing about a method of attack in the prison system, when an inmate would sneak up next to another when they were all taking steamy, hot showers and slice the kidney area of the victim with a sharp knife. Because of the hot water flowing, the method caused the prisoner to not realize a cut had occurred until blood became visible flowing into the floor drain. If a Mercy gets to this point of anger with you, make sure you're alone in the shower.

Mercys can become tiresome and burdensome to others when they are constantly controlled by their emotions. Mercys can be a lot of work. Exhausting even. Do you remember the Peanuts character who walked around in a cloud? Pig-Pen. Mercys who are unaware that their emotions are turned up so loud that it drowns out the other sounds of life around them can look like that. A Mercy cloud.

It has got to be hard at times for Mercys to not listen to voices in their heads and be defined by the fears in their hearts, but all the Gifts have equal challenges in darker areas. I say to the Mercys reading this: "Join the Gift Club." We are all facing similar mountains to climb. Hopefully, it will help you along to know you are not alone.

MERCY INTERVIEW

LOOKING INTO THE EYES OF A MERCY, I might see a softness, a yielding, a concern, or a silent desire, even a desperation to see into me to understand my feelings and intentions. Perhaps suspicious eyes that betray the Mercy believes I had some ill-will, or maybe that I thought the Mercy had done something wrong.

Most of the Gifts have a Polar Gift, one that would represent an obvious mirror inverse, strong where they are weak, weak where they are strong. The Polar Gift of the Mercy is the Prophet, which I will discuss and contrast with later.

It has taken me a long time to see and understand this, but every one of the Gifts also seems to neatly overlap another on either side of it. In other words, there is a natural circle that the Gifts form. I will explain overlapping in more detail later, but for now I will just share that the Mercy Gift overlaps with the next one we will look at and also the last one. What I am suggesting here is that there is a specific, natural, and circular ordering of the Gifts, which I call the Gift Wheel. I believe strongly that this order is a fact of nature, part of our biological structure and design that help to ensure the survival, even prospering, of the entire human race. I believe I can prove this through the reliability of this information and the inevitable truth of it, that people throughout the world can identify with one of these seven patterns on a motivational and intuitive level if they look deep enough.

I also find it interesting that there are clear and distinctive patterns in what each of the Gifts feels about The Gift System, if we could call it that.

Said differently, the predictable way each of the Gifts reacts to the existence of the Gifts is, in and of itself, further confirmation of the Gifts in my mind. Once they get past their initial mistrust, because Mercys have difficulty initially trusting anything, Mercys seem to initially like the idea of the Gifts because it can make them feel deeply affirmed, and also know that they are not alone, that there are other Mercys like them.

But after the honeymoon phase is over, Mercys get almost universally exasperated with the Gifts, I think because it makes them feel uncomfortable that their interiors are so visible. Simply, Mercys don't like having their covers blown. And over time, they seem to feel that people are looking down on them, or thinking that they are not measuring up somehow. Especially male Mercys.

If you had a Mercy daughter, and were trying to get her to eat broccoli, you may want to remember that Mercy children thrive on emotions and relationships. Mercys also tend to be visual and creative, perhaps musically. So, as silly as it might sound at first, any approach that utilizes these facts strategically is more likely to work. One approach might be to sit down together and have a feeling party about all the different feelings Mommy or Daddy has about loving the Mercy so much, and caring about her best interest, her future, and her overall well-being. Then discussing how important it is to eat well, and how it would make Mommy or Daddy feel so happy if they knew the Mercy was eating healthy foods, like broccoli. Another might be to have a broccoli day, and draw broccoli pictures together, and make up a broccoli song, and have broccoli friends over. Sound silly? Well, you can let the parent whose child is not eating broccoli explain how silly it is to you while your child is eating it.

I remember how my Mercy daughter Lauren could not recall a president's birthdate for a class test, but could tell you the exact shade of red his lips were in a picture on some obscure page she had seen weeks prior. I wondered if figuring out a way for her to draw a picture of his birthdate would be an easier way for her to remember it? Don't be afraid to be radically creative with Gift Knowledge.

Mercys make great interior decorators, graphic designers, social media consultants, kindergarten and grade school teachers, actors, singers, psychics, advocates, counselors, and especially caregivers (if they can overcome any medical considerations of those they are caring for, like blood for example, because Mercys have fragile stomachs for stuff like that). I don't in any way mean to limit by these examples and just offer these to help animate.

Mercys dream about harmony and union and relationships and sharing feelings and seeing everyone get along. They dream of a world free of conflict, where people can be happy and loving towards each other and towards them. They dream of being with their friends.

To name that Gift in one note, so to speak, watch when a story is being told that involves someone getting sick or someone being injured. If you see people in the crowd whose faces are changing different shades of green, whose eyes are dramatically living out the story as if it's actually happening to them, or as if they are actually seeing it, chances are pretty high those folks are Mercys.

If you want to mess with a Mercy, act horrified at how the Mercy affected someone emotionally. Say something like: "Oh, my gosh, I can't believe you did that to so and so. She was devastated." And then say you have to go to the bathroom really badly and will have to explain more when you get back. Let the Mercy squirm for a little bit. The worst thing in the world to a Mercy is to be (unintentionally) insensitive and also to be seen as insensitive by others. Mercys do not want to cause negative emotional affects.

When I ask myself who might be obvious Mercys in the celebrity world, one male and one female perhaps for fun, actor Jason Bateman and actress Jennifer Aniston pop up in my head. If you stop and notice it, the mention of these names tends to conjure positive emotional associations. They are both soothing and friendly in some unexplainable way. You can't quite put your finger on it, but watching their movies somehow makes you feel okay. They seem normal, accessible, and unthreatening. This may sound radical to you, but I am convinced that they both have the ability to reach through the screen and make emotional sense of the viewer while they are acting. In other words, on some level, they have already been able to emotionally intuit and visualize what you would be feeling as you watch.

I believe that Mercys are so much more sophisticated than the rest of us in terms of emotional intelligence, that they frequently know what we are going to feel way before we do. Therefore, they have a heightened ability to visualize cause and effect with respect to what the emotional need may be in the viewer, as well as what the viewer will feel in the future. And that's how Jason Bateman or Jennifer Aniston could know me, right through the screen, even though they have never met me.

Another example of the Mercy Gift in action is the Arlington Ladies.* This group volunteers to help spouses, children, and families navigate the emotional waters of losing a loved one in the line of duty with our nation's armed services. They will sit with you, stand with you, hold your hand, hug you, and let you cry in their arms. There might be some other Gifts in the group who have different motivations, but I would hope for a Mercy if I needed help there.

Woody Allen is a Mercy. Surprisingly, Johnny Carson was a Mercy. The people closest to Johnny all said he was one of the shyest people they ever knew. Johnny also wrestled with darker demons, demons that told him he was not worthy, not good enough, was undeserving of his success,

---

*The Arlington Ladies are a group of women who attend the funeral of every member of the United States armed forces who is buried at Arlington National Cemetery. The group also includes one man who is known as the Arlington Gentleman. The history of the group traces its existence to 1948, when Chief of Staff of the United States Air Force Hoyt Vandenberg and his wife Gladys witnessed young service members being buried without any family members present on one of their walks through the cemetery. Just a chaplain and a military honor guard, the standard attendees, were usually present. The lack of anyone honoring the young airman being buried prompted Gladys to form a group of members of the Officers' Wives Club to attend all Air Force funerals. In 1972, the wife of Army Chief of Staff General Creighton Abrams, Julia, founded the Army's version of the group. In 1985, the Navy also followed suit by creating a group of their own. The Coast Guard Arlington Ladies group formed in 2006. The Marine Corps Arlington Ladies were established in 2016.

and that disaster was looming for him. If you think about it, it makes common sense. Johnny Carson could read the emotions of an audience and seemed to intuit exactly what line or gesture or tone or pause or facial expression would telegraph the best emotional response from the audience. Emotional cause and effect. When Ed McMahon announced "Here's Johnny!" he was also unknowingly signaling Carson's transition into character. Johnny was not shy on stage because he was playing a different role, a persona he experienced as separate from himself.

And for any younger readers in the house, or for older readers who want to explain a Mercy to a younger person, Kermit the Frog is a Mercy. He is the most sensitive, gentlest, and most insecure of the Muppets. And he thrives on encouragement and hope. Even puppets can have a Gift.

If I were writing an ode to Mercys, I would start by reminding them that they should give themselves more credit. After all, you are not the most plentiful Gift by accident. We other Gifts sorely need you, to help us remember to feel, to be empathetic to others, and to care about our fellow man. There is a profound beauty in the Mercy Gift, a gentleness, a sensitivity, a tenderness, a vulnerability, an other-centeredness that all of us can learn from. Charles Darwin might have concluded that Mercys apply an evolutionary positive pressure on society as a whole.

Mᴇʀᴄʏ Uɴɪᴄᴏʀɴ

I ᴄᴀʟʟ ѕᴏᴍᴇᴏɴᴇ ᴀ "GɪFᴛ Uɴɪᴄᴏʀɴ" ᴡʜᴇɴ he or she is a great example of a fully functioning Gift, meaning the individual seems to have success-fully integrated the Gift into the person's inner being and adapted it to the world around them. The Gift Unicorn has become, perhaps, a best-case version of what the Gift can be. A Gift in full bloom. All Gift cylinders firing.

I think that a Gift Unicorn will also manifest the ability to use the light side of the Gift against the dark side of the Gift. In other words, the Gift Unicorn has learned how to trick the Gift in a way that results in an ability to self-repair just like doctors and scientists can use harmful bacteria to cure harmful bacteria in the right conditions, and programmers can remap computer viruses to find and resolve unwanted computer viruses. Using the strengths of the Gift against the weaknesses of the Gift.

I am picking Steven Spielberg as the Mercy Unicorn. His work in film embodies a higher form of emotional intelligence that, from my view, originates from his Mercy Gift. Notice also Steven Spielberg is modest, self-effacing, and fundamentally insecure. He is not a proud, arrogant Hollywood billionaire blockbuster filmmaker. It is entertaining to watch people question why a man of his success would be so modest and insecure, when the simple reason is that his Mercy Gift is operating normally.

If you look back at the body of his work, you will see a collection of art that reflects his ability to literally reach into us emotionally and make us feel things we may not even have been aware were inside of us. He is a master emotional safecracker and can unlock deep feelings using his Gift's power and insight.

Do you remember how his first blockbuster film, *Jaws*, affected you emotionally when you saw it for the first time? As a young director filming what became a severely over-budget and over-schedule movie, he saw what most around him likely did not, exactly what emotional impact the shark, and its constant absence, would have on viewers.

Look at a long list of his movies: *ET*, *The Color Purple*, *Jurassic Park*, *Close Encounters of the Third Kind*, *Empire of the Sun*, and *War of the Worlds*, just to name a few. The history of those movies can be seen as a tracing of a Mercy exploring and refining the art of emotional cause and effect, learning how to go spelunking deep into the psychology and heart of the viewer. His themes are common, universal, and deeply penetrating emotionally. Many of his characters embody classic Mercy traits: down-trodden, fragile, insecure, overwhelmed, deeply sensitive, trapped in various forms of inner chaos, yearning to be freed.

Inevitably, Spielberg's need and desire to be hopeful resonates throughout his work. I see him trying to calm himself and also therefore assuming that the rest of the world would necessarily need calming and reassurance as well. To his credit and the credit of all Mercys who can aspire to spreading calm and reassurance, I think Spielberg is right. We all do need it, even if we don't admit it, and even if we do not see it or feel it on the surface.

His Mercy masterpiece is therefore *Schindler's List*, the powerful film about the Holocaust. I have listened to Steven Spielberg talk about his work and his life and am convinced that he may have had an inner knowledge that all of his power would eventually culminate in a singular event. He speaks about the shame he felt towards his Jewish origins when he was growing up. Do you remember the Mercy in darkness who can set aside their personal convictions out of fear of rejection? He spoke about his feeling negative towards family members for years. Do you remember the Mercy in darkness who assumes negative motivations in others?

Yet as he grew and matured and learned, I believe he began to see that his becoming stronger and bolder as a story teller would have an even greater positive emotional effect on more people. In *Schindler's List*, all of these elements conspire to produce what might be called an ultimate Mercy movie. The black-and-white film, the frigid cold, the panicked sounds, the ashes falling from the sky, and the eyes…the eyes that you see in the film, windows to our common broken humanity. Spielberg also used his Gift to play with the emotions of the actors, jarring them throughout so they would feel the arrest of the situation, the blackness, the unpredictability, the randomness, and the hopelessness. It must have been supremely hard for a Mercy to get to a point where they could comprehend that telling a story about the Holocaust is ultimately calming and reassuring to people, even though you had to take them into a place of blackness and unimaginable horror to get there. And that is so because you can show them the way out, the light, the hope on the other side.

I sobbed like a baby at the end of *Schindler's List*, seeing all of the families in present time who were here as a result of the particular series of events portrayed in the film. I cried because of the sadness, the loss, the grief, the light, and the revenge of hope it all represented. And now I can also cry when I see it again, knowing that it was also a Gift triumph of sorts, where Spielberg could try and heal his own transgressions, his shame for his family's faith and heritage, and the negative assumptions he made about family members.

Mercy in Light over Mercy in Darkness. Using the Gift Force for good, even in telling the darker side of the Gift to take a seat. Victory over toxic shame, a malignancy that grew from the dark side of the Gift. He saw that he himself was in great need of encouragement, just as all Mercys need encouragement, and sought to encourage both himself and viewers through the language of storytelling, film, and music.

I pick Steven Spielberg as the Mercy Unicorn for one reason above all others. He has fought the dark tendencies of his Gift over time and in his ongoing attempt to overcome them and not be controlled by them, he has been able to give the world an emotional legacy of art that all common people can both experience and emotionally learn from. Good for him for not listening too hard to critics who tried to tear him down, those that have accused him of being the "McDonalds" of filmmakers, for ultimately telling all of them to kiss off through his art. Good for him for pushing through all the negative voices in his head that told him he was unloved or unacceptable.

Perhaps another gift he has left to us, beyond the films themselves, is a lesson about all of our own Gifts. It is our responsibility to acknowledge our Gift, to learn how to live in a way that is consistent with the best of the Gift, and to use the Gift for the greater good.

In Spielberg's words:

"All of my films come from the part of myself that I really can't articulate."

"I certainly have intuitive faculties, but I don't really analyze those."

"I don't really question them."

"It's like looking a gift horse in the mouth."

Exactly, Steven. It is like looking at a gift horse, a Mercy Gift Horse, right in the mouth.

When Spielberg finished *Schindler's List*, it would not surprise me at all if he could describe he had an experience that I would call a "Gift Release," a time when he could feel his Gift had come to fruition and achieved an ultimate purpose. As when you climb a great mountain, in this case one that took decades to ascend, and make it to the top where you could just sit in peace, listen to the air, look at creation and just breathe, fulfilled.

Server

Master Provider of Services

THE SERVER KEENLY OBSERVES OTHER PEOPLE towards the goal of anticipating their needs, as the Server finds value and meaning in life by providing services for others. A Server is relentless, indestructible, and tireless in service to people.

In the recent spate of hurricanes we have seen here in 2017, the Servers are the ones you see on television whose own homes have been decimated, wiped off the face of the earth, yet they are spending all of their waking hours working on other folk's homes. We ask them why. Well, because these other people need help of course.

Try serving a Server and you may see that the Server may find a way to get you to stop. Servers are more comfortable in life being on the giving, as opposed to the receiving, end of things.

Servers seem to be more on the plentiful side as well, but not quite as much as Mercys. I am guessing about 20% of the population. Perhaps it's because, in order for the bee hive to be successful, it needs lots of worker bees willing to endlessly toil for the greater good.

THIS LAST SUMMER, I DROVE FROM Chicago to Kenosha, Wisconsin, to have a simple lunch with an older woman at a restaurant, so I could hear how she was conjugating her retirement. It was a balmy day and we decided to eat out on the patio overlooking Lake Michigan.

With my Gift, I tend to leave fewer things to chance so I carry an alligator clip holder from my dentist's office in my pocket, the kind that they use to clip the paper towel over your shirt so you don't get messy. Some waiters carry them clipped on their lapels in higher-end restaurants, waiting for guys like me to try to imitate Harvey Keitel, the actor who always stuffs his napkin around his neck in mobster movies. Those waiters know how to snake-charm tips from diners using the clips. I like to wear my dining napkin Harvey Keitel-style and act like a mobster, since I have been known to eat like a buzz saw. Food was an issue sometimes growing up and I never really learned the art of fine dining. That's my excuse, at least.

So I asked our waitress, as is my custom, if there were any larger cloth napkins as opposed to the dinky, small paper ones. She said she did not think so but promised to check. A few minutes later, she reappeared at our table with a black cloth napkin. "Looks like we got lucky and found one." I said.

"Well, not actually," she said. "The woman over at the table with that younger gentleman gave it to me so that you could use it. I was right. The restaurant didn't have any." I immediately knew what Gift I was dealing with here.

Now it occurred to me that this woman may not have been entirely able to hear any of my conversation with the waitress. Her table was a fair distance. Sure, the wind could have blown and the sound may have carried as it reflected off the glass next to me. But I doubted it would have been entirely clear to her ears as far away as she was, especially with the ambient background noise of the cars driving by. It also occurred to me that people do not generally know what my alligator clips are when I dangle them in front of the eyes of a waitress or waiter, in my effort to animate my need and negotiate for a better napkin. As a matter of fact, the alligator clips could be mistaken for a lot of different things, having a lot of different uses. For the sake of decorum, that's as much as I am going to say about that.

The waitress added that the guest had walked out to her van and retrieved the black cloth napkin after she saw I needed it and had reassured that the napkin had been properly washed, as she worked in the restaurant arena herself. The guest insisted she did not need it back either. I guessed a small catering business was a more likely culprit; I was certain her van was a complete mess and had a ton of really unnecessary things in it, like freshly washed cloth black napkins waiting for guys like me who needed one.

I looked over at the woman, the woman who had gone to so much effort to overhear my expression, to study my need, and to persevere in the midst of *her* lunch to provide for *mine*. I made eye contact so I could peer into her spirit and announced in a clear voice so she and others could hear me that I was very grateful for her accommodation, that I really appreciated her inconvenience, and that I was going to have an even better lunch because of her selfless gesture. I watched her squirm a little bit, because I have some experience with how this affects Servers.

When you praise someone's Gift directly, when you speak in the Gift's language, it is powerful stuff and can affect people deeply. Remember that, in some ways, you are speaking to a person's deepest, innermost self. The Gift is who they really are, so don't be surprised if you see people responding in a profoundly emotional way. They may also be surprised and overwhelmed and not fully understand what is happening.

On one hand, she was moved that her efforts to serve were being seen and spoken to clearly. But on the other, she was ill at ease with my lengthier version of specific praise, because the Server does not serve for recognition. The goal is excellent service, not recognition, and Servers can even get pissed off if the world confuses that. Her look was frozen between these two powerful feelings. I had her Gift right in my headlights. When I finished eating, I turned to my lunch guest and said: "Watch this. I am going to have some fun."

It is entirely possible to be able to predict exactly what a person will do given a set of circumstances, because it is entirely possible to know how a Gift will respond. You can set your watch to it, just like the Atomic Clock. I quietly conspired with the waitress that I was going to pick up the other table's check, but that it was critical that she not reveal this until one table or the other left. By then, it would be too late and the Server could not cause all hell to break loose in her rejection of this service to *her*.

"Do you want to pay for her, or for her and her guest?" Good question. Which approach would cause the greater fireworks show? After all, I wanted my full entertainment value. "Both," I said summarily. My lunch guest, an obvious Mercy, was not really following what I was doing here, but I knew her Gift would be putting my emotional condition first and she just kept smiling. God bless her.

As the Server napkin woman began her waitress negotiations to leave, I heard her voice begin to rise, and then she rushed over to our table. "No, no, no..." she said. "You did not have to do that. There was no need for that. I just had some extras in the van and it was really no big deal. I have some others I could go get for you if you like, I have so many of them."

I had no intention of speaking to her. I was only going to address her Gift. I explained that it was truly remarkable that she could be capable of such great discernment when studying my particular need in the moment, especially given I was a complete stranger, and that her diligence in following through even at the price of her own convenience showed what a great heart she had.

I shared I had a sneaky suspicion that she played a similar role in many people's lives and frequently put herself aside in favor of serving others. By now, her eyes betrayed that I was speaking to her no longer. Her Gift was staring at me. It was time to go in for the kill. "I know this may be hard for you," I said, "but it is also important that you let others bless *you*, to let others serve you. I know it may not be comfortable for you, but it is also important to others that you allow them to convey to you how effective and meaningful your service is in their lives." I kept quiet after that and let it sink in.

Her eyes started welling up. Leaking. Healing. Understanding. Being known in the world. A moment of Gift Tenderness. We should all at least understand the Gifts, so we can be tender toward other people in the world when we are moved to. Lifting up others also lifts us up and helps to lift the world.

She could not speak anymore. Her lunch date who had joined us did not know what to say. My lunch guest was frozen also. There we were, four spirits, sitting on a deck at a restaurant in Kenosha, Wisconsin. No longer people. I carry that black cloth napkin today in my briefcase as a back-up. Each time I use it, I am reminded of all of it and of the importance of continuing to try to learn more.

LIGHT SERVER

A SERVER HAS A SPECIAL ABILITY TO perceive and anticipate the needs of others. Servers study people closely to see what those needs might be. They study habits, patterns, likes, and dislikes. They are driven to be there, waiting, ahead of time, so that just at the very moment you need something, they can be there to fulfill it. They are so good at this, so highly skilled, they frequently know what it is you need before you do, similar to how a Mercy can know what you will feel before you do.

A Server is a tireless worker. Servers remain self-sacrificial and selfless in their commitment to serve others in their assigned or self-assigned tasks. They are the ones who show up early and work late. They have the capacity to be literally relentless in their efforts and will toil from morning to night, seven days a week if needed.

Servers are extremely loyal people. Once a Server begins serving you and you benefit from the service, it is not uncommon for a longer relationship to ensue. Once a Server engages you in a longer-term relationship, the Server will stick with you to the bitter end, through thick and thin, through all kinds of ups and downs. Servers possess a capacity for loyalty so deep that even if you don't always regard or treat them well, they will try to stick with you.

A Server has an excellent memory for details that are pertinent to other people. Similar to a Mercy remembering dates and occasions that are special to you, the Server will download details about you as a way of cataloguing data for purposes of being able to serve you better. If you have daughters, the Server may remember you always like to give them a card and flowers for Valentine's Day, and may provide you with information on a flower sale a few days ahead of your even remembering this is the time of year for that.

A Server always remains conscious of thriftiness. Not only will Servers want to provide services to you, they won't want you to spend too much money along the way. Consequently, you will hear Servers say things like "You don't have to buy that. I have some of those at home and I can bring them tomorrow for you." Or "That's okay you don't have to pay me anything to do that for you. Don't worry about it."

A Server has a willingness to use personal funds to prevent projects from being hindered. Servers don't like things like money getting in the way of getting things done for you. If they run into a situation where a budget does not allow for something they know you need, or if they conclude you don't have the resources to take care of something that you would like to see done, Servers will pay for it themselves and insist you not make a fuss about it.

Servers hate red tape. They do not like obstacles that prevent them from serving effectively, so when they run across procedures or rules or protocols that hinder them from getting something done for someone, they can get really frustrated.

DARK SERVER

A SERVER CAN STRONGLY DISAPPROVE OF others' inabilities. Servers have to be careful with becoming impatient and frustrated with people they perceive as being incompetent, lazy, or ineffective. They can deem someone as essentially worthless if the person is not being productive or participating by doing a fair share. The Server may be saying inwardly, "Look at all I am doing and you are doing little or nothing in comparison."

Servers may overlook personal problem areas in their own lives because of being too busy serving others. The Server is essentially "other-centered" and focuses in an outward fashion on the needs and desires of other people. As such, Servers can frequently disregard looking within themselves, at areas that may need attention. Sometimes you can identify Servers by noticing that they may not be taking care of themselves enough…not enough sleep, unhealthy foods, and not enough (or any) focus on areas of personal growth and development.

A Server can find it very difficult to say no to people. When someone asks a Server for assistance, it would be rare to ever hear a refusal. I have noticed that even if Servers do say no verbally, they usually find a way to help you anyway, explaining that they are not agreeing to help you while they are helping you, telling you perhaps that this is an exception which, of course, it isn't. Or if they say no, if you wait a little bit, they will show up and ask you if you accomplished what you needed to, or if you still need help.

A Server needs to develop leadership qualities. Servers do not naturally see themselves as leaders since they are focused on putting others ahead of themselves. But Servers should also realize that there is an important concept called Servant Leadership, an idea that is replete among religions. If we see a Server in a leadership role, we are more likely to be able to understand what serving others represents and can emulate those important traits. Servers may need to consider that they can serve even more people through modeling service to others, at a greater rate of effectiveness, if they learn to lead.

Servers should become alert to areas that are not their responsibility to meet. They need to develop the ability to say no, precisely because they are usually in desperate need of boundaries. Boundaries are important to establish for emotional health and for understanding and regulating what people are and are not responsible for. Servers struggle with boundaries because they are often trying to do everything for everyone. It can be good on one hand to have fewer outer boundaries, because that makes it more likely for one to step over a line to help others, yet this can also lead to poorer internal emotional boundaries, which can lead to stressful forms of frustration.

Servers can feel rejected when their services are not needed and also have a hard time seeing the difference between their own identities and their services provided. In their emotional imagination, they are frequently one and the same. So if someone does not accept or does not need the Server's offered service, the Server can feel personally rejected. But services and people are not the same thing. I can still appreciate the offer or the intent and the person behind it, yet not need the service. As a result, sometimes Servers will impose their service on you, unwanted or not, because they don't want to feel rejected.

Servers need to learn how to delegate and to let other people serve them. If you want to watch a person sweat or squirm, explain to a Server that you are going to serve them and it is your intention to have them take a break and relax while you do all the work. They will typically break out in a cold sweat, become very uncomfortable, claim some excuse as to why they can't participate, or insist that they have to help too. A Server would be wise to understand that part of serving well is to allow people to graciously express their appreciation for the services, which sometimes could involve serving them back.

Servers often have low self-esteem. Because Servers faithfully and naturally put other people above themselves, it is a natural consequence that they can feel they are "less than" somehow. They struggle with not seeing themselves as worthy and important. But clearly they are valuable, and would do well to know and feel that.

Many Servers have lower digestive tract problems, usually because of worrying too much. Servers are world champion worriers. That's why they never throw anything out. They have basements and garages that are jammed full of what other folks might call junk, and purses and drawers that are crammed with stuff. They keep all these things in case someone else might need them, so when they do they can provide it to them at no charge. They constantly think about what other people are trying to get done…a room that is being remodeled where someone might need some extra storage space they can offer, or babysitting services for free. They live in a world of other people's needs and their stomachs can take a toll.

Don't be surprised to see some Pepto Bismol on a Server's desk.

SERVER INTERVIEW

IF YOU WERE LOOKING INTO THE EYES OF a Server, you would see two different and (some might say) opposing qualities, because a Server can look both expectant and tired at the same time. Servers are a little bit jumpy or jittery in general, and I think that is because they are constantly on the lookout for things they can help with, but they are also overworked as a result of all the serving, so they can also look a little bit run down.

Remember that I am making my way around what I see as a natural Wheel of Gifts. I am putting the Server right after the Mercy because these two Gifts have some obvious overlap, in the sense that they are both very "other-centered." The Mercy is consumed with other people's feelings while the Server is consumed with other people's needs. They both put others ahead of themselves, which is also connected to why they both struggle with self-esteem.

The Polar Gift of the Server is the Organizer, whom you have not met yet, so I will wait until I get into the Organizer Gift to discuss that.

I mentioned before that each of the Gifts seems to also have a similar reaction towards the Gift System. I have noticed that, a little bit like Mercys, Servers can initially really enjoy hearing about the Seven Gifts because it validates who they are. It seems to make them happy to be understood. But only to a point. They don't want to talk about it too much. Remember that the Server is focused on serving and they don't want to get distracted from that. They would rather serve than talk about serving.

If you have a Server child and you are trying to get your offspring to eat his or her broccoli, you would be wise to frame the matter as a service, to explain that healthy eating is a way the Server child can help Mommy and Daddy out.

I am not trying to be cute here when I say that Servers make great servers. Many waiters and waitresses that seem to really love what they do are Servers. If you think about it, that makes common sense, because the Gift gets to do what the Gift loves to do the whole shift. Servers make great support people, like customer service representatives and secretaries. And they make some of the best nurses in the whole wide world. Remember they are the worker bees of the hive, so anything that involves hard work and endless toil they are going to be good at. They are also great charity and relief workers, since self-sacrifice on behalf of others is at the center of who they are.

If you are a parent, take note of your child's Gift, because it can direct and guide. This is a good, practical example. If you have a Server daughter or son, get involved with helping out people in need, like in a food bank or homeless shelter or with poorer, elderly people who need help with yard work and grocery shopping. If there is a neighbor or a church member who is going through a rough patch with medical issues, show your Server child ways to engage. Your kid will glow with energy and purpose and start seeing and dreaming about new ways to help others.

That is also what a Server dreams about, being able to make a meaningful difference in other people's lives. Servers don't want a lot in return because in their utopia, they serve in a way that does not disrupt other people's resources too much. They just see a big smile on the faces of the people they are serving, implying they have done things well. In a Server's fantasy, the Server sees that you need a new shirt before you do, gives you the shirt off the Server's own back and it fits you like a glove because it turns out being exactly the right size.

If you were to name the Server Gift in one note, see one thing that would mark someone as being a Server, I would say that if you saw someone accidentally drop a fork off a table, or perhaps drop a cell phone to the floor while riding on the train, the person who reacts the fastest and with the most enthusiasm and abandon to jump up and get it for you, with no embarrassment or self-consciousness at all, is likely a Server.

If you want to mess with Servers, just act like you really needed their help and they just blew you off and obviously didn't care about assisting. Or another good one is acting like they blew too much of your money while helping you.

The matter of identifying celebrity Servers becomes a little bit more problematic than with some of the other Gifts, because Servers don't typically seek the spotlight, as they are content to help folks along behind the scenes. More typical ones would be public service figures, people devoted to helping others in need. Whenever I hear about doctors who travel to godforsaken, hopeless places to help people even though they put themselves in harm's way, I wonder if they are Servers.

But I think I can spot at least a couple more visible celebrity Servers. The actor Steve Buscemi is one. If you listen to him and even watch him while he is acting, you can see how other-centered he is, how he would hold the door open for you, quickly lend you a dollar if you needed one, help out a stranger, and put people ahead of himself. And you see how he is a little jumpy and watchful that way.

Gabourey Sidibe, the actress who played Precious,* has a Server aura about her. She radiates the feeling that she is willing to put others ahead of herself; that's one of the reasons she was able to play that character so well. She left you with a sad, empty feeling that she would never be put first in anything.

___

*In 1987, 16-year-old Precious (Gabourey Sidibe) lives in the Harlem neighborhood of New York City with her unemployed mother, Mary (Mo'Nique), who has long subjected her to physical, verbal and sexual abuse. Precious has also been sexually abused by her now-absent father, Carl (Rodney "Bear" Jackson), resulting in two pregnancies. The family resides in a Section 8 tenement and survives on welfare. Her first child, a daughter named Mongo (short for Mongoloid), has Down syndrome and is being cared for by Precious' grandmother, though Mary forces the family to pretend that Mongo lives with her and Precious so she can receive extra money from the government. When Precious' second pregnancy is discovered, her high school principal arranges for her to attend an alternative school, where she hopes Precious can change her life's direction. Precious finds a way out of her traumatic daily life by escaping into daydreams in which she is loved and appreciated.

Zac Brown, the country western singer, is an obvious Server. He is soft-spoken, modest, unassuming, and puts everyone else first. When you go to one of his concerts, he will even cook you a meal and clean up after you before he plays for you. He calls it Eat and Greet. He also started a summer camp to help kids with ADD and autism and he named his second album *You Get What You Give*. That's a Server album name if there ever was one.

His buddy, singer Alan Jackson, gave him a 1966 Cadillac Eldorado as a gift. He told Zac he gave it to him as a thank you for being allowed to play with him, but I'll bet you Alan saw Zac was doing everything for everyone else, and decided it was time to turn the tables on the Server, as I did when I bought that Server gal lunch in Kenosha.

Catherine Keener is the actress who played in the movie *The 40-Year-Old Virgin* and she also radiates Server. Out of all the actresses in the whole wide world, no one can play a single, working mom with way too many responsibilities, too little resources to do all she would like to do, a perpetual drive to do everything for everyone else around her, and virtually nothing for herself. I contend she can play that better than anyone else because she animates Server out of her own (inner) backyard.

In the world of cars, you can tell that a vehicle is an El Camino by knowing that if it looks like a car in the front but like a truck in the back, it is a Chevrolet El Camino. Or the other possibility is a Ford Ranchero. Have there ever been any cooler names for something you drove? *Elllll Cameeenooo. Rancherrrooo.* Something about the way those names roll off the tongue. Like *Tex-Mex.* But I bring the matter up now, how you know you are looking at an El Camino or a Ranchero, because I want to go back to the nurse on the train at the beginning of this whole tale. She was a Server all day long. A Server through and through. And she was an easy call. Can you see it now? I know it may have sounded like I was acting like a savant or just making stuff up. You just get used to spotting El Caminos, even if other folks aren't familiar with them, just like the nurse's friend wasn't, the friend who went all the way back to grade school.

If I were to write an ode to the Server, I would share that I believe this Gift is the most holy, the godliest, and the most spiritual of them all. Whether you believe in a God or not, whether you are Jewish or Christian or Muslim or Hindu, I think we all could agree that there is something universal and moving in the Jesus story, the idea of sacrificing all for another. I feel that Servers are closest to this notion of God and holiness if you can look through that lens for a moment. There is a profound beauty in setting yourself aside for another, for raising another above yourself, for giving someone else all you have and then some.

Server Unicorn

So with that ode to the Server as a backdrop, it may come as no surprise that I am picking Pope Francis as the Server Unicorn. You may be thinking to yourself well of course a reverend or a priest might be inclined to serve, because that is part of a religious calling. But that doesn't mean they are Servers per se. I am picking Pope Francis for reasons that have more to do with him personally doing things that don't come naturally to him or his Gift, like I did with our last Gift Unicorn, Mr. Spielberg.

Let me first address why I think Pope Francis appears to be a Server. Now I would imagine many priests would mainly be Mercys, Servers, or Prophets, because that would make Gift Sense…the Mercy for the motivation to be empathetic, the Server for the motivation towards service, and the Prophet (as we will explore later) for the motivation towards righteousness. This is basic Gift Algebra.

I think Pope Francis's "Gift Tell" is his frugality. When they made him pope and showed him his new palatial quarters, he summarily rejected the trappings in favor of staying in an inexpensive, spartan, modest apartment. When they presented him with limousines to ride around in, he rejected them in favor of driving around his old Fiat or riding the bus with the junior popes. And he pays for his apartment, his lodgings, his car, and his bus fare out of his own pocket.

I think it is clear that he has a strong motivation to save a few bucks for the faithful while he is being pope. He does not take kindly to priests that have accumulated wealth, Italian villas, expensive art and furniture, and unnecessarily gaudy clothes and jewelry. That is completely instinctual for a Server, part of the basic motivation. Not only are Servers driven to serve you, they are driven to do it inexpensively. If you are a self-indulgent priest wandering around the Vatican, your days may be numbered.

Pope Francis also has a gentleness to him that is not feigned. He does not seem excessively caught up in emotions of others, like a Mercy might be. He is all about service. If you watch him as he travels the world, notice how he cannot help himself but assist when he sees a need.

On a recent trip, he stopped the whole papal procession to help a woman who had fallen down. Then on the plane he was flying on, he married a couple right on the spot after hearing about their wedding they had missed due to unexpected circumstances. This pope, this world leader, cannot help himself but serve others in ways big and small. If his assistant dropped something by accident, I swear this pope would pick it up as a courtesy.

But at the end of the day, I am picking him as a Gift Unicorn because he has disciplined himself to do something that does not come naturally to the Server, and that is to lead others. You can see it in his eyes, his modesty, the absence of any desire for power or prestige, and his raising up of others above himself. It's not an act. It's as real as it gets. But in the midst of all of it, he has accepted the idea that his charge is to try and serve even more, even better, through the mantle of leadership.

I know it may sound anachronistic, but you will never see a better example of Servant Leadership, or a Server Leader, than Pope Francis. This man would help you clean your toilet if he saw you needed help with it and do it happily. Washing the feet of others is a natural (Gift) act for him.

I wish I could have talked him out of donating the white Lamborghini that was made for him, though. That was like a Pope El Camino. I would have said to him that he could have served the Italian police by playing go-karts with them so they could test out their engines and become more prepared for the real bad guys. I'll bet they would not ever issue Pope Francis any tickets when he played, eliminating any need for him to rinse off any trees.

I absolutely love it when Pope Francis asks everyone to pray for him, because that's hard for a Server, to ask others to serve him. It's no surprise that Pope Francis said love *"is the concrete service we give to each other…love is service! A humble service, done in silence and hiddenness."*

Exhorter

Life of the Party of Life

Of all the Gifts, the Exhorter is the most enthusiastic, excited, upbeat, encouraging, and friendly. Exhorters are a walking good mood and if they are not in a good mood themselves, which is generally a rarity, they will put themselves in a good mood by putting you in one.

Exhorters are antsy and anxious and restless. They want to keep moving from one thing to the next and will buck up against anything that bogs them down.

They wake up in the morning and start thinking about all the ways they can get people to like them even more. They will notice exactly what you like and don't like, in fractions of a second, and move quickly to put themselves right in the middle of what you do like.

Put Exhorters in a slow-moving research project and you may need to call the police when they somehow escape from that prison or call an ambulance when they have run out of what they consider air. Life is a fast-moving party for the Exhorter, or at least the Exhorter thinks it should be; Exhorters love being the center of attention, right in the middle of it all.

Exhorters seem to be less present than Servers, although not by much. I am guessing about 12.5% of the population. This proportion also seems to make common sense, because we need cheerleaders, encouragers, sparklers if you will, but not an overabundance of them. Otherwise, we would be partying all the time and nothing would get done.

WHEN THE CAT IN THE HAT CAME INTO the home of the two children whose mother and father were away, he brought along a box with Thing One and Thing Two in it. Full of restless energy and a complete lack of respect for authority, they came ready to start a party, light the place up, and start general mayhem by flying kites around indoors. The Things were both Exhorters.

Thing One and Thing Two also showed up at my house on a very rainy day, at the lowest point of my life. I had lost my daughter, my business, my first marriage, and the full use of my foot. My right heel had shattered when I came down off a ladder building a basketball goal for my two daughters. My father said any one of those four things could bring a man down. My darkness was deep. I tried to put out the flames of fires within me with Kentucky bourbon and red wine, sometimes together. It didn't work. The fires just smoldered.

At some point along the way, two of my closest friends decided they would have no more of it. Exhorter One told me I should move into a sister industry and start life anew. I was a natural planner, intuitively orderly, and would be wonderful in a new role. Exhorter Two agreed, and both of them relentlessly called me, stayed in touch, encouraged, and painted rosy pictures of the future. I thought they were both insane. Stone-cold crazy. You don't revamp on that scale at my age.

But for every objection I offered, there was always an answer. "Stop worrying so much! Everything will work out! Don't look at the negative, look at the positive! It'll be great!" Neither would allow me to stay in depression. They tag-teamed me like pro wrestlers and conspired with one another to help me regain my emotional and spiritual footing. My heart was weak and worn out. Maybe for that reason I was more pliable and vulnerable. I found myself starting to actually listen to them. Eventually their fervent stories started sounding less implausible to me. The picture of a hopeful future started becoming more real. I started living in their vision more and more in my mind. I was trying on these new clothes they had made for me and feeling them start to fit.

They made calls, cajoled people, fostered connections, made backroom deals, called in markers, networked, and laughed and laughed about how grateful I was going to be to them. When Exhorter Two was told there was no space for me at the proposed environ, he said: "When Michael Jordan shows up to play, you make a space." Now I had a professional sports agent, an agent who clearly found an ally in hyperbole. I found myself caught up and entangled in their ridiculous, far-fetched, fantastical wave of optimism. With their undistracted encouragement, I leaped into this new world they had described, and claimed a new role as my own. When I saw things in that new world that did not match the vivid descriptions Thing One and Thing Two had painted for me, I just assumed I would have to work a little harder to make them that way.

About six months after I had jumped, seeing now that I had made it safely, I could look back and more soberly reflect on what exactly had just happened. "You told me a lot of things that just were not true, things you could not have known, and you had no idea whether this would work out or not. You basically made a lot of it up."

"Yes, David," the Things said. "That is true, but you would not have done it if we hadn't approached it that way. You're too stubborn to have listened. You're much happier now, you're not as dark, and you have a new sense of purpose and we knew you'd figure things out. We knew you had a comeback in you. We did it for your own good."

Thank God for these crazy Exhorters. No one else would have had the heart, the audacity, the imagination, or the energy. I still can't believe it. I felt like I had been blindfolded and they said, "Just take one big step straight in front of you. You'll be fine. Just do it. It'll be great." And when

I completed that step I took the blindfold off and looked back and down and saw a precipitous drop into an infinite canyon.

"I could have fallen into the canyon," I said.

"Yes, you could have," they now admitted. "But you didn't."

Truth be told, I can't write this without my eyes filling up with tears. People on my train wonder if I am okay as I am writing. I wish I could tell them all. Exhorters see the best in us, what we can be, and they will use any lengths, reasonable or not, truthful or not, to help us get there. The Things helped me claim something that was in me, a part of me that I could not see or understand because I can't smell myself or see myself sometimes. I am standing too close to the wall to be able to look up and see the building. I'll even go so far as to say they may have saved my life. They were like Marines who saw a man down, committed to never leave one behind.

So what do you do to say thanks after all of that? Use a little Gift Knowledge. There is one thing in the physical world that an Exhorter may love more than anything else, a weakness: a trophy or an award or a plaque. Those symbolize recognition and Exhorters fantasize about being recognized. It makes them glow.

So I went to a local craftsman, the best trophy maker in Chicago, and had two identical plaques made for Thing One and Thing Two. They accepted them as if they were on the award stand representing the United States at the Olympics. There was an unexpected normalcy in their reactions, as if they knew they were in the Olympics all along, and that this was a just reward. Those plaques hang in places special to them to this day, one in a home and one in an office. They tell me they look at them as often as they can. When they do, they smile in a way that only Exhorters can.

EXHORTER
Lifetime Achievement Award

*In recognition of this Exhorter's tireless encouragement
and urging along when exalting others,
Relentless optimism (even if not always justified) on others' behalf,
Never-ending pursuit of celebrating and valuing the essence of
fellow people...
All lovingly done so that others might be able to come to a deeper
and
more meaningful place of self-fruition and contentment,
Calling on them to ultimately experience their spirits
soaring within them...
Presented on behalf of all of those you have touched.*

I noticed that the Things moved on quickly after they saw I was okay. Exhorters are antsy and they need to keep moving. They left fast in favor of the next projects they had in their Exhorter cues.

It was fun telling Thing One and Thing Two that they had made the book. They took the news just like it was a weather report, as if of course they would be written about in a book because after all, the work they do is important and worthy of recognition, just like when I presented them with their sacred plaques. I have to agree with them. It is important work that they do. Every time I see their numbers appear on my phone, I always pick up, because I know they won't let me get off the phone until they are satisfied I am laughing sufficiently or feeling good about my life in general.

I have an office next to an Exhorter these days. I saw he was studying for a test on his computer for a recertification of some sort. I did not have to see his eyes to know exactly what he was feeling. I said to his back: "Okay, imagine that you were captured by Isis and they offered you a choice. You could either be burned alive inside of a steel cage or be forced to study for recertification testing. Which would you take?" Before I had even finished my last sentence, he said to the screen: "Neither. And I would save everyone a lot of time." Even in considering the process of his own torture and death, the Exhorter is restless and fidgety and doesn't want to get bogged down and mired in details. "I would take the can of gasoline, pour it over my own head, and light the match myself."

I suspect recertification testing and Exhorters won't ever get along very well, even with extensive therapy. The Exhorter feels a strong sense of urgency driven by the fact that there are still a lot of people left in the world who have not had the good fortune of meeting them. So many people, so many hearts, so many people waiting to like them.

Time is wasting. Let's get out of here. Let's get going!

Light Exhorter

AN EXHORTER IS ANXIOUS TO PLEASE. Exhorters want to figure out quickly what makes you happy and uplifted. They will notice everything they can about you and try to pick up your wavelength quickly. They want you to like them. They want you to be their friend. They want to be friends with everyone. They don't want to let you down. They want you to be happy when you see them.

They enjoy recognition for accomplishments, success, or athletics. It affirms for them that they have been pleasing and that people like them. Many Exhorters have a special area, shelf, or room for their trophies, which they will regularly clean and keep presentable, as both a testimony to their being recognized and a way of reliving all of it.

Exhorters see the importance of the individual. They thrive on helping people learn to see themselves as valuable and trying to help bring them to fruition. They love to encourage people and to help them get to a better place, where they can become who they are capable of being, where they can truly bloom. Exhorters live to lift people up. You won't likely hear an Exhorter gossiping about someone, spreading bad news about them, stirring the pot of negativity. They don't want to tear people down.

Exhorters are natural born networkers. They will say things like "Oh…I have to introduce you to Jack. He's really smart in this particular area." They will also be the ones holding the fund-raising event at their home for the church or the kids' school. Connections. It's all about connections and connecting people with one another. The Exhorter is the network hub. All the social jacks get plugged into the Exhorter.

An Exhorter typically always has a positive outlook. Exhorters are incessantly optimistic, always preferring to look away from or past the negatives in situations. And they won't let things like facts or statistics get in the way. If you told an Exhorter you only had a one-in-a-million chance of becoming the mayor of Chicago, you would hear them exclaim how great that is because you actually do have a chance! Let's go for it!

Exhorters are quick to grasp concepts. An Exhorter has an exceptional ability to visualize new and better solutions for situations. Exhorters typically do not see themselves as being bound by things like rules or conventions, so they have an innate ability to think past predictable shapes and point to some new and different form. They are extremely creative.

Exhorters see chronological sequence and like to put things into steps or stages. Exhorters love book titles that start with "Eight Steps to..." or "Ten Ways to Improve…" They like to put things into an order that they or someone else can follow to get to a destination. They are eager to go through the steps and to help you through them as well.

Exhorters are encouraging speakers and can lift up their audience. All authentic motivational speakers are Exhorters. Exhorters are very energetic; their batteries always seem to be fully charged. If there happens to be a microphone anywhere close, the Exhorter will grab it and fire things up. Not only are they not afraid of the stage, they search for stages.

Exhorters are good communicators and can tell stories charismatically. Once Papa showed me an ancient parchment of paper, something so old you would likely only see it in a museum. It was an old award certificate from when Papa was in second grade, full of old classroom smells of chalk and aging cardboard boxes and farm dust from times past, a recognition of his special skill, kept over decades as a personal Exhorter treasure for him, perhaps his form of a trophy. It said in gothic lettering: "Special Skill: Storytelling."

All Exhorters make friends easily, so be careful of your time if you accompany an Exhorter somewhere, like to lunch or to a ball game. You may never get there because the Exhorter will stop to chat it up with any familiar face and some faces that are not familiar. You may find yourself talking to your Exhorter buddy in the elevator when he gives you a just a second signal and starts chatting up the person he does not even know who is riding with you. For the Exhorter, every life situation is simply another opportunity to make a friend, to gain someone's affection, and to have that person feel uplifted by all of it in the process.

Exhorters remain concerned about applying things in their own lives, as they do not want to be hypocritical, and want to walk the walk not just talk the talk. Typically Exhorters are responsive to spiritual conviction, meaning that they don't want to be a phony. They are hard on themselves that way and expect a lot from themselves.

Dark Exhorter

AN EXHORTER WILL BEND PERSONAL convictions in order to gain the approval of others. The internal operating directive of Exhorters that compels them to please people and to want others to like them also poses a serious threat to principles and strongly-held beliefs. The Exhorter needs to develop the ability to take a stand for what is right, regardless of the consequences and how it affects popularity.

Exhorters can develop mechanical responses, especially on topics they deem unimportant to their functioning. Exhorters typically see things like planning, scheduling, and protocols as hindrances to just hurrying up and getting things done. Don't be surprised if you hear them responding in a mechanical and disconnected tone, the same tone you might hear if a classroom teacher forced a student to say "I will never shoot spitballs again in class" out loud, a hundred times.

For the Exhorter, truth can be a gray, even an arbitrary area. Objective researchers might be inclined to let theory develop around facts but for the Exhorter, facts will seem to magically appear around a theory. The Exhorter is more focused on the moment, the momentum of things, and staying in motion. To convince others, Exhorters have a tendency to just make stuff up because it is faster and more convenient. As such, Exhorters routinely exaggerate. Some folks might call this lying. But Exhorters see exaggeration as a means to an end, more fuel for their enterprise, painting things in a way that makes their imaginary world seem completely real. Exhorters can think that the more charismatically and energetically they proclaim something, the truer it becomes. Truth can become an invention, like promotion or branding.

Exhorters can close their spirits down and become retaliatory when pushed too far in confrontations. Similar to Mercys, it takes quite a bit to get Exhorters to a point where they will blow up. Maybe that's why Mercys and Exhorters can really explode. It's like compressed gas that builds up like a pressure cooker and then blows the lid off. The few times I have seen an Exhorter get to this point have been nothing short of spectacular and I am grateful that I was not the one that set them off.

Exhorters are reserved in their personal commitment to people. While it is true that Exhorters have more friends than probably all the other Gifts combined, they may not have a lot of truly close friends. That's largely due to them feeling insecure because they don't want you to get too close and see their flaws. They are afraid that if you see them for who they really are, you may not like them as much. And they really need you to like them.

For example, they typically don't like being given presents. They want to be the one giving the present, not receiving it, similar to a Server not wanting to allow being served themselves. Both Gifts in these circumstances want to be in control.

Exhorters can be so spontaneous that they cause other people's schedules to be disrupted. Exhorters do everything on the fly. You may be on your way home from work and your Exhorter buddy might call you and say "Hey! Let's take the train into the city and we'll watch the game at this really cool sports bar next to Wrigley Field. It'll be a blast!" But then you try to explain to your buddy that it will take an hour and a half each way, that you will therefore miss the first third of the game, and that you will be home no sooner than 1:00 AM in the morning, which will likely threaten the peace of your marriage and throw a wrench in your need to be up early to prepare for an important business presentation the next morning.

Your Exhorter buddy might say: "Oh, come on, stop being such a stick in the mud! You're worrying too much! Everything will be fine. The train will be faster than you think, your wife will totally understand, and you will do absolutely great tomorrow at work! You always do! I have confidence in you man! You're the best! I'll meet you at the train station in a few minutes." Click.

And the next thing you know, your morning alarm is going off, you're hungover, you woke up on the couch, and you forgot where you are employed. When you talk to your buddy later that day, he says: "Wasn't that awesome? We met so many cool people. Let's light the candle again tonight. Where do you want to go?"

A party follows Exhorters everywhere they go. A party waiting to happen.

Exhorter Interview

IF YOU WERE TO LOOK INTO THE EYES OF AN Exhorter, you would see the same eyes that you see when you're dangling a piece of yarn in front of a cat, or holding a ball in front of a dog. The Exhorter is ready to play, always game.

The Polar Gift of the Exhorter is the Teacher and since you have not met the Teacher yet, I will defer that comparison until later.

On our Gift Wheel, the Exhorter overlaps with the Server because both Gifts are natural-born people-pleasers, only in different ways. The Server has a real strong urge to please through acts of service and meeting people's practical needs, while the Exhorter tries to please by making folks happy, by helping them feel encouraged, and by bringing about fun and folly.

The Exhorter loves the idea of the Seven Gifts in general. As soon as you explain the Gifts to Exhorters, they immediately pick up that this is a way to see more into the core of people, to understand them better, to perceive more of who they really are. That fits right into the wheelhouse of the Exhorter. They may intuitively know that Gift Knowledge may help them do their Exhorter jobs better. As I have said before, more than any other Gift, the Exhorter sees the value of the individual and wants to help bring about the fruition of that individual's potential.

That's what Exhorters dream about. Elation for the Exhorter would look like having encouraged and coached and helped someone along who then began to soar and the Exhorter subsequently standing in front of a crowd being recognized, getting an award for having helped another person to that new height. That would be an out of body experience for an Exhorter. All cylinders firing. I have seen moments like that with my own eyes, because Exhorters make the best damned coaches— competitive, endlessly energetic, enthusiastic, possessing this uncanny ability to make every player feel unique and special. So when you see a coach like that up on a stage accepting the team's award for winning the championship, take note that you are also looking at the sun's rays spilled over a bed of new-fallen snow, just like the HVAC man saw through the smudged windows of his old van at the beginning of this Gift Tale. Reverence.

If you have an Exhorter child and you want your child to eat his or her broccoli, chances are the child is competitive in something. Maybe a young girl might be involved in tumbling, ballet, or soccer. Maybe a young boy would be competing in basketball, hockey, or baseball. Or maybe all of those examples would be switched around, since boys and girls can be good at all those things. You might tap into the Exhorter's competitive nature and convey one can become an even better sprinter by eating broccoli.

Exhorters are natural born salespeople and can sell anything to anyone. No one can sell like an Exhorter can sell. Like I said before, they make great coaches and athletes and they also are great comedians, emcees, and announcers.

It's easy to name that Gift in one note with Exhorters, because they can't possibly conceal who they are, just like a star in the sky can't hide anywhere for long. As proof of this fact, I was sitting in a coffee shop between work meetings taking a pause to write in my Gift Book, when I walked into the boy's room to expel some of my coffee. I came out of my stall, washed my hands thoroughly like my mother and wife have both taught me, and started straightening my tie and training my wet hands back over my hair. A guy steps up behind me, ready to use the sink next, looks at me in the mirror with a big smile on his face and exclaims: "You look great! You got it all going on today!" Busted. An Exhorter all day long. I knew exactly who he was, so I thought I would acknowledge his Exhorter service. "Thanks." I said. "I needed that. At fifty-five, I will take that when it shows up. You just made my morning." And that Exhorter looked back at me with an expression that said he felt good about having done his Exhorter job making me feel good. Exhorters are not hard to spot.

If you want to mess with an Exhorter, wait until one is talking in front of a group of people, potentially a big gathering, and then start making visible facial expressions as if the Exhorter is saying something really offensive or hurtful. Even if the crowd has hundreds of people in it, when the Exhorter notices your discomfort, the rest of the crowd will disappear in the Exhorter's mind, and only you will be left. Then, the Exhorter will change a speech to try to lure you.

It's not too hard to come up with celebrity Exhorter examples, since Exhorters gravitate towards the spotlight. Turn on *Saturday Night Live* and you may be able to quickly see that almost every single one of the "Not Ready For Prime-Time Players" is an Exhorter, like Jimmy Fallon and Tina Fey. Comedians are almost always Exhorters: Will Ferrell, Kevin Hart, Vince Vaughn, Jonah Hill, Seth Rogan, Jerry Seinfeld, etc. Bill Murray is an Exhorter.

A very high percentage of professional athletes are Exhorters, given that Exhorters are very competitive and generally gifted athletically. By the way, don't piss off Exhorters on the athletic field, because they will wax you for it. Instead, tell Exhorters they are playing great, even unbelievably. That can distract them into imagining award ceremonies in their heads and you may see them start missing shots then. Stick a wrapped present on the tee box at the golf course before your Exhorter buddy hits and tell him you got him a gift that you want him to open at the end of the round. Watch him start to sweat. He'll likely pull his drive way to one side or the other.

Derrick Young used to work at a small company I owned some years back. I used to spend time with him after hours, listening to him share how he felt like he had not really found a vocation that really fit him well. Derrick loved good nutrition and working out and he especially wanted to help encourage others to get to a better place in these areas. We talked about his Exhorter Gift a lot. Like all Exhorters I know, he took to the Gift information like a fish to water. Derrick became very aware of the need to match his natural, intuitive impulses to a career.

One day at work, I walked into a bullpen with a bunch of people standing around in a circle. I was told to be quiet because Derrick was doing the Scorpion. I stuck my head over someone's shoulder and saw him contorted and frozen in an impossible shape. I calculated that I could probably only do about an eighth of the Scorpion.

I don't think Derrick's dad knows about the Seven Gifts, but he sure knows his son well. He was reading the Chicago South Side paper one morning and saw that a local news channel was interviewing for a traffic broadcaster. Derrick's dad told him he should go interview, that Derrick would be a natural at that. When Derrick balked, to his parental credit, his dad reminded him how the document read that was sitting down at the Cook County Recorder of Deeds offices, one that was related to the ownership of the two-flat Derrick was living in.

Derrick did really well in the interview. Everyone seemed to like him. Surprise, surprise. Out of hundreds of applicants, he walked out with the trophy. So every morning I tune in and watch Derrick as I get my coffee and straighten my tie. He is always bubbly, always smiling, and always full of energy. All the other newscasters obviously love him. They are mostly women who also remind viewers from time to time that they believe Derrick is, for the moment, Chicago's most eligible bachelor.

If I see him say something on the morning news that harkens in the direction of our shared history, some insight that only the common thread of time and friendship can reward, I text him and he texts me back. Ha-ha-ha, he says. Watching my friend on the screen as I start my day reminds me not to be a jerk, not to take life too seriously, and to see the value in others and live in the moment. And damned if Derrick didn't end up encouraging me too in my new diet and exercise protocol.

You see, these days the savvy news executives send Derrick out on all the exercise assignments and tape the playful circus that ensues. He climbs the stairs of the John Hancock Tower to raise funds for the disenfranchised, conducts disciplined Yoga poses, or takes on a marathon run, all for Channel Two Chicago. He even did the Scorpion one day in the bullpen at the CBS studios and the savvy executives broadcast it on television so everyone could see it. I am guessing I am up to being able to do about a quarter of a Scorpion these days. I know Derrick will keep encouraging me to make progress.

My ode to the Exhorter is a simple one and involves some measure of gratitude. Thanks to the Exhorters of this fine world that make it a place that is fuller of fun, laughter, and excitement. Thanks for not giving up on us when we are blue and down and sad. Thanks for trying to see the best in us and for helping us get to a better place. Thanks for helping those of us who are too intense to learn how lighten up and smile more often and live in the moment.

Exhorter Unicorn

I am picking one of Chicago's own as the Exhorter Gift Unicorn: Chance the Rapper. Chancelor Jonathan Bennett was born in a West Chatham neighborhood and used his Exhorter Gift to become a breakout rapper, singer, record producer, and actor.

Watch him perform and you will easily see his upbeat restlessness, energy, and sparkle. Chance could have taken his fame, money, and celebrity and spent the rest of his days partying hard and chasing girls and driving expensive cars, but he didn't. He remembered his roots and has developed into one of the finest models for Chicago's inner-city youth. He has also become a major philanthropist for important causes like the ailing Chicago Public School system. Not too long ago, Chance wrote a personal check for a million dollars to the CPS, a gesture that said "Shut up and put up."

One of the reasons I am picking Chance is that he has found a brilliant way to both encourage people and take a stand at the same time as a political activist. And that's not necessarily natural for an Exhorter, taking a stand that is, because taking a stand always risks alienating some people, and an Exhorter does not naturally want to do that.

I have to say that Chance is filling an important gap in today's racial, social, and cultural conversation. I for one have a hard time watching professional athletes refusing to stand for the national anthem, athletes that will leave the stadium after the game driving half-a-million-dollar supercars. I am one of the last Babyboomers and grew up in a generation where if you did not stand for the national anthem in class, the principal would come down for a visit with a wooden paddleboard. My grade school principal was Pearl Antram and her husband had some wood tools and machinery in his basement, evidenced by the fact that he was able to custom drill holes in the face of Mrs. Antram's paddleboard. That way, when she smacked your backside with it, you would feel quite a bit more of it. That paddleboard still makes my butt ache even just thinking about it.

This may be hard for younger readers to believe but, frankly, I don't see standing for the anthem or Mrs. Antram's paddleboard as bad things. Learning respect, self-discipline, and discovering the fact that there are some hard edges in life are all okay in my book. Even as a White man in the suburbs these days, when the police pull me over because I'm going too fast in my adult go-kart, I make sure and roll down all the tinted windows in the car, even if it is Chicago-cold out and stick both arms out real far so they can see them. The police have hard enough jobs as it is and I want to make things safer for all involved. I certainly would not want to be walking up to drivers I did not know all day long, especially angry ones.

We are living in a time of social upheaval, where all of us seem to be wrestling with questions of how we go about calling attention to important societal, racial, and gender issues. And to learn how to emphasize these matters in ways that don't become distractions in and of themselves. I would like to see efforts like Black Lives Matter legitimized further. That's what Chance does. He is legit, as they say. He's the real deal. Even though he grew up in more comfortable middle-class surroundings, he found his way back to people less fortunate than him. If I was at a game and Chance was next to me and he took a knee for the anthem, I would ask him if he wouldn't mind me asking him a question. I suspect he wouldn't object.

Then I would pull off my Uncle Dave's dog tags from my chest, military dog tags that I have worn for over forty years now and I would show them to Chance. I would explain to him I am an American too, just like he is, and I love this America, and would he please be so kind as to explain to me exactly what was in his heart and in his mind when he sat down for the anthem, because it brought me some pain, so I know he must be feeling some pain too. I would listen to exactly what he had to say.

Chance is the real thing.

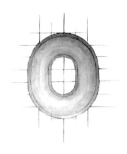

ORGANIZER

RULER

THE ORGANIZER IS ALL ABOUT ORDER, structure, focus, and planning. Organizers are intense by nature and are natural born leaders. They have a knack for being able to see where things started, where things are going, and where things will eventually end up.

If you want to get an idea of how Organizers see things, imagine a hallway that you step into that has mirrors on the walls to your left and right. When you turn to one side, you see the sequence of mirrors reflected back and forth trailing off in the distance. That's how we Organizers experience life. Organizers see the sequence in things and can be totally resolved and intractable in their focus and objectives as a result.

Someone is not an Organizer if the person is making obvious, outward attempts at being organized, like numbering socks in an attempt to wear them evenly over time. The Organizer organizes naturally and organically, so in the Organizer's world, the socks would be sorted automatically according to where they were placed in the drawer. Numbers would be a redundancy. When you tell people you're an Organizer and they perk up and exclaim that they are really organized too, they are definitely not Organizers.

Organizers, when planning and executing their plans, can easily forget that people have these things called feelings. That's our downfall.

Organizers seem to be the second rarest of the Gifts. I am going to say about 9% of the population. How many Napoleons do you really need? If you had too many Organizers, they may start killing one another off, just like cock roosters fight when trapped in the same pen.

LAST HALLOWEEN, I NOTICED THAT SOME of the neighborhood parents were staring into my garage. They would pull their little red wagons up in the driveway, moms drinking white wine and dads drinking beer, shepherding little costumed kids up to our doorstep and just stand there studying it, wide-eyed, some of them with their jaws slightly open. It took me a bit to figure out that my wife had left the garage door open by mistake. But I decided to entertain myself a little since I was stuck with candy duty. "It looks like a museum in there," one guy said.

As an Organizer, it's funny to me when folks talk about things like spring cleaning, or when office people announce that a large refuse bin is making the rounds so that coworkers can do an office clean. You see, in the Organizer's world there are no such things, because the spring and office cleanings were already done years back when the initial organizational design and layout was structured and implemented. Then it just became a simple matter of minimal maintenance and light cleaning year-round.

That's what the term *feng shui* is all about, also known as geomancy, one of the five arts of Chinese metaphysics, which posits that invisible forces bind together the universe, earth, and humanity. It's the general idea that there is balance, good energy, even peace in the proper ordering of things. Organizers see and understand the concept of *feng shui* in many things, things physical and nonphysical. We see *feng shui* in things like plans, relationships, goals, objectives, and process.

One of the women asked: "How in the world do you have the time to do that?" I guess she was imagining that every day you had to dedicate time to creating a museum of a garage. My mind was swimming, imagining the disorder she lived in, for her not being able to see that order was actually something that you could achieve. Order is finite. A place you can actually get to. I could see she could not even imagine something like that was even a possibility in her own life. Since I was dedicated to entertaining myself, I asked her: "How do you have time not to?" I explained to her that the initial investment of hours I made in planning and structuring the museum garage was far less than she and her husband probably spent looking for stuff they could not find, let alone the financial waste of rebuying things they already had but couldn't locate.

I spent that Halloween trying to spread the Organizer Gospel, but all I saw was a lot of blank faces, disbelief, and distrust. Almost every one of them could not see what the heck I was talking about. But Organizers are used to that, to people not seeing what we see. We Organizers are all okay with being alone in that way. It never really affects our course in things either. We know where we are going and will not be swayed by distractions or by people in general.

But there was one exception that Halloween. Standing next to his fairy queen granddaughter and his Batman grandson, a silver-haired gentleman with calm, assured eyes commented how he liked that I had adapted vinyl flooring components to become wall guards so that the trash and recycling bins would not dig into the drywall and mark the paint up. He said his garage looked much the same as mine and that he had balls on strings that almost magically dropped from the garage doors as they opened, so that the car aligned perfectly when he pulled in, as the balls gently touched the windshield at just the right distance. I did not tell my fellow Organizer that when Batman and the fairy princess get a little taller that one won't work anymore, because the kids play with them like tethered volleyballs on playgrounds. Especially Batman. I had those balls in my garage and found out the hard way.

My kids don't generally listen to me, but I know they watch videos so I started my own "Dad Channel" on YouTube and made a video called *Feng Shui Garage.* You are welcome to check it out. My hope was that one day they might be in a place where they could understand what the heck I was even talking about.

LIGHT ORGANIZER

ORGANIZERS SEE PROBLEMS AREAS COMING in advance and see sequence as clearly as others see the sun in the sky. They know that if you do this now, this will not happen later. And conversely, if you don't do this now, this will happen later. As such, they can see quickly what should be happening in order to achieve a desired result.

Organizers are also aware that other people do not see what they see. They're used to that. So when possible, especially if they have garnered the necessary power, they will just act in spite of what they see as other people's lack of perspective or understanding.

An Organizer is highly orderly. To others, the high degree of order and clearly established structure of the Organizer's inner and outer worlds may seem intense, but to the Organizer, flawlessly regimented environments and protocols are actually simpler and, sometimes surprisingly to others, a lot calmer.

Organizers accomplish their duties and tasks quickly and efficiently. Organizers live in a world of fiscal and mechanical cause and effect and they are all about making things more effective and efficient. As a result, they typically can cover a lot more ground within the course of any given day than others can. They can manage multiple tasks simultaneously well, much like a good short-order cook can at a busy diner. They possess a natural ability to manage use of time, so they can maintain a schedule and focus that may appear to others to be highly regimented. They may not need lists and schedules as much as others do, because so much of it is intuitive. The list and schedule are already installed in their heads.

Organizers can visualize long range accomplishments and create the steps to get there. An Organizer categorizes the business of life into short-term, medium-term, and long-term objectives. Other people may be adept at short or medium-term goals, but the Organizer excels at long-range thinking and planning. It is entirely normal for an Organizer to see what needs to happen over the next ten years, how it needs to happen, and at what pace it needs to happen, and to budget in advance for the unexpected.

It is therefore wise to consult an Organizer if you are trying to get somewhere in the long run because they can break it all down into bite-sized pieces and walk you through exactly what needs to happen. And again, Organizers are generally used to the idea that other people are not seeing what they are seeing, that others do not see the relationship between the steps an Organizer is pointing towards and why they are pointing there. People tend to look for shortcuts and faster ways to get somewhere, but many things in life do not adapt to that thinking and require methodical intentionality. Organizers typically can identify those situations. Long-term projects, to be done well, require longer-term timelines. Organizers understand timelines well.

An Organizer coordinates manpower effectively. Organizers can generally see who would work best in what situation. They can see what skills and traits a person has, what the person's temperament is like, and can match that set of facts with the proper position or role. Organizers see the need for tracking, monitoring, transparency, and involvement to keep projects and people on track. People would generally follow an Organizer leader because they can see the stock price of the company is going to double if they do.

Understanding the Gifts can help Organizers get people to where they can work best. Somewhere along the line, when I was hiring new people, I stopped asking them about prior experience and started giving them a Gift Test. If I needed a salesperson, I looked for Exhorters. If I needed internal support, I hunted for Servers, etc. By the way, Gift Tests are easy to make. Start an informal Gift Club and when you have five people that are all sure they are a particular Gift, create questions where all five of them decisively agree on the same answers. Once you have these standardized questions and answers, you can ask people these questions to see how they respond in order to determine their Gifts.

An Organizer can identify power and leverage in situations quickly. Organizers can size up fast where they have power and where they don't, or if they don't how they can get it. Generally speaking, they use this ability towards the greater good, but there are always exceptions.

Last year, a couple from Indiana and I both had our cars broken into while we were parked off the highway at an industrial farm complex that proffered a farm-fresh restaurant. Having only been inside for an hour, I was surprised when it happened since it seemed to be a safe environment. I spoke to the local police and found out that others had their cars broken into there as well recently. That's when I got upset, knowing that others had been harmed already and likely would be in the future. I had noticed earlier at dinner there were a larger number of busboys and waitresses just standing around. The manager could have easily told unoccupied workers to keep an eye on the guest's parking lot to protect the field.

So I did not take my issue to the restaurant. I flipped some stones over, found out the farm produced an organic dairy drink that a major soft drink company had branded, and then e-mailed a complaint synopsis directly to them.

I found out the name of the founders of the farm and triangulated the city where I believed their personal residence was located in. Only then did I contact the restaurant. I explained I had initiated contact with the soft drink company and that I was going to level my complaint directly to the founders personally in their city of residence if the matter was not rectified and assurances given about the future safety of the parking lot. I got an apology, an assurance, and a FedEx with a check from them the next day.

I also don't mean to imply the ability to perceive or create or mute leverage has to be weaponized. But in this case I felt it also might help protect other unsuspecting people and families in that parking lot. I tracked down the couple that got hurt alongside me through police reports and offered a clear path for them to be made whole as well, since it had looked to me like they could ill afford a large insurance deductible. Identifying leverage can also be used for purer purposes, like creating helpful incentives for personal growth, creating more opportunities for others, or protecting people against aberrant behaviors.

Organizers are extremely creative and tend to think outside of prescriptive shapes and patterns. If something is not working correctly within a system, an Organizer will tend to look at and question the entire system as opposed to trying to just tinker inside of an existing protocol. Organizers typically see that the issue may lie within the system itself and not just within one aspect inside of it that everyone else is looking at. As such, Organizers may not be talking about the same topics everyone else is talking about.

Organizers may see the need to bulldoze the whole thing and build something new and better, something that can solve not only the issue at hand, but also other problems the Organizer sees that have not become manifest yet. Organizers love to design ideas and structures and protocols that solve many different things simultaneously. They love minimalism and concise, clear, streamline approaches. *Feng shui.*

An Organizer has the ability to make decisions (completely) unemotionally and also to become less emotional as others become more so in a given set of circumstances, especially a crisis. It is interesting to me that this inverse relationship exists and what it implies for our species as a whole. An Organizer can become like a cyborg, a robot, and operate entirely mechanically while others around them appear to be losing it.

I once saw on the news a replay of a large airliner filled with hundreds of people that had lost all power, trying to make it to an airport. There was little hope that a major catastrophe could be avoided, so they laid heavy foam down on one of the runways anticipating the worst. You could hear the controller frantically squawking to the pilot that runway number six was all clear and foamed just for them. Silence. Then the pilot calmly coming on: "Roger that tower, cleared for landing on runway eight." Then the controller almost screaming: "Negative! Negative! That is runway SIX!"

Then the pilot, as calmly as Papa sipping coffee, once again: "I was just kidding with you. Runway 6 it is." And then the cool-hand pilot calmly floated that steel and aluminum glider weighing hundreds of tons in for a three-point landing and saved every soul on board.

I think I know what his Gift was.

Dark Organizer

I WAS NOT LOOKING FORWARD TO WRITING this part of the book. I feel like a dry drunk at an AA meeting. I am forced, once again, to admit I am drawn to and repelled by the darkness of my Gift. I am staring at a bottle that I know I should not drink from, just like a recovering alcoholic who has to admit he will never be cured, who must remain in the process of recovery, not drinking one moment at a time for the rest of time.

An Organizer, through pride, can become hungry for power. Organizers are generally narcissistic and overly confident in their skills. They see power as a convenient vehicle to achieve greater efficiency when implementing their organizational vision. They are convinced that everyone will function better if their plan is implemented, and will basically just take over if given the opportunity. Machiavelli was an Organizer.

Power is therefore a natural currency for an Organizer. We can comfortably oversee a large company, an institution, or a country. In our minds, we see the plan clearly, the one that can cause everyone to benefit, and see authority as a more efficient means to that end. Just let us completely take over everything and everyone will be the better for it. That's how we think.

But in the Organizer recovery meetings that I have with myself in my mind, meetings that I should have more frequently, I have to admit even though my plans may be good ones, or even great ones, there are other dimensions that are important that my plan may not account for at all… emotional, relational, and spiritual dimensions.

Organizers can become completely insensitive to other people's personal desires when they conflict with theirs. There's a part of an Organizer that just doesn't like people, plain and simple, even though we need them. People are messy, inefficient, and sometimes dumb. As a result, an immature Organizer (myself included) can basically flatten and steamroll people and their feelings in the process of organizing. Organizers can wrongly conclude that other people's expressions and ideas and desires cannot make their well-laid plans any better. The Organizer knows it takes focus and willpower and diligence and consistency to implement a plan well, sometimes a larger scale one, and can wrongly assume that it's okay to have casualties of both people and ideas along the way.

Organizers will work excessively to accomplish tasks and then expect the same from others. It is typical for Organizers to be highly functioning and effective, to overachieve. They can operate at higher levels of intensity for longer periods of time than most people and most Gifts, and then can become impatient and frustrated at others if they do not function at their same level. Passive aggression can start to form, exacerbated by the Organizer's natural impatience.

As an Organizer, I would be wise to remember that not all playing fields are level and also that a greenhouse with many different types of flowers is generally more interesting, uplifting, and even productive than one that contains different colors of just a single type of flower. Not everyone is me and I should neither expect nor desire that they should be. Diversity is a good thing, a positive force.

Organizers will tend to cause others around them to feel regimented and unloved. Because we Organizers are so plan-focused, we can *literally* forget that people around us have feelings and that emotions are, in fact, a major consideration of our humanity. It is hard for people to understand just how emotionally devoid Organizers can be, or to comprehend the level of emotional ignorance people are dealing with in our Gift's case.

I remember when I was trying hard to become more emotionally functional in my organizing, to ask people about their feelings while I was working, to try and recognize and invest in their hearts and not just focus on their immediate work product. I have to say none of it came naturally to me. I started rehearsing being more relational by stopping my number-two guy one Monday and asking him how his weekend was. He looked at me quizzically, pointed out to me that I had never asked him anything like that before, and that while he appreciated my effort, it felt really forced to him, like I had scheduled on my calendar an item that said: "Say hello to Rich and ask him how his weekend was." With my best attempt at sorrowful eyes, I lied to him and told him I felt bad I had made him feel that way. You have to start somewhere. For me, it was only requiring that I changed the way I thought, acted, and felt. No big deal. I confess that I walked away thinking it might be a great idea to schedule emotional interactions with coworkers on my calendar.

I remember once explaining this to another Gift, a Mercy I think it was, and the person said she was surprised because I seemed like a relatively in-tune person emotionally. "I am glad that I fooled you," I said. "It has taken quite a bit of work to get to this point." I still have a lot of work left to do.

Organizers can accept character flaws in others if it results in reaching goals and getting the job done. Organizers are so plan-focused and goal-focused that they will often accept people's involvement whose behavior or character is questionable. Examples of this could be people who are dishonest, morally corrupt, or in the worst of cases, criminal. We tend to be so results-oriented we put our plan above everything else and don't see how we get there is frequently just as important, or maybe even more important, than where we get to.

An Organizer, when angered, will organize the demise of another. There is no question that an Organizer can use abilities to identify power and leverage in situations, married with their creative skills to think outside of prescriptive shapes to take down someone perceived as an opponent, and to do so very effectively.

I once ordered an air cleaner through the Internet and never received a confirmation code, so I moved on to the next vendor. Two air cleaners were eventually delivered and the company that had failed to provide a confirmation code refused to accept a return, claiming my office workers could have refused delivery. To complicate matters further, the vendor was located in Canada. I began to visualize strategies to take him out. That weekend, I watched on television as the Executive Vice President of my credit card company played in the annual pro-am golf tournament at Pebble Beach. I thought, why not personally involve him? So I did. I hunted him down through layers of security and bureaucracy and subterfuge until I was on a first name basis with his personal secretary. She eventually reported to me that Mr. Executive Vice President would authorize crediting my purchase funds back if I could demonstrate the item had been returned.

Now, that was a tough one. First, it had to go through customs so the delivery costs alone would have outweighed the cost of the machine. Second, my opponent could simply refuse delivery. So my only chess move was to reject delivery of the original package, but UPS was not inclined to do that a month after the fact. Our battle had taken days and now weeks. So I decided to bring the package to its original state, wrote the words "Delivery Rejected" in big, bold letters on it, and went on the hunt for an unmanned UPS truck with open doors. With delivery drivers going into mazes of hallways in office buildings to make deliveries, a truck fitting the bill wasn't hard to find. I shoved the box in the back of one.

The next day, I printed off a document from the UPS web site that showed the original delivery to me had been rejected, implying the package was on the way back to Canada. That was just enough to tip the last card. On the evidence of my receipt and separate confirmation through the UPS website, Mr. Executive Vice President ordered my account credited. Checkmate. I called my Canadian enemy for fun and calmly explained his situation was hopeless and that he would be wise to remove my name from his customer directory. He got terrified because he started saying, "No, no, no!" I didn't understand until he explained that the shipment would now be caught in limbo in the customs area and he would be charged a fortune, on top of the other fortune that would be due UPS for all of their delivery troubles.

I knew what limbo meant because some years back I had asked my mom why I was baptized in infancy as a Protestant when we were not a religious family. She explained that her parent's generation believed that when children were born, it was important to rush them to the priest to have them baptized quickly, so that their souls would not be trapped in limbo if they died unexpectedly somewhere between birth and baptism. Limbo, she explained, was the place between Heaven and Hell and they did not want children's souls to be eternally imprisoned there if something went wrong. I still did not understand why they went to all that trouble if they didn't necessarily believe in God or the church. She said they did it just in case they had miscalculated the existence of a divinity, like when a trader hedges a bet on a stock in the options markets.

So as I understood it, my now-sobbing Canadian was indicating his air cleaner would be confined between Heaven and Hell in customs. He was pretty brittle now as he shared his business was not doing well enough to support his young family, blah, blah, blah. I calmly said I would see if I could do something to help the situation and signed off. He said goodbye with a little bit of restored hope in his voice.

I went down to Walgreens and picked out a really nice pacifier. I got the upgraded version in case one of his kids actually wanted to use it. I sent that pacifier UPS of course, straight over customs and directly to the Canadian, no note, no missive, as I felt the pacifier spoke for itself. But I made sure the sender's identity was written clearly.

Organizers are real good at evening out scores or taking someone down. But notice I have put this trait on the Dark Side, and not the Light. Sure you could argue that this skill might be helpful in taking down someone like Osama Bin Laden, and I think that's reasonable, but the trait also has a darker tint to it. As much as I don't like to look at this, either in the outer or inner worlds, I have to admit that Adolf Hitler bears all the traits of an Organizer gone berserk.

I have given this some thought and I also think that some countries have overall Gift flavors. For example, I think Italy is mostly Exhorter. France is mostly Mercy. And I think the Huns are mostly Organizer. In Germany, there exists a culture of cleanliness, order, and efficiency, all marks of the Organizer. I have had recurring dreams of working in the Porsche factory in Stuttgart, all joking aside.

So when I think about the cold, senseless, inhuman, Germanic planning The Final Solution required and the orderly efficiency of it all, I conclude that not only was Hitler a member of my self-same human race, he was also very likely a member of my Gift Tribe. We Organizers have to be very careful in this area lest we go too far down some crazy planning path, forgetting that people have feelings, even possibly relinquishing our humanity for the sake of the plan.

ORGANIZER INTERVIEW

IF YOU LOOK INTO THE EYES OF AN Organizer, you're only going to see one thing: resolve. Maybe my mind is playing tricks on me, or maybe I am seeing things more lucidly than others do, but I would swear that every single Organizer I know or see has the exact same set of eyes. The exact same look. Look closely at some of the pictures of Organizers mentioned in this book and see if you can't see it too. Right or wrong, there is an unmistakable self-assuredness in every Organizer's eyes. They all look like they are going to go (calmly) right through you if need be, just like a hot knife goes right through butter.

The Polar Gift of the Organizer is the Server, as they are mirror opposites. While the Organizer naturally lords over, the Server naturally serves under. And that is exactly why these two Gifts would do well to try to emulate the other, for Servers to try to develop leadership qualities, and for Organizers to get off their high horse and learn to subjugate themselves and their egos on behalf of others.

Surprisingly, the Exhorter Gift overlaps with the Organizer Gift, and you would not think so because Exhorters can be so carefree and not intense and totally unorganized in things. But the Gifts share a very strong commonality that no other two Gifts share and that is an ability to be uncommonly creative and visionary. Organizers and Exhorters are not contained easily by other people's shapes and forms or by society's conventions. They can see both possibilities and solutions others don't typically, but for different reasons and different motivations. The Exhorter visualizes new possibilities to help free and encourage other people, while the Organizer does so for the sake of a newly-formed plan for the betterment of all, for efficiency.

Organizers naturally love and employ the system of the Seven Gifts, or other templates like it, because it helps Organizers delegate people into roles more efficiently. It's no surprise then that your author of *The Seven Gifts* is an Organizer.

If you have an Organizer child and want your progeny to eat their broccoli, just tell them what my mom always told me, that my good soldiers needed it to combat the bad soldiers within me…broccoli for efficiency, a short subject in any childhood Organizer mind.

An Organizer dreams about developing a plan for everyone to follow that will make everyone's lives better and then running it, managing it, refining it, then tending it like a garden to make it all stay in full bloom.

I will add here that learning about the Seven Gifts has helped me to form new dreams, and hopefully better ones, with added dimensions and layers…dreams that involve organizing things in a way that lifts people up, that stands for what is right, that makes people feel better, that exalts people who serve, and that appreciates thoughtful study and research. As a younger Organizer, I had dreams that were blacker and whiter, but now I can have dreams in colors, dreams that are hopefully more expansive and aspirational as a result of knowing the Seven Gifts.

To name that Gift in one note, so to speak, one would need to pay attention around the holiday season. If you see a Christmas tree tightly and neatly wrapped up and put out by the front curb within two days of Christmas being over, you can readily assume an Organizer resides in that abode.

If you want to mess with an Organizer, just do something that disrupts their plan. I would guess that at least once every two months, one of my work associates will sneak into my *feng shui* office and move picture frames a quarter of an inch, or put my computer mouse cord to the left side of my phone holder instead of the right. My first suspects are always Exhorters.

I'll throw in a Gift Tip here for you at no charge, an arbitrage opportunity for you. If you ever want to buy a used car, try to find one that an Organizer is selling. Don't look at the car, look at the garage. You won't need to waste any of your hard-earned money having a mechanic look the car over for you. It's just fine. Buy it. I figured that one out when my oldest daughter was about twelve years old. I knew I would need to buy her a used car when she turned sixteen and I needed a new set of wheels myself at the time. So I asked her to come along and pick out the colors of the outside and inside. I reasoned that I would be the best person to buy a used car from four years down the line.

Occupationally, Organizers can be world leaders, CEOs, managers, and military officers. We also make good planners, architects, designers, and craftsman because we are not interested in perfection, we are interested in *absolute* perfection.

Celebrity Organizers would typically include world leader types and athletes that have achieved legendary status. I believe Barak Obama is an Organizer and I can say that based on the look I see in his eye alone. Organizers recognize other Organizers quickly. When Obama speaks at times, I can see him looking beyond the present circumstance, or looking back behind it in his mind's eye. He is considering the sequence of things, both what happened to get us here, and where things are headed. Sequence.

Remember that I shared Organizers like their privacy. A lot of folks criticized Obama for not spending evenings schmoozing and socializing and chumming it up with political types so he could grease the wheels of Washington to get more stuff done. Obama liked time alone with his small family instead and enjoyed time by himself, precious hours of solitude, so he could reflect, work on matters more thoughtfully, read ten personal notes sent to him by fellow Americans each night, and respond to many by his own hand. For those of you who criticized Obama about that, you ought to take a look in your own Gift Mirror, recognize that there are natural ways that you were designed that may have purpose, and not throw stones when you live in a glass house. Obama was just doing his Organizer thing, in a manner that made sense to him and that suited who he was.

Batman is an Organizer who enjoys organizing the demise of criminals. Tiger Woods and Michael Jordan are both Organizers. In order to achieve their legendary status, they had to escalate their focus to an almost android level. Organizers will clearly see what is required for them to become a historic player, to compete on a level that is past current time and space, and to dial in like a heat-seeking missile to do what is necessary to get there. You want to see what resolve and focus and commitment really looks like? Watch an Organizer in that set of circumstances.

You may recall I mentioned Minnesota Fats earlier (see Volume I), the famous pool hustler. Minnesota could sink a few balls at the same time with one stroke of a cue. Here's my trick shot. To prove both that Tiger is an Organizer and also that Organizers like their privacy…Tiger has a yacht that he named *Privacy*.

Some farmers and scientists did a study on chickens some time back, but I don't think they were aware they ended up doing research on Organizers. Someone noticed that out of every pack of chickens, there seemed to be some that performed better and produced more eggs than other chickens did. Super-chickens. They reasoned that if they took out the super-chickens and bred them, they could triple egg production. But when they grouped the super-chickens together, the theory collapsed because they all started pecking at one another, trying to kill off the other ones.* Like I said, that study was really about Organizers. We generally don't play well in the sandbox with other Organizers, because we have plans that we are dead certain about and don't appreciate interference or ideas that we may see as competing for attention and resources. That's sad if you step back and think about it.

---

* "Forget the Pecking Order at Work," Margaret Heffernan, TED Talk.

At my age, I have a few more miles on my chassis, so hopefully I have learned a few things about this stuff. I hope so anyway. The biggest single lesson I learned came from the world of music. I became a fan of the famous cellist Yo-Yo Ma some years back and was fascinated how he would openly and voluntarily collaborate with other musicians who may not have had any obvious relationship to, or sympathy with, his own musical idiom. Yo-Yo has a musical clarity and precision that did not need to be cluttered up by anyone else's mess, I thought. Yet he traveled into bluegrass, tangos, traditional Chinese melodies, and the music of Brazil. He even collaborated with the late Ennio Morricone, the Italian composer who created the soundtracks for American spaghetti westerns. Yo-Yo proved at each turn that something new and unexpected could happen, something inevitably better. When I work around other Organizers like myself these days, I try to think of it as collaboration like Yo-Yo Ma's musical ones.

If I were to frame an ode to the Organizer, I would simply say enough with the odes. We give ourselves enough odes with our natural self-importance and usually get enough odes from people whose stock values have gone up due to our planning, or from gentler Gifts who praise our self-assurance. We don't need any more of it. Organizers need to learn how to live without odes and to become more emotionally operative and gentle, like our Mercy brothers and sisters. Most of all, we need to take some cues from our Polar Gift, the Server, and learn how to be selfless and other-centered and self-sacrificial.

There is an interesting concept called kenosis, which deals with the idea of emptying out yourself, your will, and your identity completely, so that you might make room for something bigger and larger and perhaps other-centered to fill you anew. Organizers don't need any more accolades. We're already full of ourselves and need to embrace some form of functional kenosis to empty out some.

Organizer Unicorn

I HOPE I CAN DRAMATIZE THAT YOU can pick up on people's Gifts even if they are historical figures, figures not around to talk to or to watch. That's one of the reasons I am picking Frank Lloyd Wright as the Organizer Gift Unicorn. Yes it's true that, if you think about it, an architect as powerful and skilled as Frank Lloyd Wright represented one of the best examples of an iconic Organizer in that he created his own world, his own universe, his own order through the language of his design and architecture. In some ways, you might even say he become a god of his own order, able to lord over physical space through the ordering of form.

That's what Organizers are built for, to impose form and order over the environment around us, to try to make it better, to improve it, so that all can benefit from our vision, our plan. And it is pretty spectacular to see physical evidence of that drive expressed through stone, glass, steel, wood, light, and shadow.

I am lucky to spend time in Racine, Wisconsin at the SC Johnson campus that Wright fathered and at The Rookery here in downtown Chicago where he designed an elaborate lobby that simultaneously spoke to the history of Chicago's World Fair of 1893. The Rookery has a lovely shop in it run by the faithful of Frank Lloyd Wright's historical society. I make sure to spend some of my pocket money there.

People may not generally know that Wright's mom gave him a special set of building blocks when he was in kindergarten, blocks that allowed him to play with the world of geometric shapes...rectangles, triangles, and circles. Wright suggested later in life that much of his sense of order came from those blocks, that when he organized new forms through his architecture, he was essentially still just playing with those same childhood blocks. This is a great example of parenting to a child's Gift. In homage to grandmother, Wright's son designed Lincoln Logs for kids and adults to play with too.

Wright loved interesting cars with a passion and had a weakness for women. Like many Organizers, Wright was reportedly very difficult to work with. He once said: "Early in life I had to choose between honest arrogance and hypocritical humility. I chose the former and saw no reason to change." He also refused to join the American Institute of Architecture, even though they awarded him a gold medal. He offered them this explanation: "Feeling that the architecture profession is all that's the matter with architecture, why should I join them?" Leave it to an Organizer to see a need to reimagine an entire profession and do so arrogantly. I mean confidently.

But I am picking Frank Lloyd Wright because I think he may be one of the few of my Gift Tribe who was able to cross over a mighty river into the world of emotions. I think Frank Lloyd Wright eventually saw that the real hidden beauty in the world of order actually lay in the realm of feelings.

When you walk into a Frank Lloyd Wright space, or you wear a tie that bears his shapes that The Rookery shop sells here in Chicago, you feel the stillness, the peace, the fragility of his sense of order. That could never have happened by accident, because he contemplated and authored it so consistently throughout his world of design and form and color. He learned, against all odds with his Organizer Gift in tow, to collaborate in all ways with the world of emotions, just like Yo-Yo Ma collaborates with other musicians and composers, shattering his own potentially perfect sense of order into little pieces so they could be reimagined and reshaped into new reflections of our humanity.

There is a striking feeling of humility in Frank Lloyd Wright's shapes, an undeniable sense of selfless service parked right alongside bold forms of order. I believe Frank Lloyd Wright's designs are a living body of work that illustrates and displays a fusion of many of his talents and also of many different characteristics of the Gifts. I see harmony with humanity and the environment. I see the Gift Wheel. I see the unmistakable eyes of an Organizer when I see his picture, and even with all of his Organizer flaws, flaws as pronounced as my own, I am inspired to grow.

PROPHET

PROTECTOR OF TRUTH AND RIGHTEOUSNESS

THE PROPHET IS THE UMPIRE OF RIGHT AND WRONG, calling balls and strikes all day long, every day. This Gift monitors everything seen in life, especially other people, and is willing to point out unfairness, a lack of justice, or hypocrisy.

Prophets will boldly stand up and confront issues if needed. They will fight what they see as the good fight all the way to the end and they generally don't worry if they break some pieces up along the way. They are all about causes and fighting for the causes they see as righteous.

Prophets are masters at detecting sincerity and authenticity in others generally and can spot a phony a mile away. Similarly, they can also discern if someone is resolved and authentic.

My Prophet friends, especially males, have to be careful about being insensitive to people's feelings. They can be a little bit like the proverbial bull in a china shop in that regard.

Prophets may represent about 20% of the Gifts in the population, about the same proportion as Servers I conclude. Maybe this is because we need a lot of policeman, so to speak, and people that are generally tough and strong and opinionated. It ensures the rest of us don't stop thinking about right and wrong and that we don't get out of line. It helps us stay accountable, since we know we are being watched.

IT IS DIFFICULT FOR ME TO SEPARATE THE Prophet Gift from the Civil Rights Movement, for it is in that realm that I have come to know most about this Gift. In the mid-90s, I began working in the South Side of Chicago, traveling the world of non-profit and community organizations, trying to marry commerce and social development. Given how and where I grew up, I felt both prepared and comfortable moving around in a virtually all-Black world.

I met Yesse Yehudah, a man who ran a large non-profit called F.O.R.U.M., an acronym for Fulfilling Our Responsibility Unto Mankind. I had learned fast that there were some shifty characters in the whole non-profit world and that not all people or entities that claimed to be on the side of goodness actually were. Yesse was sincere and serious about improving standards in neighborhoods ravaged by impoverishment and drugs. He had a scar that ran down his face and shared stories about his prior drug abuse, evidence that he had seen many sides of life in the streets of Chicago. He told me he had been rescued by Reverend James Bevel, a man who worked personally and closely with Dr. Martin Luther King. Bevel was portrayed by the actor/rapper Common in the movie *Selma*.

Yesse seemed to immediately trust me and began dealing with me as if we had known one another for years. I made the early mistake of using the term "African-American," whereupon Yesse made it clear he never wanted to hear me say that again. "I am an American," he said, "just like you." Made sense to me. Yesse eventually ran against Barack Obama for a local senatorial district seat and lost. Obama is the same age I am, graduated a year before me down the street from my school in Providence at Harvard in Boston and traveled the same neighborhoods and met many of the same people I did on the South Side of Chicago.

Yesse taught me to always hold my own when I was the only White man around, to never pander to race issues unnecessarily, and that Black folks try to get over on people just like White folks do. I already knew most of that, but it was fun and fulfilling to practice and learn more. Yesse invited me to be part of the organizing committee for the National Day of Atonement, which was the follow-up to the Million-Man March…the first open, public, national reckoning of Black male identity since the days of Dr. King.

I eagerly accepted and was probably photographed by the FBI through telephoto lenses as I entered the Nation of Islam, right down the street from Reverend Wright's Baptist Church, a place made famous from controversy involving Obama's attendance. As an aside, Wright's fire and brimstone was par for the course on the South Side. The Obamas would not have been able to attend any church housed on those streets without being in the proximity of preachers like Reverend Wright. Frankly, it was no big deal. Church settings like Wright's were where folks could express their emotions, their pain, and where they worked through inner issues, only they did so out loud and in public, unlike Whites generally.

Entering the domain of The Nation, I saw young men who were dressed smartly with bowties and who treated me with respect, although they avoided cordiality as well as my eyes. I understood they were probably guarding their souls. They could not have known there was no need for them to. I was the only White man in the proceedings except for Father Michael Pflager, the revolutionary Catholic priest of St. Sabinas Catholic Church, a priest made famous by Spike Lee's film *Chiraq*. Minister Louis Farrakhan sat a few feet away facing me.

Now I am well aware this latter gentleman has said some things that any reasonable person would consider racist, especially toward Jewish folks. And that is wrong-minded. Papa used the N-word too from time to time and when I was old enough, I called him on it. I pointed out that although he may consider it a generational thing, it was still wrong, and it made even less sense because I had never once seen him treat a person of color with anything less than the highest level of respect, concern, and love. As a matter of fact, I could see Papa may have liked Black people more than he liked White people, found them more interesting and compelling in general, and went way out of his way to be tender and kind and generous in his dealings with them. I explained all of that to Papa and appealed to him he was wrong to use language like that.

He laughed it off, like I should have known not to take him too seriously or literally, but I let him know I did not think it was a joke and that I did take it seriously. Half of my buddies at college were Black and I had learned of their deeper pains in my close friendships and conversations with them. I felt pain when Papa said words like that. My Black friends' pain had become my pain and even my deep love for Papa could not eclipse that.

So I am glad Mr. Farrakhan got to see me, perhaps noticed that a few of his Black comrades trusted me, and that I was alert in being respectful to him and The Nation. You can't play ball if you just sit up in the bleachers. Reverend Al Sampson, perhaps Chicago's version of New York's Reverend Al Sharpton, introduced me to the group as a righteous White brother. When he met me, Yesse knew I was real because he is a Prophet and a Prophet can tell pretty fast generally who is real and who isn't, who is strong and who is weak, who is committed and who isn't. Yesse said once to me: "If you're going to stand up, you have to be ready to do battle. I can tell you are on a mission."

Dr. Martin Luther King was a Prophet because he was willing, against all odds and in spite of personal danger, to be counted in this life standing up for what is right. South Side Congressman Bobby Rush, the Black Panther leader of yesterday, is a Prophet willing to fight with new weapons, political ones. On the West Side of Chicago, Congressman Danny Davis is also a Prophet, standing up for his tribe. Dr. James Bevel, Yesse's mentor, was a Prophet who was willing to march across the bridge with Dr. King and take on the entire South. The late Congressman John Lewis, who walked the bridge as well and served in our nation's capital, was a Prophet, willing to risk being beaten to death to make his point for righteousness. Jesse Jackson is a Prophet, an aggressive spokesman for keeping hope alive.

In a twist of fate, I was invited to a special dinner for Jesse Jackson by Reverend Bevel. You see, many in the Black community had for years derided Jackson for representing that he was in proximity to Dr. King when he was killed and had stood over his body after he had been shot, while many believed he had not. Those detractors felt that Jackson was being a phony, that he was capitalizing on the specter of King's assassination.

I brought my Prophet daughter Liza with me to the dinner, so she could feel what it was like to be the only White face in the room other than her dad. Bevel had located the only known photograph of Jesse Jackson standing over King's body nearly forty years later and he meant to surprise Jackson with it in a rare moment of historical redemption.

As we were entering the room, Liza walked up to Jackson and threw a fastball. She asked him a really tough question that dealt with racial equality, personal responsibility, and accountability all wrapped up into one. Jackson looked at me as if to say he just wanted to eat some dinner. I looked back at him as if to say *You are on your own bud; she asks me tough questions too.* He looked back at me as if to say, *So you're going to subject me to her on my day off?* I looked back at him as if to say, *You are a Prophet, Jesse, and she is too, one of your tribe, and you know better than I do your soup is going to get cold if you don't get to it.*

Liza just glared—I mean looked intently at him—as he and I had this nonverbal discussion. Jesse finally put his back into it. Liza got quiet and just nodded her head as he was rounding third base on his way to home. "Quiet" meant she was satisfied with what she heard. I looked at Mr. Jackson as if to say *sometimes keeping hope alive takes some overtime.* He looked back at me as if to say *I understand but I'm hungry.* I looked back at him as if to say *I think you will find your effort was worth it and I hope you enjoy your surprise and sometimes vindication has a price and it was nice talking to you like this*. As I walked past him, I said out loud: "Good evening." He said in return: "Glad the two of you could make it." After that evening, the stain of stigma surrounding that subject vanished for Jesse Jackson. I know you won't mind if we put that Forrest Gump moment in Liza's column, not mine. She would have appreciated it.

The needle of our nation's history would never have been moved without Prophets in the area of Civil Rights. Our collective reckoning, our admission of slavery, our process of absolution would never have begun. I attended the Day of Atonement, had lunch with Dick Gregory, another Prophet, and tried to contribute what I could. I was told that I would be part of Dr. Bevel's security contingency, as he would be speaking just before the keynote, Minister Farrakhan. I put on my black tee shirt and pants and donned mirrored sunglasses to match my security brothers. That morning, I stepped out of our hotel with Bevel at my side, rounded the corner and saw a straight path extending down the street about a hundred yards long to the bulletproofed podium that sat below us. The concrete lane ahead of us was clean and bound on either side with flawless lines of Nation of Islam followers.

On my left were all women, beautifully dressed in formal gowns and dresses that suggested African origins holding kaleidoscopes of vibrant color...reds, yellows, greens, blues, and royal purples. Their faces were modest but elegant. They stood motionless, a living symbol of unity and purpose and strength. On my right were the men, set like marble pillars erect in immaculate, identical positions, white shirt collars peeking through pressed suits at precise intervals...powerful, rigid, immovable, and firm in their stance and commitment.

I have never seen anything like it before or since, in any community, among any race, even when I was in boot camp with the United States Marine Corps at Quantico, Virginia, when F16s proudly cracked across the sky above my platoon so close I felt like I could touch them. The sun glinted off the face of the windows of the United Nations' skyscraper and hit my sunglasses. I felt the heat of the sun's nuclear fire on my face.

Space-time froze again for a moment, just like it did at Papa's white Formica table. I wondered if Papa would have even been able to comprehend the moment that now surrounded me, far from his front porch in Columbus. Then, incomprehensibly, a bass beat began that shook both my hair and my frame. I did not know from what bowels of the earth it was emanating, but it filled the world around me and infiltrated every molecule of air. I slowly began familiarizing the thumping and realized it was Stevie Wonder blasting through a sound system that could have flattened every building in the entire city of New York.

Living for the City. The song that appeared for the first time in my life on my father's turntable when I lived at the Laundromat with him. I wondered if a wormhole buried in the blackness of space had spit me out somewhere unexpected and improbable all these years later. Even though this was the thousandth time I had heard the song, that morning it seemed the first and only.

We began walking slowly and languidly with the beat of Stevie's anthem to Urban Black America. I felt suspended in the bass, as if I were in a thick liquid. I was present in that moment with the pimps, the butlers and maids of my youth, and the entire lineage of Black friends who had traced my entire life.

I was proud, ashamed, cleansed, convicted and for a moment, immaculate and perfect as well, with all of my new beautiful Black brothers and sisters. Now I clearly saw that my activist Prophet friend Yesse had been absolutely dead-center correct this whole time. These proud, aspiring, colorful, gorgeous, and glorious people were, in fact, all my fellow Americans, each and every one of them without exception.

I sat in the front rows, a surrogate VIP, and looked back at the sea of tens of thousands behind me. I noticed sharpshooters with telescopic sights on their rifles speckled on the surrounding rooftops, watching the crowds as Farrakhan threw lightning bolts out of his makeshift, bullet-proof cage. I looked beside me a few chairs down and Geraldo Rivera looked back at me. I saw in his eyes that he thought it was unusual for a

White guy like me to be a part of all this but, rather than inquire—let alone interview me—he concluded I was not an important player. Geraldo, it turns out, is also a Prophet. He had sized me up quickly and accurately.

America is a small place. Years later, Stevie Wonder came here to Chicago to perform a concert, so I bought tickets and took my wife. I saw Jesse Jackson standing in line and it took me a minute or two to understand that he was staring at her. His eyes moved over to mine and he looked at me as if to say *Oops*. I looked back at him as if to say, *Don't worry about it, she's really pretty and I understand.* He looked back as if to say, *Thanks, Dave.*

Stevie lit the place up with *Living for the City* and I danced and moved with my date in the United Center with all my fellow Americans once again.

LIGHT PROPHET

PROPHETS ARE ABLE TO DISCERN TRUE commitment in others. They can spot a phony a mile away, someone with questionable intentions or okay agendas. Their radar starts going off with noises and lights automatically. They are quick to say they don't trust a person if they sense dishonesty and quick to confirm that someone is reliable if they detect sincerity of purpose. Prophets are great people to consult with if you are trying to make a decision about whether you should move within closer proximity to someone. Ask Prophets what they see or what they think and you will find yourself looking at an X-ray revealing intentions and character.

A Prophet is aggressive in speech. Prophets tell it like it is most of the time, with little filtering and no reservations. They are completely unafraid and unabashed in their expression, usually involving what they believe is right. They can also be loud, as they are typically intense, and they have endless, boundless energy to share their view of things. Prophets are strong-minded and strong-willed and have no problem getting in front of a crowd to lay down what they see as the law.

Prophets tend to have higher IQs and seem to be able to grasp things quickly. Prophets are mentally nimble and can clearly see paradoxes, contradictions, and ironies. They can deduce the center of things, the core of the matter. Yet it is important to note that the center they see in most things usually deals with right and wrong, or with what is just, or whether something is fair and equitable or not.

A Prophet is generally long on memory and can recall things you did or said a while back with a high degree of accuracy, with elephant memory as they say. A Prophet's more powerful intellect also helps with testing scores. Prophets are good students and learners in general, presuming of course, they have determined studying and learning is the right thing to be doing.

A Prophet remains willing to be condemned for what is right. Prophets are unafraid to stand up for what they believe in regardless of the consequences, sometimes including death. They are the fittest among the Gifts to walk the line and stand for righteousness without regard to public opinion or popularity. Not only are they capable of not being distracted by others in their cause of righteousness, they can also be encouraged even more by the presence of opposition. Prophets typically will not shy away from conflict and can be energized even further to stand firmer by the presence of it.

A Prophet possesses a powerful desire to inform others. Once Prophets determine what they believe to be the truth of things, they show endless motivation and energy when getting the word out to others, spreading the good news, just like a fiery, evangelical preacher. Prophets have an inexhaustible supply of energy to talk and talk and then talk some more in an effort to help other people see the light. They will take all the time needed to let even strangers, or especially strangers, know the important information they have to share.

Prophets can be responsive to conviction if they feel they have been shown they are off-track. I can't say that Prophets are prone to immediately correcting themselves if an error in their approach is pointed out to them and of course I can't say that about myself either, but I can say that eventually if Prophets see their error, they can have a sincere experience of being convicted. When you see a Prophet get to that point, which may take a little longer than with other folks, it is truly a thing of beauty, because you get a strong sense of how authentic and thoughtful it all really is.

DARK PROPHET

A PROPHET IS QUICK TO JUDGE, ALMOST instantly and reflexively in all areas of life. If you're watching the news with a Prophet or eating in a restaurant with one, no matter what the situation, don't be surprised if you hear from the Prophet, "Look at that guy. He is not supposed to be doing that." or "That woman is being a hypocrite," and so on. A Prophet notices things like that and sees a lot of life through that lens. Most of the time, there is some truth in what Prophets are pointing at, but they can also get overheated and see things in black or white terms. Sometimes their quick judgments can also overlook other important aspects of situations. It's important for Prophets to temper their judgment and to understand that life is usually more complex and colorful than monochromatic declarations allow.

Prophets look for negatives and, as such, can be overly critical. A lot of the judgments Prophets make—maybe you could call them *verdicts*—tend to be negatively charged. That can be exhausting to others around them. I know that I am not God's gift to pleasantry either, but I will say that sometimes you can start feeling tired just by knowing that a Prophet is walking towards you to talk, or that one is calling you on your phone. Prophets that are not aware they have the capacity to be critical and judgmental can be real tiring.

Prophets need to become alert to the reactions of others, to see the effects they have on other people, especially in the moment. I am grateful that there is another Gift that may be even more insensitive than my own.

Maybe. Thank you so much, it's nice to not be decisively at the bottom of the Emotional Gift Food Chain.

Prophets are not usually very emotionally operative, as they can see emotions as hindrances or irrelevancies to the matter of truth. Prophets can be extremely unaware of negative emotional impacts they are having on others.

Prophets can be intolerant of other people's pain, even to the degree that they can conclude that others deserve suffering, presuming that the discomfort might be a learning tool. If Prophets do become aware that people are being affected negatively by them, their attitude can be along the lines that not only do they not care about your feelings, but also that you probably had it coming and needed to feel it so you could learn a thing or two, and that truth is more important than emotions are. Similarly, if Prophets see someone suffering, they may be prone to look for bad decisions that person made that could be said to have resulted in the person's current consequences.

Prophets can also become prideful in their personal abilities and, as such, do not typically struggle much with self-esteem. They know they are generally capable and smart and strong-willed and therefore can some-times start to feel like they are superior to others in intelligence and skill. It may be true that they sometimes are, because they typically have all those positive attributes, but it doesn't help matters if people start to develop a sense of superiority for a lot of reasons. It doesn't set things up well for focusing on areas of improvement, like becoming more emotionally operative and sensitive to others.

All Prophets need to develop meekness. I am convinced that the hardest thing in the whole world for a Prophet to do is to manifest meekness…to be humble, quiet, apologetic, reflective, vulnerable, open, tolerant, and willing to be led. When you see a moment of meekness in a Prophet, enjoy it because it is a wonderful thing, like a double rainbow after a spring rain when the sun lifts colors out of the hidden spectrum around us and reveals a thing of rare beauty that is present but invisible to the naked eye. When I witness and experience a Prophet being meek, it makes me feel humbled before the universe. It helps me to see the grandeur and impossibility of existence. It happened to me last week—I saw a double rainbow and a Prophet in my environ burst color all around me in his meekness. I fought tears and gave him a big hug.

What else could I do?

Prophet Interview

WHEN YOU LOOK INTO THE EYES OF PROPHETS, you see strength and you also get the sense that they are looking to see if you are going to say something wrong, almost like they are paying attention carefully to point out something that you missed or were misguided about. Strong and reviewing eyes.

The Polar Gift of the Prophet is the Mercy, as the two lie at opposite ends of the emotional spectrum. The Mercy is generally in the background and operates in a world of empathy, while the Prophet confidently steps out front and knocks people around generally without too much caution while causing emotional concussions.

The Prophet overlaps with the Organizer in areas of both strength and leadership. People would follow Prophets for their energy and declarations, while folks would follow Organizers for better efficiencies.

The Prophet remains the most skeptical of all the Gifts of The Gift System. Usually, you get a pretty strong critical and judgmental opinion from Prophets about all of this Gift stuff because their first reaction is usually based on looking for negatives. Their consistent objection centers on the idea that people are more than one thing or category and that attempts to deduce and simplify are misguided. In essence, they are saying "Don't try and label me, reduce me, or tell me who I am." I do think there is some validity to this concern, as is the case with most concerns of a Prophet. I agree with them in general terms that people should not ever be pigeonholed and they should always seek to be better-rounded. But I don't see these legitimate concerns as being at odds with, or inconsistent with, the Seven Gifts.

First of all, I wish you good luck in arguing with nature. Seaweed is seaweed, and scallops are scallops. Our natures are distinct for biological purposes and are embedded in our species purposefully. Second, I think you will see by the end of my Gift Tale here that I argue strongly that not only are recognition and knowledge of the Gifts *not a way of limiting or constraining* identity; these are *a way of freeing it.* Third and finally, it should come as no surprise to you, now that you are familiar with Prophets, that once Prophets determine that the Gifts are true and righteous because they can bring about greater truth and understanding, Prophets can become the most enthusiastic supporters and proponents of this body of knowledge. In another Gift Irony, it is precisely their skepticism that can eventually lead them to commitment. Rigorous skepticism and questioning can temper steel belief and fidelity.

If you have a Prophet son or daughter and want your child to eat broccoli, buckle in for an hour-long debate to convince that eating healthy is the right thing. If you are a religious family, bring God into the picture, as Prophets who are religious have a natural respect for a deity and will therefore be more likely to follow when one is involved.

Use interrogatives instead of declaratives; try the Socratic method of revealing the quality of ideas through questions instead of making statements. If you need to make a statement, at least frame it as a rhetorical question, since it is harder for Prophets to get traction to disagree with you. Questions like: "Do you think it is important to take care of your body?" or "If you had a choice between a healthy food and an unhealthy food, which one would you take and why? Which would be the right choice?" Keep squirting oil on what they are trying to get purchase on with their grip, so their hands will keep slipping. Stay resolved. Expect conflict and confrontation. You may even walk away from the table with the impression that you didn't get through and that it was a lot of time and energy wasted. But don't worry. You did. Prophets just usually don't let on until later. They have to be convicted by their own, independent thinking. That can take time.

Prophets can make really good managers, coaches, politicians, activists, judges, priests, policemen, firemen, and first responders. A lot of that has to do with the idea that Prophets are extremely "situational." If there is a blank slate, nothing to start with, they generally don't do all that well designing the ballfield, laying the sod, building the bleachers, and turning the lights on. Organizers are good at that. Prophets generally aren't. But put Prophets on a pre-existing ballfield and they will light right up. They need situations they can respond or react to. If you get into a car wreck, you would want to have a Prophet around so that someone would quickly and fearlessly respond to the situation.

Speaking on behalf of the Organizers across the world, I hope our Prophet brothers and sisters know that you can consult with us if you are trying to reach a destination, to achieve a goal, or to build something new. We know you need us and, if you don't piss us off ahead of time, we would be more than happy to lend an organizational hand. We enjoy organizational consulting and would be happy to help. You would be wise to take us up on this offer.

A Prophet dreams about standing up for what is right, for a good cause, for another person or peoples, and fearlessly confronting and fighting off the force that is a threat. Prophets dream of winning the battle and seeing smiles on the faces of the people they stood up for. They dream of people coming up to them and saying: "You were right all along. Thanks for being willing to stand up for the truth."

If you see someone at a ball game yelling way too loud, chances are you are looking at a Prophet. That's how you can name a Prophet in one note.

If you want to really mess with a Prophet, then go to an expensive restaurant and start commenting on how pricy the menu is. Prophets are typically very cheap—I mean cost-conscious—and may not like the prices. They also love free stuff and don't mind at all if other people pay for them. So if you want to mess with them, money is a good way to do it.

Identifying celebrity Prophets is not hard. Just look for leader figures who are also outspoken. Oprah Winfrey is a Prophet, an advocate who will take up a cause despite opposition. I think Oprah is an example of a healthier Prophet because she has learned how not to give into the darker forces of her Gift. She does not go after people personally she does not care for; she goes after ideas she does not favor instead. In the movie *The Color Purple*, one of the reasons her performance was so very powerful is that all of us recognized her Prophet nature subconsciously, that she was a strong woman who would never bow to any tangible force of darkness. So when she was broken by her captors, it revealed the enormity of the radioactive evil of slavery.

Rosie O'Donnell may be an example of an unhealthy Prophet, because she tends to obsess over and fight people personally. Superman is a Prophet. Hulk Hogan is a Prophet. So is Miley Cyrus. You can see she is tough, edgy, and confrontational in her music and performances. She almost dares you to criticize or reject her, or put down her art, so she can double down and take a stand against you. In retrospect, Wild Child, the car customizer, was a Prophet (see Volume I). He made sure I never sanded the pimp's car when I worked at his shop. He wouldn't let me touch it. To him, that would have been wrong.

I lovingly share here that Prophets may be the most predictable of the Gifts, as they may have the strongest Gift Reflex. If I were to start a YouTube Channel with Gift Pranks as a theme, I would certainly start by filming Prophet subjects. Start the video cameras rolling…"Watch what Therese does when I say this to her!"

Let's take political loyalties out of the equation for a moment, shall we and, hopefully, have some fun here together. Donald Trump is obviously a Prophet. What is fun to watch is all the misunderstanding about why Trump acts the way he does, what his words mean, why he is in conflict all the time, and what his ongoing need is to keep making pronouncements about trivial—I mean, less important—matters. And to watch all the other governments trying to figure him out, so that world leaders everywhere could try to understand what the hell is going on, and to better know how to read and interpret this unusual figure. Think about the millions of dollars being spent all over the world in intelligence circles, hiring analysts, behaviorists, psychologists, and psychiatrists, all in an effort to try to decode Trump.

From my seat in the movie theatre, from a Gift perspective, Trump is functioning very consistently and predictably inside his Prophet Gift. Over 90% of what he says and does can be seen clearly, understood, and possibly even exactly predicted if you look at his Gift. Trump can't seem to help himself but blast controversial statements about disproportionally small issues because he is "calling balls and strikes" in Prophetland. He regularly engages in conflicts, instead of dialogues, because he sees battle as a (primary) method of dialogue. From his frame of reference, through instinctive conflict, he can acquire needed information. He is like a blind man tapping a white cane trying to see. His confrontations are his way of tapping.

Don't at all be surprised when you see Trump befriend an enemy. Like any functioning Prophet, if Trump determines you are strong and resolved, perhaps through his conflict with you, he can be free to be open and vulnerable to you and potentially adopt your position. When Trump says things like: "I like a good fighter," he's not kidding and he's not bipolar. He's just a man who has blind spots regarding how his Gift is operating, just like me and you.

Your Gift will usually respond for you unless you are aware it is functioning all the time and unless you take steps to mediate it.

Let me offer the President of France, Emmanuel Macron, a little bit of advice as I watch him try to convince Trump to reenter the Paris Agreement, the international climate accord. By the way, Macron did exactly the right thing from a Gift perspective by clamping Trump's hand in a death grip until Trump had to free himself when they first met. Notice how positively Trump responded to that. It even started a bromance.

If I were Macron, I would remind myself first that meek lion tamers do not survive long in the cage. I am sitting right next to Trump, staring right into his eyes, unwaveringly. I explain that I have a powerful resolve deep in my soul. It is so strong, the only way I can explain it is for Trump to imagine that my platoon has been trapped behind enemy lines and that all of my fellow soldiers have been wiped out by a legion of Nazi Stormtroopers, bombed relentlessly by the Luftwaffe from overhead.

I say to Trump I am the only one left alive and as I look out over the bodies of my dead comrades, I do the only logical thing left. I load up as much ammunition as I can and then…I launch my attack. Even though, Monsieur Trump, I would surely not survive, I would wait until the first soldier came over my bullet-ridden body and then take a shot at the Nazi and then announce: "That was for reneging on the Paris Agreement, you bastards." Then I would strongly grip Trump's arm, too strong, and switch gears really fast by saying that Melania looks lovely this evening, that he is a sly dog for marrying up four levels above himself, and that I hope Trump enjoys the really good steak he and the others will have with the wives in tow at the Eiffel Tower restaurant.

My guess, after all of this, is that Trump would chuckle and smile and say that he really likes Macron, that he still does not like the accord, but is still looking forward to dining, of course. Macron would need to then grip Trump's arm, again too hard, staring into his Trumpian eyes, and say: "Oh, I forgot to tell you the very last part of the story. After the other Stormtroopers shot me again, after they shouted they would never consent to the Paris Agreement, I would shoot the dead soldier one last time for good measure and shout, "Vive La France" before I died a glorious and honorable death, defending my passion…something worth dying for." And then Macron could finish with a question.

"What are you willing to die for, Trump?" Nothing like a good interrogatory to clank around in the Prophet's head, just like an old-school pinball getting shot up into the machine, where it can bounce around the bumpers and lights for hours. Come on, Trump, grab Melania and let's get to our dinner now.

The Prophet loves strength and conflict. But don't walk too closely in front of the bull. Let the Prophet see you taunting other bulls. Above all else, never, ever, under any circumstances, show weakness. I am imagining, after Macron asks Trump if there are things he would die for himself, Trump might just say he should look at the Paris Agreement again. Good luck, Monsieur Macron. You can call me if you need any other input in exchange for dinner at the 58 Tour Eiffel Restaurant, of course, with our lovely wives who are three or four levels above us, too.

If I were to frame an ode to the Prophet, it would begin with an appreciation of the animal self. Prophets truly are lions, champions of the cause, fearless and headstrong and fixated. Thank you for your boundless energy and your zeal for life. Thanks for bulldozing when we need it and for being the blasting dynamite to clear new paths.

Prophet Unicorn

Malala Yousafzai, the young lady who has been standing up for women's education rights in Pakistan since she was a little girl, is my pick for the Gift Unicorn of the Prophet. Malala claims Muhammad Ali, another Prophet, as one of her role models. In her native country, the Taliban seeks to ban girls from attending school, but Malala did not sit for that.

At the ripe age of eleven, she became an activist for education access, wrote blogs, participated in the making of a documentary about her life's conditions and challenges, gave interviews, and enjoyed growing recognition as a result of her shining a light into the darkness of the inhuman, evil restrictions the Taliban sought to impose. Speaking at a local press club at that age, she said: "How dare the Taliban take away my basic right to education?"

The Taliban continued efforts to terrorize girls, teachers, administrators, and parents. They issued more edicts and destroyed more schools. By the time Malala was fifteen years old, she was an embarrassment, a voice that had to be silenced, a target. She received published threats in local newspapers, in social media, and in notes shoved under her door at home. She kept going to school. She kept riding the bus. One day in early October, a Taliban gunman climbed on her school bus and shot her through her head, neck, and shoulder. They used religious scripture to justify what could reasonably be called an assassination attempt.

In short, the Taliban had no idea what they were up against in this young girl because not only did she survive, she has been kicking the Taliban around in ways they will never comprehend, mainly by ignoring them and not getting in the mud with them, which diminishes their power, all the while lifting up young women across the planet, in the tradition of great Prophets like Mahatma Gandhi and Martin Luther King.

I also thought it may be nice to have a younger Gift Unicorn, to underline the point simultaneously that a Gift is timeless and has no physical age. At the age of seventeen, Malala won the Nobel Peace Prize. As I write, she is only twenty. If you are a member of the Taliban, you have a long road ahead of you. She's just getting started. In her words:

> *"The terrorists thought they would change my aims and stop my ambitions, but nothing changed in my life except this: weakness, fear and hopelessness died. Strength, power and courage were born...I am not against anyone, neither am I here to speak in terms of personal revenge against the Taliban or any other terrorist group. I'm here to speak up for the right of education for every child. I want education for the sons and daughters of the Taliban and all terrorists and extremists."*

The light side of her Prophet Gift did exactly what it was designed to do…double down, triple down on good against evil. All of the historically significant, mature, humanitarian Prophets have done exactly what Malala is doing here. They avoided obsessing and over-focusing personally on the people they would challenge and soared right over them to accentuate and accomplish an ideal. Before this is all over, when she has banked some more experience and life wisdom, this young woman will be running the country, leading a whole new and different revolution and not just on behalf of women, but of a generation of people across the globe. Her father, who is difficult to notice, will continue to help her get there.

Ziauddin Yousafzai, Malala's father, is an obvious Server who has no interest in the spotlight himself. He stays in the background as much as possible…modest, helpful, and self-sacrificial. He set aside his career in favor of serving his daughter's needs and interests and has made it an important focus of his life. As a result, Malala is able to experience an unusually high level of assistance in furtherance of her mission, in support of her life's work. When folks ask him how he taught his daughter to become so courageous, he just says: *"Don't ask me what I did. Ask me what I did not do. I did not clip her wings. That's all."*

Now isn't that a sunset to look at? A full moon at night? A Server father assisting his Prophet daughter so that she might be able to lead the world. Ziauddin may be doing some important parenting work here too, modeling to his daughter how to function in furtherance of one's natural Gift, showing her it is good to be who you were designed to be, regardless of society's labels, regardless of age.

Together, they are the most stunning father/daughter Gift Team I have ever seen.

Teacher

Auditor of Information

TEACHERS ARE DRIVEN TO NEVER ACCEPT information at face value, preferring to take a methodical step back and pour through any and all qualified available data to determine efficacy and accuracy. For a Teacher, thorough research is as natural as the act of breathing.

As such, Teachers are driven to learn and learn more. They willingly accept the challenges of obtaining degrees and advanced degrees, perhaps more than one of them. They see the acquisition of knowledge as an end in and of itself and consider information basically just interesting but useless unless it is qualified and filtered and tempered by analysis.

Teachers are generally really interesting people to sit down and have a beer with, as they generally know a lot about many different things, have inquisitive minds, and remain open to looking at most any subject as something to enjoy, discuss, and learn more about. They are even-tempered, calm, and rarely excitable.

As for the rest of us, we wonder when a Teacher is going to stop questioning everything and just get on with it. *For God's sake, just pull the trigger and get going,* we tend to think when we see them engaged for what seems like way too long researching something. Teachers drive Exhorters crazy.

Teachers seem to occur in about the same proportion as Exhorters, about 12.5% of the population. Research and accuracy are important for the tribe, but not in overabundance. Nothing would get done if there were too many of them. We need them to ensure accuracy and they need us to do things, so they can have more things to study and apply their research to.

MANY YEARS BACK, AFTER I HAD JUST learned about these creatures, I found myself on the South Side of Chicago presenting some ideas to a non-profit organization concerning projects involving both the production of affordable housing, as well as work apprenticeships for troubled youth. The efforts in question were grounded in a long-standing government-based program that I had retrofit with a component for youth mentoring and training, potentially in the trades—carpentry, masonry, roofing, heating and air conditioning, etc.

I laid out the pieces of the puzzle to the group, having had some background and experience with all of it, and demonstrated that the non-profit could approach the whole matter in an expense-neutral fashion and could even produce some funding for itself along the way. It was the days of Bill Clinton and many non-profits were under a lot of pressure to become self-funded. So there was excitement in the room when they heard that financial part, as there usually was when I spread the good word to groups like this.

My audience was the board of directors, so I was in the presence of decision-makers. I animated my topic to them thoroughly, as an Organizer would, and incorporated specific elements of their existing capacities into this new vision, this new possibility. As I rounded the last corner of my presentation, they had all but started the first project. It fit perfectly into who they were and what they were trying to get done. My asking if there were any questions at the end seemed a distant redundancy. Even the director of the group had an expression on her face that said there was no need to offer a chance to ask questions; we were done and moving along to the starting line.

Then a gentleman raised his hand and asked me what year the government agency that shepherded this program had been founded. Through the name alone—the Department of Housing and Urban Development—any adult would have ascertained it may have been around since the Hoover Dam was built, the days of the New Deal. But he wanted a birth year. The impact of his question was hard to describe. Imagine you have gone to the latest and best *Star Wars* movie and it blows your mind because of the excitement, the color, the special effects, the passion, the humor, the imagination, etc. And everyone walks out of the theatre laughing or crying or talking too loudly about how amazing the movie was and someone turns to you and asks, "What film speed do you think they shot the movie in?"

I guess the best way to describe it is to say that while all of us had felt that the conversation was *ending*, it was clear that this gentleman thought it was *only just beginning*. Said differently, while everyone else in the room had reasonably accepted what I described and laid out, especially since it was a government-related enterprise, the inquisitor had accepted exactly none of it. I could tell from the rest of the table's reaction that this was not the first time they had experienced this from their learned board member. There was a sensation that he had just popped a big balloon in the room and the air was now rapidly leaking out. I saw looks of exasperation on people's faces that basically said, *Here we go again. Nothing is ever easy. Nothing is ever going to get done. Delays, delays, and more delays.*

Well, I knew that our researcher was a Teacher, so I just buckled up my seat belt and strapped myself in for the ride. I made a gesture, a wave of my hand that basically said no worries. "Well, the group here must be very blessed to have a member who has a mind that can ensure accuracy and one who cares so much about the mission that he is willing to sacrifice time and energy to investigate and validate any possible endeavors thoroughly."

The Teacher looked at me with an expression that said, "Well, of course, what other reason could there possibly be?"

The rest of the group looked at me like I was categorically insane.

"Let me dedicate myself to writing down each specific question you may want me to field that I can't answer concisely this evening so I can follow through tomorrow and provide you with exact answers," I said.

"Now let's get started with all of your questions" I added, as I sat down next to him.

The board knew, as I did, that such projects required unanimity, so there was little for the rest of them to do except retreat to their homes. I sat with him at the table for the next couple of hours. He was an interesting man and I realized I was also getting a free personal training session as well in furthering my Gift Education of Teachers. The way his mind worked was completely different than my own. I became aware that conversations were just beginning points for Teachers. They had no intention of walking through a door you were holding open for them. They would back away from the door and start walking around the building to study it before deciding to return and possibly walk through. I knew that if I kept at it, there would be a reward for all involved, so I did.

I followed up the next day, listed out the unanswered questions and the corresponding answers, threw in a few periodicals and passages from the CFR, the Code of Federal Regulations, and exactly one specific Section of the Act. A couple of days later I got another list of questions back. *Impressive*, I thought. I would have fallen asleep if I were him. Perhaps slipped into a coma.

A week after that initial gathering, my inquisitor invited me back to meet with the board again for the purpose of getting started. He also asked me if I wouldn't mind too much speaking to two other non-profits he had lined up, sister organizations that he believed could benefit as well. I told him I did not mind. When I returned to the group, I smiled and said I was happy to have survived all the questions, which got a few knowing laughs from the audience. The Teacher didn't notice because he had his head buried in papers.

Teachers are not trying to irritate you. It's just how they are. Don't even try to persuade, or sell, or use charm or charisma; that would be a complete waste of your time. Teachers won't change their process for you, ever. They don't do anything on the fly under any circumstances other than dire emergencies. They are the all-time masters of a lack of spontaneity. But when Teachers eventually accept your information and then qualify you as an expert, take the rest of the day off because you can be sure they are out doing your work for you at that point, sharing a lot of your good information with others that has passed a quality control process. Call the office and tell them you'll be in meetings the balance of the afternoon. Buy yourself a nice lunch and then treat yourself to the latest science-fiction film at your favorite matinee. You deserve a hooky day after all of that, a just reward for your endurance.

Light Teacher

A Teacher delights in detailed studies. Teachers love research and see thoughtful and careful analysis as an essential part of any noteworthy decision-making process. They take to the Internet like a fish to water, as it is a natural domain for things like Wikipedia, online libraries, and the like. They will take whatever time and effort is necessary to dive all the way down the rabbit hole of a subject and follow it all the way to the end even if it takes weeks, months, years, or a lifetime.

Teachers have serious natures and tend to be more focused, which enables them to study and learn and research endlessly. Distractions to that end are things Teachers avoid like frivolity, poetry, and the world of emotions. Teachers always seem to have multiple areas of inquiry and learning and research that they are engaged in, so they tend to be centered on those interests at all times. It takes a focused and enduring nature, for example, to get degree after degree. If you meet someone who went to law school, then went to medical school, and then maybe decided to pick up a Masters or PhD in history as a third degree along the way, chances are you have just met a Teacher.

A Teacher has a quick mind for deductions and uses logic and reasoning as naturally as breathing air. Teachers are fact-driven, objective thinkers and will go wherever logic leads them. As such, they are comfortable in the world of syllogisms: If this is true and that is true, then this must also be true.

A Teacher is not dissuaded by charisma, sales talk, charm, or persuasion. They devalue those interactive elements in favor of more facts, more figures, and more spreadsheets. I think one can see the value in this trait if you think about times when everyone believed something that turned out to be totally wrong, like when humanity discovered the world was actually round and not flat. Teachers figure stuff like that out because they follow facts and empirical observation, not social convention, trends, or customs.

Teachers have mellow and even temperaments. Teachers are perhaps the calmest of Gifts, because they have the ability to step back from things and experience life through more of a research or curiosity lens. I have not seen a Teacher get sideways before or ever witnessed one lose it; they are calm, collected, studious, and thoughtful in general.

Teachers are interesting conversationalists for those who are searching. If you ever get trapped in an airport bar due to a delayed flight, it is best to hope you can sit next to a Teacher if you have a few hours to kill, because they are really fun to talk with. It seems like no matter what topic you want to start with, they can follow right along and keep up and then start adding colors and dimensions to the subject. They can take you down side roads, back roads, and related subjects. And they love to do it too. They are like walking Wikipedia reference material. They get to that point because they are interested in everything, want to study it, and probably already have looked into it to some degree so they can be verbal about it. The effect is a little like how jazz players just join in and start improvising. Bring up any subject with Teachers and they will catch your tune and start jamming with you.

A Teacher is self-disciplined. Teachers are naturally able to commit the time and energy needed to get the study and research done. They accept it as a given, just as a long-distance runner accepts that long hours of training are part of winning a marathon. They don't complain about hours spent in the library, on the Internet, or in the production and refinement of spreadsheets. If they have a massive scientific project, an engineering challenge, a medical mystery, or an advanced degree in their sights, they just get to it and start grinding it out. I have never seen or heard a Teacher complain in that set of circumstances. They may tell you that they haven't eaten or slept properly for days, but they will make sure to share they are making good progress, and say it with a smile on their faces.

DARK TEACHER

A TEACHER CAN CONCENTRATE ON THE facts and details of things to the detriment of personal application. Like every other Gift, Teachers can get lost in the focus of their natural skill set, in the forest of research and study, and not notice that they haven't taken a shower in three days and others are beginning to smell them. They should learn to notice they haven't gone out to play with the kids or taken their spouse out to dinner in a while. They can get so caught up in the knowing of things that they can lose sight in the doing of things. You can only learn about construction projects and describe them so much. Then there is a time to get the hammer out and start building. Teachers have to be careful to be more proportionate and balanced between the worlds of thought and action.

Teachers think that others will be better off when informed by their learning and thinking. Because Teachers have so much faith in research, data, learning, and study, they naturally think you would or should as well. Sometimes when you ask them a question, you can tell by the first sentence or two their answer is going to be a half-hour long. As such, Teachers can operate from the premise that you also need to understand everything that they do, so you can benefit from the results of their analysis. But that's not true in many instances, as the rest of us know. Life is not a test tube and it is important for Teachers to be aware the rest of us may be drawn to the unknown, the unexpected, and the improvised. Poetry, love, romanticism, and art may not be related to study and research, for example.

A Teacher can become more interested in research than people. Teachers can become so consumed with data and facts that they overlook human beings. Teachers would be wise to remember people are also research projects, in and of themselves, and you can learn a lot of things by studying people and learning about what is inside them. People carry around whole worlds in their interiors…interesting and amazing worlds.

Also, there are different kinds of learning. Teachers are very good at cognitive learning, but there are also social learning and emotional learning. There is experience too, which has forms of learning… relationship, dance, athletics, etc. A Teacher would be wise to remember that our humanity offers many bandwidths of experience and learning, not just the more linear or academic ones.

Teachers can feel they are the ones who will determine who or what is to be, based on their qualifications. Because Teachers are capable in areas involving research, it is common for them to erroneously conclude they are the ones best suited to qualify who is supposed to be considered an expert, or what should happen next in a given set of circumstances. Teachers should remember sometimes folks don't want someone who is the most technically skilled, they may want someone who has charm, or charisma, or a special energy…more ephemeral considerations than black-and-white skills or academic knowledge. Maybe sometimes people want something undefined or unpredictable to take place next, something new and unexpected.

TEACHER INTERVIEW

IF YOU LOOK INTO A TEACHER'S EYES, YOU'LL see calm and friendly generally and then you may also start to become aware that you are seeing complete and total disbelief. I'm not going to say mistrust here, because that is something more in line with what you might see with a Prophet. Disbelief in the sense that the eyes say they are certainly willing to listen, but they will not accept or act on what you are sharing until after they have checked it all out. It's actually a little hysterical to the rest of us, because we are already on the raft, floating down the river, and we turn back and see that the Teacher is still on the shore waving at us all.

The Teacher overlaps with the Prophet, as we continue around our Gift Wheel. The Prophet is motivated to determine the truth, just as the Teacher is motivated to find out what is accurate. The truth, or what is right, is awfully darn close to accurate. Different, but close. And both Gifts love to share what they have determined with others.

The Teacher is really interested in listening to your soliloquy of The Gift System, similar to any new subject worthy of discussion and perhaps investigation. Then, like Teachers do with pretty much everything else, they mention how it will be great if there were actual studies done to prove scientifically that the Gifts exist. In other words, they likely won't accept any of it until it is proven through research and possibly spread-sheets.

Teachers make great teachers (naturally), especially in drier subjects like science and history and mathematics. They also make great engineers, computer programmers, compliance officers, scientists, doctors, and researchers (naturally).

A Teacher dreams of being able to make a discovery of great value for others as a result of analysis and then of going about the business of informing others of this great, qualified information. When you see a scientist getting a Nobel Prize in physics as a result of having been able to prove a theory after years of trial and error and research, that's a good example of what a greatest moment would be for this Gift.

If you want to name that Gift in one note with regard to a Teacher (as I previously mentioned) just know that when you see someone with an advanced degree in not just one field, but two or more, there is little question who you are looking at.

Celebrity Teachers are harder to find since they don't seek the spotlight, so the public figures you tend to see of this Gift may be more along the lines of scientists, scholars, computer nerds, and folks that formally do research for a living, like in the area of medical breakthroughs.

A good example of a Celebrity Teacher or public figure would be "Sully" Sullenberger, the now-famous pilot who safely landed his airliner in the Hudson River off Manhattan after it had been disabled by a flock of Canadian geese immediately after takeoff, the man who saved every one of the 155 souls on board in the process. Sully is not sullen. He's a Teacher, measured, calm, even.

If you have ever seen him interviewed, you get a good sense of just how steady and undistracted a Teacher is. People ask him how in the hell did he stay calm enough and know what was involved with setting down that massive steel object in an insane set of impossible circumstances. Sully just calmly rattles off a lot of facts about pilot training, the weather conditions that day, and how the shape of the plane lent itself to acting both as a glider and boat, not a paperweight or an anchor. He explains it all in monotone syllables as if it were a science fair project. His mind and therefore his speech are directed at what was involved to solve the puzzle.

I was not surprised to discover that Sully had a very high IQ, got grades high enough to finish at the top of his high school class, and that he earned two separate master's degrees in two totally separate subjects,

Industrial Psychology and Public Administration. You're busted, Sully. We have your number.

It seems like Sully has only recently become freer to enjoy his deed, maybe because he now sees all of the people and families his actions saved. Almost like he has been convinced by those facts over time, the evidence and statistics if you will. I think everyone who was on that plane should say a prayer of thanks for Teachers, calm and studious as they are.

I hope any women reading this book will forgive me in advance for a brief story involving Tony Rampino, the husband of a Server woman who worked in my employ. Tony was a Teacher of Italian descent and was a little more freewheeling and expressive than most Teachers I know. I actually thought Tony was an Exhorter when I met him, but his wife quickly corrected me. I asked her how she knew he was a Teacher and she proceeded to laugh at me. Wives typically always know exactly what their husband's Gifts are after you explain the Seven Gifts to them. How could they not know? Who else has studied husbands more?

She told me that she had recently provided Tony with a whole stack of brochures on roofing materials and options for installation for the purpose of having the roof replaced on their home. After she paused, I said I did not find anything remarkable about that. Then she shared it was to have the roof replaced five or seven years from now. She had learned being married to a Teacher it would likely take him several years of research to eventually get to a place where he would actually make a decision to do something. She confirmed my suspicion that the roof was basically just fine right now. She had calculated the remaining roof life before the roof needed replacing and guessed at how long he would need to study the matter. I was convinced now.

So I was sitting with Tony the Teacher and his wife and daughters at a table after one daughter had just been married, when all of a sudden all of the (Italian) females in his family started arguing and fighting with one another. Tony tried to intervene and help everyone calm down, but when he did, all of the women turned on him, like the dogpile I mentioned earlier in this Gift Tale (see Volume I). Tony calmly looked at me and asked if I would like to accompany him to refresh our drinks. As we were walking away, I looked at him with questioning eyes, and he said: "Don't try to figure it out, Dave."

The Teacher had done all the research he could and determined there was no answer to this one. I had just witnessed a Gift Moment for the record books. It is impossible for me to count the number of times I have forgotten that Teacher's admonition, only to remember later after I had done some damage that I had forgotten what he taught me that night. Don't forget the Gift Tip we learned here either. If you ever want to know what brand of roofing to buy, or what company would be qualified to do a roof job, you know what Gift to ask. And think of all the different topics this applies to. Who needs *Angie's List* or *Consumer Reports*? Teachers are the best folks to consult.

I was lucky to have a Teacher as a doctor recently, a man who had followed the string of data all the way to the end. Thank goodness for his efforts. His story may be a good one to tell as I try to share who these people are and how important they are to all of us. Back in 2003, I fell off a ladder building a basketball goal for my daughters and shattered my right heel. It's a really bad injury, because your heel is actually shaped like a fist and hollow. So putting it back together is similar to trying to reassemble a broken egg inside of a plastic baggie filled with water.

Last year, I had my eleventh surgery, a procedure that included bolting on more hardware. This time my exhausted skin, flesh that had become mostly scar tissue, gave up and would not close the incision. To boot, a strange inflammation began creeping up my leg. None of the doctors I went to could figure it out. They had me rubbing all kinds of ointments and antibiotics and steroid creams over all of it, which only pissed off my foot even more.

I finally hunted down the best doctor in the matter I could find in Chicago, Doctor Joaquin Brieva, who explained that his medical approach was entirely "research-based." He also shared that he would not be giving me any superficial or speculative diagnoses and would only comment on my case when the entire battery of completed test results were in his hands. He said "research-based" about fifty times in my first visit to his office, as if to underline what his Gift was. I got the message.

After the test results came back, he called me in and explained that my condition was not caused by any external forces, as in a rash or bacteria, and that all the prior diagnoses had therefore been incorrect.

"Well, what is the solution?" I inquired.

"Diet. You have to change the way you eat. You have some military in you and so do I. I was in the Army when I was younger and I have lost 80 pounds myself. If I can do this, you can too."

Now, this was a shock to me on a variety of levels. First, the good doctor was a handsome, fit man and I could never have imagined him 80 pounds heavier. Second, I could not see how changing my eating was going to supposedly fix all of this. These were medical issues and this guy was talking about something completely different: food. What about new ointments and new creams and new pills for me to take? I wondered to myself if this doctor guy was like Bill Binney, a fellow Teacher, the mathematician who focused on behavior to solve math problems. So could this guy be a doctor who focused on food to solve medical problems?

I explained to Brieva that the only thing I understood about food was that I liked it. I loved greasy-spoon breakfasts so much I could probably write a popular diner blog on them. I lived close to Palatine, Illinois, where Weber barbecues are made, a place where there are probably more diners per capita than anywhere in the world.

He said he had adopted a "plant-based diet" and had stopped eating carbs, dairy, sugar, and red meat. I wiped my brow at his red meat comment, being that I am from Kansas City, the world capital of beef and barbecue. I considered that maybe my stupidity concerning food could be my advantage. I had to change, so I threw Brieva's four-way filter in place and went Marines Corps on it. I stopped eating fish and chicken and pork as well about three months after I had begun, as a result of watching cautionary Netflix documentaries.

The inflammation rapidly left, my wound healed, and I lost 72 pounds. My foot modeling days are over, but I can live with that. I was on nine medications, which included some higher-octane pain medication, anti-inflammatories, high-blood pressure, pre-diabetes, and cholesterol pills. I have not taken any medications in months. Nurses tell me my blood work is better than the answer key they use and ask me how I did it. My regular doctor unchecked all of my negative diagnoses and cleared my medical chart.

Bill Binney would like Doctor Brieva, I think. They would have coffee together—no cream, of course—and talk about how much fun it is to look up and see the building that is connected to the wall.

But remember that Brieva's story is a Teacher's story. Brieva was willing to follow the research wherever the data led him. He was ultimately able to see past the predictable world of medicine and into an entirely new venue because he trusts research and embraces the data he unearths. I would never have believed that eating vegetables and fruits would close my wounds and heal my body.

I went back to Dr. Brieva over these last holidays, a year after his admonitions to me, for his sake not mine, because I felt he deserved to see the validation of his research and the fruit of his work. Surprisingly, he remembered me. I told him all the things that had changed for the better in my life as a result of eating right, things we had never discussed and things I could never have guessed at.

His knowing eyes looked exactly like my friend Nick's, my New York City tour guide, when I was telling him all about my adventures in Studio 54 and my revelations about the crazy and wonderful and interesting world of various sexualities, among many other things I saw that night. Like Nick, Brieva already knew what I was going to say before I said it. I became aware the doctor spent his work days trying to tell people about things they would likely never fully believe.

He shared that out of the thousands of people he calculated he had seen over the years, I was only the second who had actually accepted his counsel, implemented it, and then returned later to share the results with him. The first guy carried over 300 pounds when he started and returned at 180. I was glad I had a little bit of an edge knowing from the outset that Brieva was a Teacher. We closed our moments together with the doctor proudly showing off pictures of his healthy-looking daughter, a young doctor who was using healthy eating as a core in her medical practice. The family tradition of research-based medicine continues.

If you want to mess with Teachers, accuse them of being reckless and sloppy and ill-informed about something. Ask them when they are ever going to learn to slow down and get their facts straight before they just fly off and do something on a whim.

I have found that many writers will try to find a way to drop the name of a favorite author in one of their books and that usually it's an excursion well worth taking to discover what they are pointing at. James Lee Burke is my favorite American author and his detective character, Dave Rochibeaux from New Iberia, Louisiana, has a soft spot for research librarians because they are so helpful in solving some of the puzzles he is faced with fighting crime.

And so I offer Detective Dave Rochibeaux's informal ode to research librarians as our Seven Gifts ode to the Teacher Gift:

So where do you go to find a researcher who is intelligent, imaginative, skilled in the use of computers, devoted to discovering the truth, and knowledgeable about science, technology, history, and literature, and who usually works for dirt and gets credit for nothing?*

---

* From *Last Car to Elysian Fields* by James Lee Burke

TEACHER UNICORN

SAL KHAN IS MY PICK AS THE TEACHER Gift Unicorn. He's the guy who I think has figured out how to use technology in the best of all possible ways. Salman Khan went to MIT and obtained a Master's of Science degree, becoming proficient in areas involving mathematics, computer science, and electrical engineering. Then he traveled to Harvard and obtained a Master's of Business Administration. Two advanced degrees.

When he was about 20 years old, he went about trying to tutor his cousin, Nadia, using the Internet. After other relatives sought him out as well, he started a YouTube channel in 2006. Three years later, because of the success of Khan Academy, as he called it, he quit his job as a financial analyst to pursue educational tutorials. In the first few years, his channel garnered almost a half billion views.

He charged people exactly nothing, preferring modest sponsorships that avoided the entanglement and distraction of monetization. Khan Academy's mantra is: "Learn almost anything…for free." The videos are prehistoric by today's tech standards, campy even, and feature hand scribblings and old-school diagrams. Khan narrates many of them personally and never shows his face as a way of keeping the subject focused on the topic and not him. He recorded many of them in his sound booth, his closet at home, with his high-tech equipment, his $25 Logitech headset. His topics include math, algebra, geometry, science, economics, and social science.

In the earlier days, Nadia told him that she did not want to talk with him on the phone anymore, that she only wanted videos. That way, she could go at her own rate, not have someone looking over her shoulder, and could review more difficult concepts by replaying them over and over without embarrassment. Khan realized that he was less popular in person.

Microsoft founder Bill Gates helped to get the Khan Academy party started by singling out Sal's efforts at a public ideas forum, which got passed around in the form of a video file. Khan's response was: "I shit a brick when I saw that." Gates is ferocious when it comes to math and has pointed out that his foundation's research shows that math skills are a significant stumbling block to employment.

Which brings us to 2018. Khan Academy has accumulated over 6,500 educational videos, over 3.8 million subscribers, and in excess of 1.5 billion views. Sal Khan was named as one of *Time* magazine's 100 most influential people in the world and was featured on the cover of *Forbes* along with the story, "$1 Trillion Opportunity."

What I like best about Sal Khan is not just what he did do but what he did not do. He recognized that the purity and innocence of his endeavor, which began with tutoring Nadia, did not need monetization to flourish. Most people in his position would have capitalized the business and walked away billionaires and then some.

But Sal didn't. He started a brick-and-mortar institution, Khan Lab School, as an adjunct to his online efforts; he only accepts what would be considered smaller-scale compensation by any standard for a man who could easily make a windfall fortune off a movement he has begun. The joy of research, the discipline of learning, and the empowerment of knowledge won the day because of Sal's renaissance thinking. I have never seen a better use of technology to further the minds of youth in our world.

GIVER

CHAMPION OF SOCIETY'S ADVANCE

OUR SEVENTH AND LAST GIFT, THE GIVER, SEES broader patterns in both our race and in society's history, and acts to advance larger-scale efforts and societal causes to make things better for all of us, present and future. Givers are very large-scale thinkers and see their purpose as one of moving things forward for us all.

Givers have a knack for financial dealings, so it is common to see Givers sometimes accumulate massive amounts of wealth. Even if Givers do not personally accumulate larger scale wealth over the course of their lifetimes, the endeavors they dedicate themselves to usually end up becoming extremely valuable in financial terms. I'll try to give examples of the differences between direct wealth and indirect wealth.

Givers have to be careful to not start operating from the premise that nothing is as important as their broad-based effort and also to not become prideful in the gifts they give to society, or on society's behalf.

Givers are by far the rarest of the Gifts. I am guessing less than 1% of the population, at best. You have to travel to a rare rainforest in the Amazon, hang in the trees, and hide with binoculars to see one.

* * * * *

I HAVE FOUND IN THIS LIFE THAT THE LAST job is usually the hardest. I tell that to my wife, kids, and those in my charge frequently. If you are painting a room, cleaning up a basement, moving a friend, or doing a project at work, the last part—the finishing of things—usually becomes the most difficult part. At least it seems that way to me. So it is with explaining the Giver to you. Here's my fundamental problem: I don't know that I have actually met one in person and therefore have not been able to study this rare bird up close. If I did meet one or know one at some point, I was not aware of it.

But I sure know them when I see them from a distance. I can spot them a mile away through a telescope. So I will go about explaining things a little differently as a result of this quandary and start with the Light and Dark sides of this Gift.

* * * * *

L IGHT G IVER

A GIVER HAS A KEEN DESIRE TO see humanity's causes advanced and a unique ability to imagine matters for what they represent for humanity as a whole, not just an individual, and certainly not just for self-interest. Givers intuitively see a much bigger picture than the rest of us do and concern themselves with our society's broader benefit. As such, they will be able to see bigger implications in most anything: technology, art, exploration, history, etc. and they will be able to see ways to improve these topics for our entire species.

Givers typically have financial keenness, which can manifest in the short or long term. A Giver will typically engage in activities that reflect an acute sense of financial insight, skill, and acumen. It seems a Giver can even manifest financial acumen intentionally or unintentionally. Maybe it is precisely because the focus is so large in scale that one is frequently able to achieve larger scale financial success, directly and indirectly.

Givers feel their personal needs are secondary to the needs of others. While many Givers will engage in activities that create immense wealth, they typically do not personally benefit from all of it. Givers are not personally greedy, but are greedy for success so that wealth can be created to further benefit mankind.

Dark Giver

A GIVER CAN BECOME PRIDEFUL AS A result of the gift given and has to be cautious about identifying too closely with the gifts given. Feeling good about gift-giving is one thing, but being prideful is quite another. Building self-esteem through gift-giving can sometimes go too far.

Givers can build personal power through the giving of things and should therefore be careful about building their influence through their ability to give gifts. Givers should also not use people's desire to receive gifts from them as a means to leverage personal power.

Givers can sometimes determine the value of others according to their wealth and evaluate folks based on how Givers evaluate themselves. Since so many Givers are financially savvy and successful, they can begin to see others in the same terms and assess people's value or importance based on how much wealth others have accumulated.

Givers can presume they are able to see a need and a solution. Because they are naturally able to comprehend larger considerations that are relevant to humanity as a whole, Givers can develop a sense of presumptuousness in terms of what they see as both a problem and a solution. While it is true that it is important to have humanity's interests at heart, it is also true that part of our humanity involves smaller-scale matters, matters that may relate to an individual, or an individual's set of circumstances.

Much like a Server can feel rejected when services are rejected or not needed, Givers can feel personally rejected when the gift they wish to give is rejected or not needed. Problems can arise when they align their sense of identity too closely with their gift.

* * * * *

SO NOW THAT WE HAVE WALKED THROUGH the Light and Dark sides of this final Gift, I am going to share three short views of Givers, ones I can spot from a distance. I am going to start with a familiar one who has amassed one of the largest personal fortunes in human history and then share two more that are good examples of Givers who have not sought to accumulate personal wealth to give, but have engaged in broader causes that have created great value, both in societal as well as financial terms.

It is important to understand also that not every person of great wealth is a Giver, even though they may be engaged in various forms of philanthropy. Givers have a specific bend to them, a bend you can see clearly manifest in their focus and approach.

* * * * *

JEFF BEZOS, THE FOUNDER OF Amazon, is a Giver. His industry, the creation of the world's largest scale Internet-based provider of goods, as well as the largest provider of cloud infrastructure services, suggests that he is motivated to provide on a scale that can result in the betterment of lives for an entire world. He also founded an aerospace firm that focuses on space exploration called Blue Origin. His efforts are also amazingly financially lucrative, as he has become the wealthiest person in the world recently, depending on Amazon's stock price.

So clearly he has the initial markings of a Giver, but what seals it is the nature of his efforts outside of his industries, the character of his carefully selected philanthropic efforts. I think it is important to note that some people have questioned the depth of his heart for charity, expecting that Bezos would follow in the footsteps of Bill and Melinda Gates and other familiar billionaires like Warren Buffett and contribute to the Gates Foundation or perhaps his own.

Bill Gates is a Giver, too, but Warren Buffett is not. In Gates, you can see the mixture of financial acumen and a drive to see society's causes advanced. In Buffett, you see a good old American Prophet, a man who is long in IQ and reserved about the matter of money. When I say reserved, I am pointing at his Gift Tell, his ostensible frugality.

Buffet still lives in Omaha, Nebraska, occupying the same house he bought in 1959 for $31,000. He is known to only buy slightly used cars, some marked down due to hail damage, and drives them around for years and years without any driver. Buffett would not be able to avoid the sale shelf at the local supermarket and may still insist that his wife clip coupons from the newspaper. He goes to McDonald's regularly and claims that he splurges there occasionally. When he feels like treating himself, he buys the more expensive version of the breakfast sandwich, the one with egg and cheese, for an extra 50 cents. On lesser days, maybe when his IBM stock is down, he buys only the all-sausage version for half a dollar less.

Now that is true freedom. Having over $80 billion and being free to fully savor and enjoy a splurge of 50 cents. Consider that proportion carefully for a moment. If you consider the exact distance between 50 cents and $80 billion, you may also be looking at the exact measure of this man's ability to be who he is, which is worth much more than all the money in the world. Gift Freedom. So Buffett is a Prophet as sure as the day is long and a pretty cool one at that. I have grown to have a lot of respect for people who are unabashed in the open and visible expression of their Gift. I see it as a blessing to all involved. Buffett is donating almost all of his vast fortune to charity, but for an entirely different motivation than Gates is. For Buffett, simply, it is the right thing to do.

If you look carefully at one of the philanthropic projects Bezos has sponsored, the 10,000 Year Clock, you will see the unmistakable character and motivation of a Giver. The clock is 500 feet tall and powered by the earth's thermal cycles. It is designed to tick exactly one time each year, the century hand advances exactly once each 100-year interval, and a cuckoo shoots out exactly once every millennium. The project was conceived by a man named Danny Hillis back in the late 1980s. Bezos got involved within the last ten years to provide both funding, as well as the remote mountain to build it in. On the surface, the clock is both a poem and a technological marvel. But if you look deeper into its design, you really start to see the Giver Gift.

Carved into the mountain are five room-sized chambers for each of the following checkpoints: one year, ten years, 100 years, 1,000 years, and 10,000 years. The one-year chamber is a special orrery, a word that means a model of the solar system, and contains depictions not just of the planets and the earth's moon, but also of all the interplanetary space probes our race launched in the 20th century. The Clock will activate and run the orrery once a year on a predetermined date at solar noon.

The ten-year chamber is still under development. You can even send in your best shot, your grandest idea, and they will take it under consideration. There are no plans to animate the remaining chambers, as they are leaving the invitation open to future generations.

Not only is Bezos about advancing humanity, he is creating a project that will literally marry us in time and cause and illustrate in the process how we can merge the two across the arc of space-time and future generations. It may be both the most ambitious and rudimentary attempt at time travel, a thought that may be seen echoed in the name of the non-profit organization they formed to support the project: The Long Now Foundation.

Bezos wrote in a blog: "It's a special Clock, designed to be a symbol, an icon for long-term thinking." If Bezos had asked my opinion, I would have told him to rename it the "Giver Clock," as there may be no greater poetic axiom than this project that emblemizes the Giver aspiration. The name Giver Clock also embraces the notion that we will all need to come to grips with our own Gifts and the Gifts of others to advance our race. We need to make sure renaming it is okay with Danny, of course. I have to remember to be sensitive to people's feelings while I am organizing things.

I am going to venture a Gift Prediction here. Bezos is a radical thinker and is in no hurry. He is going to take his time and wait for the right set of ideas, or formulate some of his own over time. He will eventually come up with a most unusual and imaginative use for his fortune on humanity's behalf. Not only will Bezos knock the ball out of the park, he will take the cover clean off when he hits the big one. I predict it will be an event in human history in and of itself. I hope I live long enough to see it.

* * * * *

HERBERT VOGEL, A LEGENDARY COLLECTOR who amassed 4,782 works of fine art, was a Giver. He was born to a Russian Jewish garment worker from Harlem, never finished high school, worked in garment industry sweatshops, then served in the U.S. Army during World War II. For his entire professional life, Herb worked nights as a clerk sorting mail for the United States Postal Service and never made over $23,000 per year. He had no other source of personal income or wealth.

He married Dorothy, the daughter of a Jewish stationery merchant from New York. Dorothy got her bachelor's and master's degrees in Library Science and worked as a librarian for the Brooklyn Public Library her entire career. They never had children, inhabited a one-bedroom rent-controlled apartment in Manhattan's Upper East Side, lived extremely frugally, and shared their small living quarters with cats, fish, and turtles named after famous painters. I am convinced that Dorothy possessed the Teacher Gift and that her ability to research and analyze was a key driver in the couple's ability to thoughtfully amass this collection.

They both loved painting but realized they were not good enough at it to pursue it themselves, so they cultivated their love of art by trying to buy pieces from little-known artists who would allow them to pay in very small installments. They used Herb's income to eat and pay rent and Dorothy's to acquire art. Before Dorothy showed up, Herb spent a lot of late nights at Cedar Bar, a storied artists' hangout in Greenwich Village, listening to artists converse, learning with fascination. "I never even asked a question," Herb once shared.

Dorothy and Herb bought their first piece in 1962 using two basic criteria that went on to be used for decades in the future. The first was that they would only buy what they liked, which makes sense given that collecting art on two civil service incomes might be a little difficult, and the second was that they had to be able to carry the piece home. Fitting nearly 5,000 pieces of art in their one-bedroom apartment was no small challenge, so they gave up things like closets, couches, and chairs while learning to do the polka around all of the paintings.

Some of the artists, many of whom became famous later like Christo and Roy Lichtenstein, recognized intuitively that the Vogels were amassing an important collection, especially given their dogged dedication to the cause. The artists likely sensed that the purpose behind Herbert Vogel's drive was larger in nature and recognized Herb was out for humanity, not himself or his wife. The artists cut the Vogels better and better deals as a result. Right or wrong, all involved avoided the overhead of galleries.

The Vogel collection became, over time, a standard-bearer for minimalist and conceptual art and also included some post-minimalist work as well, all quite different from the pop art that generally reigned during the time of their acquisitions. The Vogel's collection gravitated towards simplicity, essential forms, nothingness, and monochromatic surfaces.

They had no retirement savings when that season came. Their collection could have yielded millions of dollars in investment profits, yet they made it clear they had not produced the collection for monetary gain and insisted that it remain intact in its entirety. They never sold one piece. In 1992, they gave the entire collection to the National Gallery of Art based on the condition that 2,500 of the works be evenly divided into 50 lots of 50 pieces each, with each lot then donated to one of 50 states. *The Dorothy and Herbert Vogel Collection: Fifty Works for Fifty States.* They made it clear that their objective was to ensure that all of the art belonged to the public. They specifically found a gallery system that would never charge admission to people who wished to see the exhibitions.

In Herbert Vogel, we see the Giver Gift in full bloom, propelled to push society forward, to collect, preserve, and revere its cultural and artistic treasures, a selflessness and order that is hard to even comprehend. Because of his largesse of imagination, he also created an enormous financial windfall opportunity which, in this case, he (and Dorothy) gladly gave as a gift to all of us.

* * * * *

NELSON MOLINA, A NEW YORK CITY trash collector, is a Giver. Nelson is a life-long New Yorker who began picking up people's refuse in 1981. Instead of just clanking heavy bags into the backs of municipal trash trucks, Nelson kept looking and looking, just like Herb Vogel the art collector kept listening and listening.

What Nelson saw was treasure. He noticed that people pushed great things to the curb, items that were not only perfectly fine, but pieces that were also sometimes beautiful and valuable. He saw that, as a function of our human condition, circumstances could prevail where refuse and beauty could become interchangeable. Sometimes there was no easy place to donate, or perhaps an object had become vexed by bad memories or feelings or history, or maybe folks just did not understand what it was.

Nelson Molina's industry also seemed to require him to possess insight into the psychological, emotional, and financial nuances of the inhabitants of the borough he served...larger insights about the industrialized, material, consumer society we live in and the erratic nature of value and possession and meaning within it. It's also quite a dramatic commentary on wastefulness.

Nelson started bringing things back to the warehouse, the same one the trucks drove out of. He cleaned the pieces, claimed the abandoned second floor as his own, and started laying things out for display. The sanitation workers are not allowed to pilfer things for personal use, but his efforts were still within the Department of Sanitation guidelines since the items never left the shop, and Nelson was and is an honest man. And he has higher purposes.

Other workers, even ones outside of Nelson's borough, began contributing as well, as Nelson had started a good game, an easier way to pass the time on the job, something fun to talk about on the routes. Items in his vast collection, which now numbers above 50,000 pieces, include paintings, sculpture, guitars, furniture, toys, clothes, jewelry, clocks, cowboy hats, stained glass windows—almost anything you could possibly imagine. A tapestry as varied as society itself.

The city relented and surrendered the second-floor warehouse space to him, as they did not have adequate funding to open a museum to hold the items, although many university professors, anthropologists, and art curators voted for the museum approach. There is a big sign that hails at the entrance to the exhibition: *Treasures in the Trash…A Special Tour With Nelson Molina.*

Some say that Nelson has an almost mystical sixth sense. Nelson says: "I love this job. It's one of the greatest jobs in the world." With respect to the formal standards of his curation, he claims: "It does not matter what it is. As long as it's cool…" I believe Nelson when he claims that he has a knack for knowing when something is valuable, perhaps by the way something poked out of a bag, or by the weight, or the sound the trash made when he picked it up. I also believe him when he says he can tell the difference (sight unseen) between a wine bottle and vase by a simple ping.

Someone needs to explain to Nelson that although he may not have a formal teaching certification, he could easily speak to behaviorists and anthropologists and historians to add to their research parties. He has created a museum, a collection, an archive, and seems to have done most all of it by sheer intuition and street smarts. Nelson groups things together by theme just like a director of a national gallery would. The gathering of works has to have financial value, so the city has ended up with an unexpected reserve, a little hedge. The place is not open for public viewing at present, except if you are part of a specially arranged tour for a group, or perhaps a reporter. Maybe someday it will be. I sure would like to see this Giver sanitation worker's present to humanity.

GIVER INTERVIEW

LOOKING INTO THE EYES OF A GIVER, I THINK you might pick up the sense that Givers may be in the moment with you, but are not of it. In other words, they may be functioning here with us in the physical world, in the same space, but may be operating mentally and emotionally in a different realm, almost in a slightly different dimension of time and place. They seem to have an extraordinarily long view of things, so the moment may not hold their attention well.

There really doesn't seem to be a Polar Gift of the Giver, and since there are Seven Gifts, an odd number, not everyone gets paired up. Maybe we could say that the Polar Gift is a spouse, since opposites usually attract and tend to balance us.

The Giver rhymes with both the Teacher and the Mercy. Givers manifest a calm, steady calculation in pursuits, so they overlap with Teachers that way…methodical, disciplined, and curious. Givers also possess a distinct empathy for others, which overlaps with Mercys, except that the Giver channels this care towards humanity itself, towards humanity as a whole, unlike Mercys who direct empathy towards individuals. So now we can bring our Gift Wheel to a close and make the grand circle complete.

I confess I don't know what a Giver might think of the Seven Gifts, but given Givers general sympathies towards our race, I am guessing they might enjoy this body of information more than the average Gift, if Gifts could ever be averaged.

I don't know either how you would ever know if your child was a Giver. Perhaps you would see a strong bend towards global issues. When you needed a Giver child to eat broccoli, you could mention it would empower one to do a better job aiding the lot of us. But I think that it probably takes a long time to see if someone is a Giver, almost like it takes a long time for a good wine to age.

Occupationally, Givers make great innovators, inventors, curators, collectors, explorers, investors, developers, and entrepreneurs. I am also guessing a lot of students at MIT may be Givers.

Givers must be dreaming in visions that will bring our race forward, creating resources necessary to propel those visions ahead, and providing resources for others who are engaged in those objectives as well, resources that can be massive in nature, as big as a solar eclipse.

To name that Gift in one note, if you see a situation in the newspaper, or on your smartphone these days, where some seemingly average person who lived a modest life had passed away and donated a million-dollar-plus fortune to an institution of higher learning, a fortune that no one knew about or ever would have guessed at, then you likely just saw a Giver pass through our world. The person had a long-term, hidden agenda to advance things and turned out being a lot more financially savvy than the Giver ever let on.

I guess if you were to mess with Givers, you could razz them about not caring about anyone but themselves, about not being concerned about where our race is headed.

If I were to write an ode to Givers, I would thank them so much for their radical ingenuity, masterful creativity, and prescient overall insight. As an Organizer, I have to say I am humbled by a Giver's ability to see beyond my longest view of things and the competence in planning well beyond the limits of my own skills.

GIVER UNICORN

I AM PICKING ELON MUSK AS THE GIVER Unicorn. He is so fired up and energetic about advancing humanity that it seems like he makes even his own head spin. Elon, an avid fan of science fiction, taught himself computer programming by the age of twelve. One of his favorite science fiction series, Isaac Asimov's *Foundation* books, shares the lesson that "you should try and take the set of actions that are likely to prolong civilization, minimize the probability of a dark age and reduce the length of a dark age if there is one." Musk appears to have taken the lesson to heart.

Elon founded and sold a couple of software companies early on and did really well as a result, but his first big moment came when he co-founded and then sold PayPal, the sale of which brought five billion dollars. Musk, however, was just getting started. He founded SpaceX, the first large-scale, successful private space transport company and then co-founded Tesla, the first large-scale electric car manufacturer. Both are now household names. He inspired SolarCity, a company that provides solar services to households, which then also became a subsidiary of Tesla. He also cofounded OpenAI, a non-profit organization dedicated to studying and promoting safe artificial intelligence for both today's and tomorrow's worlds. If all of that wasn't enough, he co-founded Neuralink, a company that utilizes neurotechnology when developing brain-computer interfaces. Then he started The Boring Company when he got pissed off about California traffic and decided he was going to tunnel under the hardpan and build a hyperloop.

He is building self-driving electric semi-trucks and wants to get started on electric supersonic jets soon. His express vision is "to change the world and humanity." Before all of this is over, I am guessing Tesla and SpaceX and SolarCity will have their logos on things sitting on the face of Mars.

I like three things about Elon Musk quite a bit. First, he still finds time to court a lot of interesting women while he is changing the world. Second, he openly shares a lot of proprietary knowledge and technology as an open invitation to other innovators to further humanity's cause. And third, he has a legendary sense of humor.

Recently, on one of his usual quarterly earnings calls, he told a lot of analyst types to stop asking him dumb questions. He said: "Boring bonehead questions are not cool." He also sold a bunch of flamethrowers for fun and then for April Fool's, announced that Tesla was filing bankruptcy. But my favorite was when he threw a Tesla Roadster on top of a SpaceX rocket, put it in orbit, and then livestreamed it while David Bowie played on its space stereo. It is fun to imagine what aliens would conclude if they ever found that one. *What in the hell is going on down on that planet?*

Musk's sense of humor is clear evidence he is not in the moment with the rest of us. He is somewhere else entirely, seeing way past what the rest of us see. Maybe Bezos and Musk need to have a couple of cups of coffee together. If these two Givers combined forces, they could nudge the direction of our planet's orbit.

* * * * *

I WOULD BE REMISS IF I DID NOT TELL a Chicago story here. My buddy of 25 years, George Clos, operated an automotive shop on the Northwest side of Chicago called Nortown. Our kids went to school together and the day I first met him, his whole family seemed to appear around my youngest daughter when I was dropping her off at school one morning. There may have been ten or more of them that poured out of oversize SUVs carrying camcorders and appearing to be highly energized, almost like a network television crew late for an important event. Turns out their oldest, George Jr., who had his hair neatly slicked back that day, intended to present my youngest daughter with a ring and the family was there to support him.

The whole family was shorter in stature and the patriarch had Elvis Presley hair. He asked me if I wouldn't mind moving a little bit so he could get a better camera shot. I looked around and my better instincts told me these were really good people, harmless people, and I actually started to see the virtue and nobility of young George's effort. Strangely, I found myself rooting for him. He did, after all, have very good taste. I stepped out of Elvis's way and suggested he get a different angle for better lighting. My Mercy Lauren, darling that she is, accepted and George Jr. turned magenta.

Since then, George Sr. has taken care of my cars and has understood me well enough to allow me access to his garage so I can walk around, smell the grease, talk to the mechanics, inspect the cars and all the medical procedures underway, and tinker on my own ride. It's like being in Skeet Murowski's garage, only the go-karts are bigger, faster, and more expensive. George even has Gojo hand cleaner (see Volume I).

A few years back, Tesla had opened up one of its first brick-and-mortar locations just west of the Loop. So one day, I asked George what he thought of the Teslas. Were they reliable cars? Had he seen many in the shop? George shared he thinks they do pretty well and that he hadn't seen many since Tesla handles all service as part of the purchase. He went on to mention that Tesla called him recently to make a deal with him. He explained that many Tesla owners buy after-market wheels, which we used to call "mags" growing up, and that Tesla's shop equipment could not conjugate the different wheels to balance tires, and so on. Tesla wanted an arrangement where they could shuttle all those situations to Nortown for a seamless Tesla-like service experience.

As George is telling me this story, he can tell I am very interested. He is, after all, a Server and notices stuff like that. He slides the pink message slip under my nose as collateral material for his tale, to show that Tesla did in fact call. I look at the name on the message.

"Is this who you spoke to?" I ask.

Yes, he spoke to that gentleman.

"What did you say to him?" I ask.

George explains that he told the Tesla person that he had no interest or need in making any deals because he ran the best tire shop around and he was going to get the business anyway, arrangement or not.

"George, do you have any idea who this is? Do you realize who you were talking to?"

No, George was not familiar with Elon Musk, the name I was looking at on the message slip. I looked around the garage. None of the mechanics knew of Elon Musk either.

"Do you know who Thomas Edison is?" I ask.

Yes, of course George knew who Thomas Edison was. So did the mechanics, whose heads were now solemnly nodding. "George…You just told Thomas Edison to fuck off."

I started laughing.

Only in Chicago.

Only at Nortown.

Now I can't count this as a Forrest Gump story for myself, because I had not spoken to Musk personally. But if I had, I would have counted it for sure. Years later, I texted George a picture of the Tesla Elon Musk sent up into space. "Are you getting a better picture now of who you told to screw off?" Truth be told, George remains nonplussed by it all. No one is going to get in his way. He is on a mission to serve, space rockets or not. He knows how to take care of your car and of you as well and won't be distracted from that by anything. I have watched him work with the same level of care and precision on a teenager's car that was worth less than a $1,000 as he would on a $200,000 Lamborghini.

Customers of his would just drive to his shop some days to sit in Nortown's lobby for a few hours and be around him and his wife Della, despite their cars running just fine. I suspected some of them made up mechanical problems just to go there. Some of his customers just drove over and sat in his waiting room like it was a coffee shop or something. He always had time for you, would let you pour out your troubles, and lend you an ear. The phones and the impatient rich guy with the platinum credit card could wait until you finished your story about your dog or your family or your childhood. Sometimes I think George is a therapist masquerading as a car mechanic. I call him the Oracle of Nortown. George would just listen as he served all day. He only offered advice if you asked for it.

Elon, if you are reading this, next time call me first before you talk to George. You may have to form a line behind the French president for my advice, but it'll be well worth it. You have to learn how to speak "Server." If you had approached George differently, he may have listened.

First and foremost, I would have suggested that you explain that there were a lot of people who needed his help, that you wanted to try to provide a clean path straight to him, and that you felt like it would be more cost-efficient for customers that way. You may have underlined the idea that you had confidence that all the Tesla owners would be in capable hands. As it was, he may well have concluded adding Tesla to the mix would have impaired his ability to serve people directly and more cost-effectively. Had you approached him that way, he might have tried to serve you and ask if there was a formal arrangement that may be helpful to you and to Tesla, now that he could see your better intentions.

Call me next time, Elon. My only ask will be a Tesla Roadster for the day. Not one in space. Here in Chicago. A black one. Black on black. With mags that only George can service.

Life is full of ironies and so is Chicago. When the old man with the Elvis haircut, the father-in-law, died recently, George's Nortown was forced to close down and Tesla ended up buying the property. I am sure Elon Musk probably did not make the connection.

In another irony, Tesla had to turn right around and sell it, due to the fact that they were bleeding some cash and could not develop it into a higher-end coffee shop, restaurant, lifestyle-oriented, Tesla repair place like they had planned. Tesla made a cool couple of million on the flip.

George didn't care. He drives his Mac Tool truck around the Denver area now, serving mechanics everywhere by not only selling them tools, but teaching them what they need to know to use them right. Serving people so they can serve others, using his Gift just as it was designed. I know why he drives for Mac, as opposed to Snap-on, even though I never asked.

You see, Elvis was driving the motorhome on country back roads pulling a trailer with a race car in it a while back, but neglected to connect the hydraulic brake cables from the heavy trailer. The brakes on the motorhome failed under the forces of stress and age, and the set jack-knifed irreparably around a hard curve.

The accident was nearly fatal for both Elvis and George, Jr., but the race car survived almost unblemished because the Mac Tool straps did their job and held it in place. The two of them might have been hurt worse if the race car had unleashed. Eventually, George took the time to send Mac Tools pictures of their success in the matter, to share that their equipment functioned exactly as advertised, and had served them well because the accident could have been worse had they not. Mac thanked George and asked his permission to throw an explanatory video up on their website. George obliged and Mac sent him a set of replacement straps as a courtesy.

That's how George rolls. That's how he keeps score in this life. And that's exactly why he drives for Mac Tools instead. He doesn't care about money. He uses a different currency. He cares about people, not status. When George had to shut down Nortown, I considered selling my hot rod, my adult go-kart, or keeping it and moving to Denver. He remains the best car man I have ever known and I miss him terribly.

Elon Musk was lucky to have met him, if only by phone.

* * * * *

GIFT PROPORTIONS IN HUMANITY

 Mercy 25%

 Server 20%

 Exhorter 12.5%

 Organizer 9%

 Prophet 20%

 Teacher 12.5%

 Giver 1%

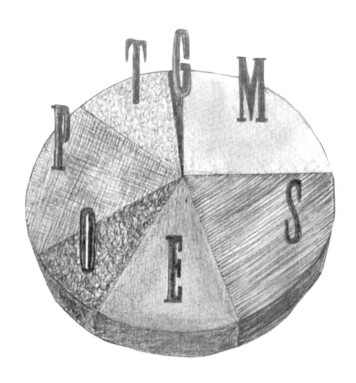

Love and Sexuality

Feel free to tear out these pages if you have a younger reader.

THERE HAVE BEEN SOME AMAZING books written about Love Languages. These books have always strongly reminded me of the Gifts as I see parallels. I would suggest that this Gift Knowledge also can land squarely in the realm of love and romance. Gentlemen, if there is a young lady you want to court or maybe take to the prom, you would be wise to ask yourself what her Gift is, and also to know your own, as it may allow you to see what parts of you fit well with her parts.

Let's say the young lady you want to take to the prom is a Mercy and you are a Prophet. You may be wise to tell your more insensitive impulses to take a chair, as these could be very unappealing to her. You may also, during an encounter, share a story about a time you stood up for someone who was being mistreated, because you both believed and *felt* it was the right thing to do. Being strong and stable and consistent around her may also be helpful, as all of these things might naturally draw a Mercy woman to you.

They say that opposites attract and I think you see this in the Gifts generally too...Prophets with Exhorters, Organizers with Mercys, Teachers with Servers, etc. It can help not only to know that we are different, but also specifically how we are, and also what we can do to enhance intimacy within those differences as opposed to being torn apart and imprisoned by them.

In an interview, the singer Tim McGraw once said: "In the car, I drive. In the relationship, she drives." His wife, singer Faith Hill, added that she liked to fight, that she loved a good fight. Think there is a chance he is a Mercy and she is a Prophet? Sounds to me like Tim has figured out some helpful things, blessings to the both of them. The dance between a man and a woman, or between partners, is a complex and rich and turbulent one. But knowing the tendencies of my own Gift and my partner's can take a lot of steam out of the hot iron and lead me to better ways of understanding and approaching things.

When I was a young boy growing up, I noticed that sometimes a couple seemed mismatched to me. I saw, at times, a beautiful girl who was hitched to a boy I may have thought was nerdy or less than her somehow. I'm sure envy had something to do with this but, in retrospect, maybe there was a Gift Dance that the young man knew better than I did, a dance between his nature and hers, a way of corresponding to one another that I did not yet comprehend.

If there is a mate you desire, man or woman, someone you may think is three or four levels above yours, find out what the person's Gift is and swing for the fence. Go for broke. Pick the sweetest girl, the smartest boy, the most beautiful woman, the kindest man. Do it sooner than later. It is only a matter of time before this all makes its way to Match Dot Com. Buy your real estate now, while the prices are a little cheaper.

I met my wife because of the Gifts. We were in a class that included little breakout groups that centered around the Gifts and found ourselves looking straight at one another, two of the only three Organizers in the whole field. Within seconds, we looked at one another differently, since we now knew deep, parallel secrets about each other. It is hard to describe the power of feeling understood, even appreciated, for the natural impulses you were Gifted by creation. In a moment, all the qualities that may have been mocked or critiqued by others in the past became rich, meaningful, and nuanced powers.

The joy of a clean kitchen. The serenity of a tightly made bed. Cleanly scrubbed teeth. A gleaming car, vacuumed, with two or three coats of tire shine. More than one shower or bath a day. A straight line. Adhesive price labels carefully heated and removed on new objects. An orderly drawer. A new Sharpie. Costco. A freshly sharpened pencil. The sounds of washers and dryers running. The marks on a carpet a strong vacuum cleaner makes. Good lighting. A brand-new razor blade in your shaver. Lint rollers. The smell of Windex.

We were in Heaven together in just moments. Heard. Understood. Appreciated. Affirmed. Yet it is still a mystery that I cannot yet comprehend in my Gift studies that I have never seen any other example of two of the same Gifts as a married couple outside of my own marriage. Inevitably, I see Polar Gifts everywhere, but never two Mercys, never two Prophets, and so on. I wonder why that is. I still have not wrapped my head around it.

Perhaps, as part of my Organizer Recovery, my self-created and self-induced twelve-step program, I may have to admit that it could very well be narcissism, pure and simple. Maybe the Organizer has so much self-love that it is capable of marrying itself. I openly admit in advance that this is a sideshow, but I feel compelled to share how I was able to get my beautiful wife, a siren, a woman three or four levels above my own, to accept my wedding proposal. And the fact that I owe a lot of it to "The Duke," Monsieur John Wayne. The tale has been a secret to this point. What is the purpose of a good story, after all, if not to tell it? All human understanding is based on narrative. Why not narrate to better understand?

When I was five or six years old, watching Westerns on black-and-white television, I saw how the wild horses of the American plains ran free, both beautiful and chaotic. There was something eloquent and magical in watching them snort and pound their hooves across the prairie, their manes crashing against their elegant shapes. Yet there was also entropy in it, as they were unprotected and subject to the whims of both nature as well as ill-intended men.

In the John Wayne movies, there seemed always to be a grand moment when his tenderness and toughness collided, as he both drew a wild colt to him while shoving a bit into its mouth and a bridle over its head. In the movies, the wild horse ultimately became happier because there was now protection from the elements and from others…food and structure. And the horse could still run in large open fields and go places and do things it had not before, now appreciated and loved and stroked and ridden.

I saw my future wife the same way as the wild colt. She was both beautiful and chaotic. I endeavored to come up with a way to propose to her. I reasoned I had to figure out an approach to be both tender and tough. She was also, after all, an Organizer Woman and had in her femininity, as well as an appreciation for directness, decisiveness, and clarity. So I bought a wedding ring and slid it under our bedroom pillows. I rehearsed in my head what I wanted to do, as this was going to require both forethought and a lot of self-discipline.

That fateful night in our lovemaking, I made sure the pillow hiding the ring was close by. I controlled myself, took a deep gulp of air, and dove down under the surface of her warm waters, held my breath and saw the glorious colors underneath, gently touched surfaces of elegant suspended plants and brushed against otherworldly underwater creatures who looked at me with the same wonder as I them. I focused, and waited…waited until I felt the waves tremble and undulate around me, until the arc of her agony and ecstasy arrived.

As she was lost in it, lost in time, lost in us, lost in the moment…I grabbed the ring from under the pillow and jammed it on her finger. I shoved the bit in her mouth and threw the bridle over her mane. She had no idea what was happening, nor did she feel me force the ring on, her body having succumbed to her inner being, the release of all of her femininity. As she continued to recover, she finally looked at her hand and saw the ring. "What is this?" she asked.

"Hello, Mrs. Whitacre," I greeted her.

She never took it off, so I guess it worked. One of the nicest side benefits of all of this was the fun I had when her girlfriends found out that I had proposed to her and would then naturally ask her how I had gone about it. She tried hard to navigate that one. And when she stammered, looked at me, and said: "Why don't you tell the story, Honey?" I just hit my Jimmy Connors two-handed backhand and sailed the ball back over the net. "Well…I don't know, Sugar Toes. It was a little bit unexpected, almost traumatic, wouldn't you say?"

I then excused myself from the conversation of the ladies, went to the boy's room, and left her to proceed with the explanation. On my way, I could feel a little bit of Papa's static electricity in my hair. The world is full of gifts and of Gifts and I can truly say that watching your wife trying to explain this method of proposing is a gift that just keeps on giving. I'll even bet Jean Harlow would have appreciated it.

On my wall at home, I framed a poem for us by Robert Louis Stevenson, the writer of *Treasure Island*, one of my childhood favorites. It contains these words:

> *I will make my kitchen, and you shall keep your room,*
> *Where white flows the river and bright blows the broom,*
> *And you shall wash your linen and keep your body white*
> *In rainfall at morning and dewfall at night.*
>
> *And this shall be for music when no one else is near,*
> *The fine song for singing, the rare song to hear!*
> *That only I remember, that only you admire…*

A Gift Poem, if there ever was one, written for an Organizer couple.

Discernment

A GIFT IS A VIBE THAT YOU CAN START to intuit in others. When you start practicing with the Gifts on a conscious level, eventually your subconscious catches up and can take over. Now some folks might call this "observer bias," where what you see can be the result of what you expect to see or what you want to see (in others in this case). What I find a little amusing about this, though, is that it is usually always Prophets who point out this possibility.

I think a better operative concept here was put forward by the great writer and thinker, Malcolm Gladwell, who raised the notion of "thin-slicing" with respect to our experience of other people. It is the idea that we, at almost an unconscious level, form the vast majority of our eventual conclusions about people in the first few nanoseconds of encountering them. The definition of the term thin-slicing finds its roots in classical philosophy and psychology. It means the ability to find patterns in events based only on "thin" slices or narrow windows of experience.

But I have found that while you can get people's Gifts right most of the time, you can't get them right all the time and, in some people, it can take years to figure out which one the person possesses. This can be true when one was influenced very heavily by a parent, for example. You might see someone, let's say, who seems extremely patterned, organized, methodical, willful, and strong and start to conclude the person is probably an Organizer. Only later, it might become clearer that the father was an Organizer, that the person has been imprinted pretty heavily with Organizer traits as a result, and the person is actually a Prophet underneath all of that, a Gift that also displays obvious strength and willfulness. The example here is my son, Max, when he was about seven. It took me a few years to realize what I was actually seeing.

Maybe there is also such a thing as Gift Fate, because it was my daughter Liza who cut Max's umbilical cord to release him so that he could fully engage in this world, and perhaps Liza's Gift knew we would not have long enough with her, so it knew to pass through the shears to enter Max so that we would have an echo of Liza, a remembrance we would always be able to see and feel, a form of her energy still among us.

Another situation where making someone's Gift is particularly difficult is when an individual is exceptionally well-rounded. A young lady I know named Kelsey is a great example. Kelsey has the ability to be strong and resolved, she loves to compete, can be very focused, and watches carefully and notices things in others. She can also be relentless, as I personally experienced at her hands across a ping-pong net. It was not pretty, even with my old tennis skills.

When I met her, I made her as a Mercy since most of her bells and whistles seemed to sound off when she worked with disabled children and raised money and awareness for a like-minded charity. But I lost confidence in my diagnosis over time since she exhibited all these other traits. A few years later, I returned to my original conclusion and decided to double down. I gave up speculating and just asked her if she thought she knew what her Gift was in the paradigm I share with people who are interested or willing to listen.

"Yes," she said. "I knew right from the beginning I was a Mercy."

So I asked her why she didn't let on to me then that she was, since she knew I was having problems ascertaining it. *Leave it to Mercys to be coy about their Gift*, I thought. That was Kelsey's Gift Tell all along and I missed it.

"No particular reason," she responded. *Sure*, I thought.

"Maybe just because I think it is good to try to be rounded as a person," she said.

Yes, Kelsey, of course you are right about that one. It is important that we be rounded, that we be multidimensional. Thank God I still have people in my life willing to mess with me. It keeps me on my toes.

I also think some people can identify their own Gift right away. Other folks may need time to discern theirs. It can be a really freeing process I think, because it can help people distinguish between innate and learned behaviors, between behaviors that were observed and assimilated, versus those that are natural and instinctual.

But once you drill down and hit your Gift, you will know it, the fresh spring water from this well will unmistakably start bubbling up to the surface.

The Gift Compass

THERE IS A GIFT LEGEND THAT HAS BEEN passed around for who knows how long and by whom. It goes something like this. Imagine a person walking out of a grocery store carrying an armload of paper bags filled with food. The bags begin tearing apart, but the person is carrying too much to be able to contain the spill. It is said that:

The Server would dive to catch the groceries as they fell, having noticed the matter in advance and anticipated the assistance that may have been needed.

The Mercy would initially look away, not wanting to make the shopper feel embarrassed or humiliated, and then gently start to enter into the matter of helping clean up, offering soothing words of comfort while doing so.

The Prophet would think *Well, you got what you deserved, and hopefully you will learn from this.*

The Teacher would stop and pick up pieces of the bag, hoping to identify the manufacturer, to avoid this label in the future, and to inform others of the same when the opportunity arose.

The Exhorter would immediately smile and laugh and turn the situation into a playful joke, asking for a name and neighborhood of residence, seeing the opportunity to network and make a new friend.

The Organizer would walk straight around the person and the mess towards the store, proceed to hunt down the manager, then explain that there was a problem on the grocery line, that the manager should consider double bagging from now on, the source problem now located and addressed.

The Giver? Well, I don't know what the Giver would do since I don't know that I have met any Givers yet. Perhaps he or she would consider if there was a larger cause here and then conclude that no, there was no larger cause. I hope that there might be Gift Explorers who come after me, who are better and smarter than I am, so there could be some finer light shed on the Giver situation.

No offense to any church, synagogue, or mosque folks, but religions are like metaphor field days, like the field days of grade school, where all the parents and some alumni come and sit in the stands, and flags and banners wave about. Religions have some of the most beautiful and elegant and rich metaphors. Not only can objects and symbols stand for many things, so can people, as in historical and religious figures. My discussion has dealt with the variety of Gifts among different people, yet there is a deeper metaphysical and spiritual aspect to all of this. Ultimately, my goal should be to become all of these Gifts at once, to be able to emulate and learn and incorporate all of them into my inner and outer being.

Christians talk about the idea of "One Body." I think one could reasonably argue that each of these Gifts spread among different people in a community creates a sense of wholeness, completeness, balance, unity, and function. Maybe Christians in their lore would also say that Jesus had no singular Gift and possessed all of them. It is also said that the notion of *oneness* is a gift of love, the eternal truth shared by all religions, Christianity, Buddhism, Judaism, and Islam. And there are other senses of this important word: the *oneness* of time, the *oneness* of force, the *oneness* of purpose, and so on. The art or practice of the Seven Gifts is not a religion; it is a set of ideas, like a socket set in a toolbox that has different sized sockets to gain purchase on a shape—in this case, the general motivational nature of a person.

The Gift Compass represents the possibility of all the Gifts coming together in one person. It embodies the pursuit of this ideal, this form of *oneness*. It means that the Gifts are not just exterior-facing, existing in the world around us, but that all of them have the possibility of living and growing and maturing inside of us.

Knowledge of the Gifts can also guide us. We can use our Gift Compass, just as we would a real one, to help us navigate in life. I think of True North as one's primary Gift.

I may be able to accomplish something or approach someone better by asking myself what a Mercy would do, or a Teacher? I can look at my Gift Compass and choose to chart a Gift Direction and manifest something new and better. The Gifts are all pieces of a more perfect whole, each having its own identity, purpose, role, and function, a tapestry that is perfectly balanced.

We are actually all one, together on this planet. Racial divides, gender matters, religion, and politics all melt in the light of the Seven Gifts.

Our Youth and the Authentic Self

WHEN I HEARD THE FOLLOWING WORDS for the first time and began to comprehend them, I felt I was standing in the shallow ocean, frozen, watching a large wave appear that was gaining momentum towards me, overwhelmed by the dark implications of it all.

Buying likes.

My stomach reflexively tightened and wrenched when I heard the utterance come out of the young boy's mouth. I did not fully understand why I was impacted so much in the moment, watching an interview on a news program about the dangers of youth and technology, cell phones, and social media. I have always been and remain deeply suspicious of technology, as are so many of my generation and those that are left of the generations before my own. Many of us are not convinced our race is moving forward.

When the young fifteen-year-old boy told the interviewer that he spent eight to ten hours a day between his cell phone and computer screens, I felt the same nausea I usually do. But when he said that he had started "buying likes," something shifted deep within me. I felt sickened, like some dark force was trying to suck the life out of me. I knew then, as I do now, that all of this has gone way too far. I have an ongoing debate with my son about what areas of technology truly improve our lives, versus areas that may cause regression. Maybe my smartphone helps me navigate while driving, since I am not good at directions, and maybe it has successfully replaced the daily newspaper I loved to read once. Thank God Papa had his job when he did. I haven't seen a paperboy in decades.

But kids now think that cell phones have replaced their parents for understanding the world. A large part of the business of my youth was my need to rely on my parents to explain things to me: what a fine restaurant was, how to be cautious with propane, what tire dressing worked best on the car, how and when to hold a door open for a woman, not to eyeball people on urban streets, what a line of cars driving slowly behind a hearse with their lights flashing meant.

When I watch lovely, unsuspecting young women using dating apps, when I see the triumph of the virtual self over the actual self, when I observe that many youth believe *I post, therefore I am*—as opposed to *I am what I am*—I become discouraged. But when I heard of "buying likes," some form of personal hell broke loose in my soul. I had known this exact feeling before, from some unknown place in my personal past, as it also felt familiar to me, yet I had no way of placing it. For many days and nights, I felt troubled by this darkness. Then I remembered the gravitational wave detector.

In recent years, a group of crazy Teachers—that is to say, scientists who clearly possess the Teacher Gift, built an antenna miles long on Earth's flat surface to try and validate Einstein's Theory of Relativity. You see, Einstein always believed that gravitational waves existed in our universe meaning, simply, that gravity produced waves much like sound waves or radio signals. So the Teacher-scientists, in their fierce and intractable drive to research, set up the biggest antenna our planet has ever seen to try and detect any such waves. Essentially, the antenna was the flat shape of a "V" on the ground, with each prong extending about two and a half miles out. A grand research V. And soon after they fired it up, the V detected some of the waves they were searching for, the same ones Einstein had foreseen. Then they turned Earth's most powerful telescopes back where the pulse emanated from and scanned into the deepest part of our known universe to see back billions of years ago, so they could eventually know that the gravitational waves began with the destruction of a black hole in deep space. Sometimes, you have to build your own gravitational wave detector and wait. It's the only way you are ever going to be able to know what is going on in your soul. I built mine, and waited.

One night, I was flying down Wisconsin country backroads, windows down, smelling the loamy fields…the scents a sweet and sour mixture of manures, peat moss, embedded rains, flowers, rotting animals in ditches, and turned soil…savoring the opera music lightly playing in the background, my gaze lingering on the fireflies etching the dark night like Papa's Ohio Blue Tip matches striking when he lit his Camels, glad to be back close to the openness and freedom of my Missouri farm spaces in a different part of my America. The rear-view mirror revealed the back of the car submerged in a suspended cloud of road dust, my rear taillight imprisoned within it, animating forward motion that suggested I was traveling through space-time.

My subconscious must have floated back to my childhood days because in the darkness of the countryside under the Wisconsin moonlight, I felt a strong pulse hit my detector. The long amplitude radio signal in my soul, emanating from my deep past, had finally caught up to me in present time. I slowed the car and turned off the music. I turned my strongest telescopes on and tried to see back in time, to tune in the faint message.

We are strange beings, collections of memories and time and places and people and feelings, and we don't properly fathom all the information we hold within us. The plates shift, the tidal waves launch underwater, the molten lava spews, and we strive to keep our air passage free above the surface, to suck precious oxygen and to hope. The long amplitude wave wasn't from billions of years ago and did not involve the death of a black hole. It was from 1974 and I could now see exactly the moment I first felt this precise, dark feeling that had been troubling me in the present. Back in that year, I had been sitting on a carpet floor, hidden between rows of books.

At age twelve, as an outcast during my first years at the prep school, I sheltered in place in the forest of the vast and expansive campus library during my free periods. I wandered around that place and discovered I could pretty much run unchecked on any subject since I could choose to stay anonymous by simply not formally checking anything out and leaving a library card footprint. This was new to me, this method of freedom of knowledge and inquiry, and I quickly saw I could travel into subjects that were clearly not age-appropriate. Perfect, I thought. This was like the sweet sin of Papa teaching me to swear, or when he handed me his unfiltered cigarette to try, or when he pushed a little piece of Red Man chewing tobacco under my lip.

I looked at forbidden picture books of people with medical deformities, naked African women, serial killers and their victims, and eventually the Nazis. One day, I turned a page and the exact same feeling had slammed into me—the "Angel of Death," Dr. Josef Mengele, the Nazi doctor who had experimented on Jewish children. When I first studied the words on the page, looked at images of the children, began to comprehend the stagnant, putrid evil of the endeavor on these innocents, I felt a diamond drill tip hollow out a new place within me that had not been there before. Unimaginable human evil imagined and realized, coupled with the simultaneous shock in understanding that I was of the same species.

Many adults today are conducting psychological and financial experiments on our children. Generations to come may not be able to look back on black-and-white pictures in libraries, photos of experiments and horrors past, because no decent standards will be left to compare them to, as all of those standards will be bent and then lost to the powerful sands of time. We won't be able to see images of measuring instruments, sharp tools, and sick engineers with pickled hands and liver spots on their faces because this damage, these wounds, are interior—not exterior. They are not physical and are instead psychological, emotional, spiritual, and metaphysical in nature. The wounds are only visible indirectly, only on seemingly unrelated surfaces, manifesting as depression, weight gain, a disproportionate degree of gender and sexual confusion, anxiousness, unfamiliarity with the physical world where trains can hit you and cars can collide, and an inability to understand and foster intimacy with others.

I mean to poke a sharp fork right in the eye of this monster. Tarzan would have stabbed it. The Duke would have hit it with a carefully placed rifle shot. Dirty Harry would have used his .44 Magnum. The billionaire tech barons who are using their Internet-based industries of social media and Internet commerce as weaponized delivery platforms for social, behavioral, and mind control focused on children should be convicted for crimes against humanity, just like the Nazis were at the Nuremberg Trials.

To those barons I say this: I prefer the pimp to you any day. The pimp has more integrity because he is not disguised. The pimp shows his car, his fur coat, and his gold teeth. He has the presence and criminal dignity to be honest about his nature and intentions. You are lower because you hide behind hoodies, faux torn jeans that are actually expensive and not really from Goodwill, and you carry yourselves as fake advocates, so-called disrupters, progressives, and fabricated social change agents. You are none of these.

Take the cards out from under the playing table. I am already familiar with some of the arguments and larger justifications that you use…that the Internet is a form of a utility, that you can't impede or monitor how some people might misuse your platforms or devices. That thesis doesn't hold water because we all know you are talented in the extreme. If you can construct virtual worlds that can predict, in advance, what color button a person prefers and would be more likely to press, you can certainly apply your skill sets for better purposes. Essentially, you are running a large virtual summer camp for children across the world. Children leave their parents as they dive into devices. Adults running summer camps have practical, legal, ethical, societal, and moral obligations to protect children.

But to be able to enforce reasonable and moral standards legally, laws will have to be passed first. In the financial sector, Dodd-Frank impugns "unfair, deceptive, or abusive acts or practices." Isn't that language at least good enough for our children's protection? In the meantime, I pray for your financial demise. I hope you are sucked up in a smothering tsunami wave of public awareness and indignation.

We are living in a masterful time, the time of the "Me Too" movement. Women are finally experiencing a long overdue and blessedly deserved watershed moment, driving the world to awaken and look into the cold stare of sexual harassment and workplace abuse. I have so much admiration for the women who have risen to this moment. Let's hope that the cause remains as pure as it can, just like Dr. Martin Luther King did his best to keep the cause of nonviolence on track in the civil rights movement. Strong men need to speak out with these brave women. I know there is an army of true gentlemen out there, men who will lay it all on the line to stand for what is right, who have been taught and self-taught to tell their baser instincts to take a seat in favor of their sacred role towards the preservation and uplifting of their eternal sisters, daughters, and moms.

My mother taught me about the Me Too movement when I was eleven years old. I insulted little Nicole Romine, the ballet dancer, across the street in her front yard by telling her she was stuck up. Her mom called mine and that night I was told to get my jacket on after we had finished our dinner.

"Where are we going, Mom?"

"Over to the Romines so you can learn how to be a gentleman."

I was forced to humiliate myself. In front of all the parents and most importantly, in front of Nicole. I had to fess up to exactly what my insult contained and then spell out clearly, loudly and slowly, why it was exactly and precisely not true.

Tears streamed down my face, while my mother made sure that no one would touch me or comfort me during my delivery. She wanted me to know the turtles were near (see Volume I). Truth be told, I thought Nicole was cute and she eventually became the very first girl I ever kissed. Looking back, I am pretty sure she didn't kiss me because of my insult. My humility drew her. My gentlemanly apology beckoned. So Nicole taught me something my mother did not bother to mention to me, or perhaps felt I may have had to learn on my own, that there are sometimes other unexpected benefits to being a true gentleman.

I think one of the ways we can honor these brave women is to be as honest as they are about abuse. When I was five years old and living in the small college town of Athens, Ohio, I was molested by an older boy. It was not one of those boyhood situations where you showed one another your private parts, trying to make sense of what seemed to be taboo. He lived down the street on Sunnyside Drive and, in retrospect, really did a number on my parents by manipulating them, acting like he was courteous and respectful in public, while intimidating me in private. I did not understand it all, but eventually my mom sensed something was wrong and I told her as much as my five-year-old capacity would allow. He was then quickly and summarily banned from my life.

When I hear people complaining about why an accuser did not come forward earlier, when I hear a defense attorney self-righteously questioning a woman's credibility, I see that none of them know what they are talking about. As human beings, we are built to try to survive tragedy and trauma. We protect our hearts and psyches as best we can to make it through. Some of those primal mechanisms are within our control and some of them are not.

It was almost fifty years after my exposure to this abuse that my spirit began buffeting from the ugliness of it. I started to get mad and began nursing on more Whistlepig whiskey than I should, my lighter fluid of choice. I realized I could even the score, go Marines Corps on him, and use my Organizer Gift to provide order to his demise. I shook the remaining ice in my drink just as a Las Vegas craps dealer shakes the dice, floating in alcohol and fantasies of retribution.

My history teacher at my prep school later tried to convert me to his victim of sexual abuse. He knew I was in deep water emotionally because of the turbulence of my parent's divorce and began regularly closing the door when he helped me by talking about these matters. He said he wanted me to have a safe place to share, a shoulder that I could lean on.

One day, his hand started moving up my leg as he sat close to me. It was slow and deliberate, almost like a test. I froze. I thought he was just socially awkward at first, as if he did not understand guys did not do that. I maintained my strength and let my eyes convey that I was streetwise. I did not buckle. I think I was also sad and disappointed as well, because his efforts seemed to me to be a needless complexity. After all, it was helpful to be able to talk about things with someone. It was also ambiguous and confusing. He had two sons who were close to my age in the same school. None of it made any sense to me and still doesn't. I slowly steered away from him after that, as opposed to telling anyone about his action. I heard years later that he was eventually exposed as a predator at a different school where he was fired from, then eventually convicted.

As human beings, we try to assume the best about people and situations mostly, we give people the benefit of the doubt mainly, just like we would want others to give to us. Thank you to the women who have inspired this unique period of honesty and accountability and change. You all certainly have inspired me. I also hope we don't have to live through decades of cyber-pain and cyber-abuse, only to end up with a "Kids Too" movement.

Billions of dollars in profit, personal power, and prestige aren't anywhere near the value of the soul and mind of a child. Our youth can't ever individuate or self-actuate successfully when adults with evil intentions manipulate their minds and self-worth and seduce them into believing that they are not actually themselves, they are a virtual representation of themselves instead, and the only way they can make themselves presentable and acceptable is for them to enter their debit-card number and "buy likes."

Evil is evil, no matter what neighborhood you live in, no matter what cloaks you are wearing, and no matter what the conventions of society say you are. Five years from now, there will be entire industries dedicated to unplugging you, just like the smoking patch, with folks cancelling your honorary degrees and taking your pictures down off of walls everywhere.

I read a newspaper article today about some enterprising Primary Thinking parents who arranged for an intervention for their beloved son. He was shuttled off to a facility that disallowed cell phones and computers and the Internet for a sobering month. Social media had hacked his brain and he could not see out of it, nor could he distinguish between what was real or virtual. The boy was depressed because all of the things he projected online did not line up with his interior. When he came out of this treatment—some might call it normalcy—he could breathe again on many levels.

If you don't see fit to change your ways now, make sure and stop by Party City and pick up some favors. The party is just getting started. We will come for you. It is a matter of time. Change your ways now, before you become the next Dr. Josef Mengele in our human history. If you want to repent and get on a better path, I'll offer to help things along. I'll give you some shoe-shining pointers and you can go over to Sal Khan's house and start with a few of his favorite pairs. Make sure you snap your rag for him so he might enjoy the service more, but expect no tips.

Just like the City of Chicago Police Department can now predict your likelihood of being murdered as an urban gangbanger, I believe the Gifts are so predictable in our human behavior that the categories could easily be automated by a Gift Algorithm. Artificial intelligence could be trained to speak to us in the language of our Gifts. I imagine this will eventually happen, because forms of it are already shaping, as more people discover the veracity of these specific patterns in our nature.

Like any power or any knowledge, this is neither good nor bad in and of itself. It all will just depend on how this powerful information is used. I believe that an app could be developed that could summarily determine one's Gift.

But let's hope that one does not come about. It's much more fun deducing them yourself. Discovering, learning about, and practicing the Art of the Gifts can represent a return to the authentic self. The Art of the Gifts is a force against the displacement of reality by the virtual world. The Gifts can ground us again. They can help return us to the real world, where real people reside, and move us away from the constructed virtual, social-media self.

The Gifts also represent a sound pathway to actualization. You cannot hone, develop, and become your true Gift on a screen. You have to breathe in the real world. The Seven Gifts are a prayer, a plea, to become actual, real, and authentic in our connection with ourselves and others. Think of the X-man or X-woman who gets a unique power for the first time and does not yet know how to use all of it or contain it when needed. Beginning to know your own Gift is similar to that. You have to train.

Knowing one's Gift is ultimately about how to focus energy. What we choose to channel. I had a wonderful professor in college who taught me much of what I know about energy, only he was not teaching in a classroom. I eventually concluded he had likely never graduated from primary school. His name was Larry, a stone mason of Italian descent. I worked with him over the summers, in what was called Plant Operations, a collection of union carpenters, roofers, and craftsman who took care of the Brown University physical plant, much of which was (and still is) well-aged.

I was the only student—to my knowledge—allowed to be part of them. They let me operate heavier equipment, pour and smooth boiling tar on flat roofs, and drive the long-bed, brown king-cab work truck around the campus. I insisted that they allow me to buy a Plant Operations uniform so I could feel their skin. My dad once told me that you need the right tools and the right uniform to do the best job. They graciously relented. I couldn't keep track of all the rules they regularly broke where I was concerned.

But Larry the stone mason was different than the others. He was an immigrant who had never bothered to learn English, for one thing. His media were powerful rock and heavy stone and I suspect he did not think of ignoring an entire national language as a significant matter. He was the only mason entrusted with the care of sacred pieces of historical rock and stone dating all the way back to 1764, the year the university was founded. He was recognized as a master craftsman, an artist of sorts, hailing from the working-class neighborhoods of Providence, Rhode Island.

Larry the mason saw my skills as a helper, a number-two man, and quickly claimed me. Working with my father as he built things had taught me to anticipate well, to intuit where he would want to go next, and to be there ahead of time with the right tools and the right attitude. Larry was short, powerfully built, and carried a head of raven-black hair that projected testosterone. Yet his iron, calloused hands were also simultaneously soft. I felt them as we handed things back and forth. The micro-dust from the stones and rocks from the prior day's job seemed to linger and cling to his clothes, hair, and skin. He always smelled like he was freshly showered. "Deodorized," Papa would say.

I spent many afternoons in the hot coastal sun with Larry on various stone missions. We would singularly be dropped off from the union truck in the middle of nowhere, in parts of the campus I never knew existed, once to resurrect a stone platform that held a patina-bronzed sculpture of the Brown University Bear. Our only instruments were a large metal pail filled with water, which Larry carried as if it were a feather, a mallet, a hammer, a chisel, and some gentle white rags. I quickly saw that Larry had a system of ethics that would take years to unravel. He looked like Anthony Quinn playing Zorba the Greek. When we worked, he would grunt and spit and gesture. I was expected to interpret. I measured his intensity and got fairly prolific at reading him. I learned what interpreters felt like, ones who don't formally know sign language, but are charged with explaining to the rest of the world what someone who can't speak for themselves intends.

What Larry taught me about energy eclipsed most of my formal philosophy lessons. He walked up to the stone base and began humming as he moved his hands over surfaces. He moved around it like a ballroom dancer, like The Duke, like Papa, like my dad steered the El Camino with one hand. He turned his head a little to the side, like a wave breaking, and shot me a sideways glance as he smiled. His innate software had run some breathtakingly complicated calculation that told him something about the molecular structure of this object, a calculus that I truly doubted a supercomputer could reason, a vast equation that had a ridiculously simple and direct solution.

But it was lunchtime first. So Larry sat down under a tree, bronze-skinned and content, enjoying the simple pleasure, the elegant custom of a peasant's workday. I sat close by at the correct respectful yet available distance, kept one eye on him, and also looked to see if there were any young women strolling anywhere near. Larry would occasionally explode in a grin and laughter and look at me as if I had told a great joke or as if he had told me one. I began to understand that in his mind, he had, so I might as well enjoy the moment as well and indulge with a broad smile. Then Larry would become quiet, maybe even a little melancholy, and I knew his heart had wandered somewhere in his memories, maybe a place of grief, sadness, or yearning.

Words are so important, so critical, to our ability to create meaning. And words are so unimportant, so irrelevant, to our ability to create meaning.

After our lunch, Larry returned to touching the stone, moving his fingers slowly over the broken piece of quarry rock, rubbing his hands on his face unconsciously as he considered the fault lines. He was taking it all in…absorbing through a mason's osmosis the depth and weight of the fractured piece, the context of its frame, and the eventual goal of its seamless recovery and replacement.

He grunted. I immediately put the chisel in his hand. His brow was sweating now. He took the clean, white towel I offered. As he wiped off his forehead, I watched his eyes register an athlete who was training close by at a track-and-field area. The strong, young man he saw was bathed in sweat and held a piece of railroad timber on his shoulders like a cross for added resistance. I watched Larry watching his muscular back working as he climbed stone stairs. Larry threw his hair back, looked at me and then said the only word I ever heard him speak the entire time I knew him. "Stupid…" he muttered. His air was one of a feudal lord or an aristocrat or a world leader.

Then he broke focus, probed the head of the chisel until he found a specific spot in the rock, shoved the chisel snug against it, slowly took a breath, and threw the anvil of the steel hammer. His forehead veins swelled as he hit the head of the chisel with such an explosive force that I felt the air move. Even after the blow, he kept his body rotating towards his focal point, as if he were throwing a javelin or a shotput and wanted to transfer even more energy in his follow-through, just like an Olympic athlete.

I saw a crack appear across the stone that looked like a lightning bolt that would tell of pending tornadoes in Kansas skies. He rappelled, as a rock climber pushes off the face of a cliff, and then moved his hands over the quarry rock, stroking it as a living thing, reminding me of the kind veterinarian who stroked Blackie's fur, our beloved Labrador, before he laid the needle in him to put him down. But before Larry could find his next point of energy transfer, the entire piece of stone split open like a ripe watermelon, and the fingers of cement that had held it in place vanished into dust. Larry looked at me, having now become a ghost of stone dust, mouth wet and blood red, and laughed loudly.

It is said that university professors without tenure must "publish or perish." I saw that Larry had written me a metaphysical essay on existence, purpose, and energy. I had read every word of it carefully. He knew that I knew. It was my job, after all, as a stone mason's assistant, to read the mason's thoughts. Larry had written extensively about the flawed nature of wasted purpose and energy and argued towards a calculated, intense, and effective focus of will. Time is short on Carl Sagan's blue dot in black space and 99% of our effort should be given to intuition, feel, observation, and thought, so that we can apply a pure and exhilarating 1% toward impact and execution. Laser focus. Maximum efficiency. No waste.

Looking back, I can see Larry was from my Gift Tribe, a fellow Organizer. The tea leaves were there for me to read. His metal pail was always wiped and prepared for the day, his worn tools clean and simple and ready; the white cloths freshly washed; all done to anticipate and eventually counteract the brute forces implicit in the physics of quarry rock and stone. His choice of that singular word ("stupid") betrays an Organizer's erroneous sense of superiority and his channeled, intense focus against the immovable material of rock suggests he is up to the challenge and measure of forces like physics and gravity, penetrating the impenetrable. He believes he is also like the stone.

The Brown Bear statue still stands today and the small podium embodies Larry's essay to me that we should be careful, thoughtful, caring, and even loving in how we expend our energy. Learning to focus the power and energy of one's Gift promises the same purity and freedom. I also hope that the designers of our Internet summer camps for our youth read Larry's essay and think carefully and soberly about how and where to channel their energies.

.

Origins

I WAITED INTENTIONALLY TO THIS POINT IN my Gift Diaries to share with you where the Gifts came from because I wanted to make all of this about knowledge and not religion. That's not to suggest that religion is bad or to say it is not possible that sometimes there can be great knowledge in religion, or great religion in knowledge. I say more power to folks who gravitate towards religion, as long as it is not a cult. And more power to folks who gravitate away from it, as long as they do not lose their natural sense of spirituality. As my mom used to say to me: "That's why there are 31 flavors at Baskin Robbins." You get to pick what you want in this life.

If you are not religious, you would be wise to study religion at some point in your life and if you are religious, it would be smart for you to study atheism and perhaps some forms of existentialism. I did not grow up in a religious home. Our religions were art, poetry, writing, music, and design. In my childhood world, right or wrong, formalized religion was considered a crutch, a weakness for people who could not think independently for themselves.

The closest I ever got to an imaginary or potentially otherworldly figure was Boo Radley in *To Kill a Mockingbird*. Boo Radley, not Jesus. The only time I saw Jesus regularly was on the face of a plate that hung on Papa's wall, but no one in my family ever mentioned that fact, let alone emphasized it. So I am not trying to evangelize here. Believe me. I used to mumble the *Pledge of Allegiance* in Catholic church services I attended with my kids, since I did not know any of the language concerning the sharing of the sacraments.

The Seven Gifts were lifted straight out of the Good Book, the Bible, which is also a great work of literature. The best information can sometimes come from the most unlikely of places, like from Caleb, the janitor who supervised me, with whom I worked side by side at my university as I continued cleaning inescapable toilets.

Caleb was an elderly, overweight Black man who was jolly, insightful, patient, not formally educated, and completely at peace with his existence here on earth, unlike many I saw around me. He was like a figure from *Alice in Wonderland* because his King's English was absolutely flawless. He spoke with a diction and clarity that suggested he was actually a famous Shakespearean actor in real life, a thespian, and was only pretending to be a janitor as some sort of method acting exercise.

He addressed me as Master David as a nod to the fact that I was a first-born male, like Papa used to emphasize. He always patterned the utmost courtesies, as when I handed him back the vacuum cleaner, the "Thank you, sir," the "Top of the day to you, Master David," and the "You are truly a gentleman and a fine man." You would have thought I was the mayor of a grand city and had just ceremoniously handed him the keys to it, as opposed to a dirty, overused industrial vacuum. Caleb daily animated how to conduct oneself with dignity and humility in the midst of a complex environment layered with issues of class, wealth, and higher education. He showed me that respect, dignity, and class have absolutely no relationship to wealth, education, vocation, or social status.

I did not quite know how to react when Caleb eventually would tell me to leave my shift early, insisting he would take care of the rest of my duties for me. "You have much better things to do with your life, Master David," he would say. "You have a majestic future ahead of you. It is my pleasure to handle the balance of your menial duties so as to respect your work commitment to the university, so I will be pleased to punch out for you at a later time, so that you can honor your financial obligation to yourself, your family, and your future."

I noticed that Caleb's language was slowly becoming more detailed and flowery, ever since he found out I was an Honors English student, and had learned I possessed a growing love of words. He was twirling his bat a little bit for show now. But I also saw the great joy I seemed to bring him, like a greater sense of purpose.

For ethical symmetry, Caleb also made sure to explain that he would be working just a little bit harder than usual to cover my end after I left early. He wanted to be sure I understood that no one was gaming the university time clock (excessively), that no one would lose out here. His more intensive work periods were, strictly speaking, his gift to my future. I believe he was sensitive to what he modeled for me, as he was a very principled man. He could have been a humble nation king, formal philosopher, or public ethicist in another life. Or certainly a famous Shakespearean actor.

After graduation, I ceremoniously presented Caleb with a key to a grand city, a very expensive bottle of his favorite, native, Jamaican rum that I had saved for with dollars earned playing Frisbee out on the Campus Green while dear Caleb shuffled and vacuumed. It was the least I could do to show him how much I had come to love and admire him.

I make Caleb as a Server, as a detective would make a perpetrator, based on my memory of him. When I see unreasonable acts of kindness and service, like when a workingman walks ahead of me coming up on a large line at a great breakfast place, but then graciously pauses and opens a door so that I might step ahead of him, acting as if somehow I am doing him the favor by allowing him to inconvenience himself, I think of Caleb, another fine tenured professor of Brown University.

My point is that sometimes you can learn the best information from the oddest of places. You can learn stuff about food from Netflix documentaries, an unlikely but powerful source. It is entirely reasonable to me, then, to think that the Good Book is a place where you could learn something that is really unexpected and good too.

We have different gifts, according to the grace given to each of us. If your gift is prophesying, then prophesy in accordance with your faith; if it is serving, then serve; if it is teaching, then teach; if it is to encourage, then give encouragement; if it is giving, then give generously; if it is to lead, do it diligently; if it is to show mercy, do it cheerfully.*

Primary Thinking dictates one of the oldest surviving and most complete works of literature in human history could contain the most poignant, insightful, and accurate personality typing system known to our race. It makes common sense also because in earlier times, without the intense distractions of technology and our modern world, people may have been able to take the time and care to peer into one another more deeply. Perhaps they also needed to fundamentally for the sake of necessity.

As you know, the word *Gift* can mean many different things in many different contexts. It can also be a noun or a verb. Even the Good Book throws the word around quite a bit in different ways in various situations. I made the decision to capitalize this version of the word Gift, as I believe it is worthy of it.

If you Google the general topic of this book, you will quickly see that Christians claim this knowledge and generally see concepts involving gifts through the lenses of godliness, duty, salvation, and redemption. I think that is all well and good and I want to be careful as I walk around these subjects of religion, out of respect for people's right to believe what they wish and to find allegiance to ideas that connect. Yet I think this Gift information is much more profound and universal, calling for a broader view of things, eclipsing just one lens, religious or otherwise. The Seven Gifts are at once secular, practical, religious, philosophical, psychological, emotional, and spiritual. A person might say that one's Gift comes from a higher power. Another might say one's Gift is a form of a higher power. Maybe both are true.

---

*The Bible, Romans 12:6-8, New International Version (NIV)

I walk around feeling like I found a hidden Michelangelo painting at a garage sale. If you want to, for fun, you can think of finding the Gifts in the Bible like I do, like it is a secret DaVinci Code or a previously unknown Bible Code, like an inner sanctum or hidden chamber.

Very, very cool stuff.

Future Giftologists

MARION STOKES COULD NOT STOP TAPING. Over a 35-year period spanning 1977 through her death in 2012, Marion videotaped the world's largest known archive of television news programs, representing literally hundreds of thousands of hours of footage. Her collection consisted of 24/7 news coverage by C-SPAN, FOX, MSNBC, CNN, CNBC, and various others. She kept eight VCR machines running in her home and timed family meals, outings, and vacations around the ability to have the six-hour tapes in the machines methodically changed at exact intervals.

Stokes' son, Michael Metelits, said that the advent of 24-hour television news networks acted as her "triggers." He said that his mother became convinced there was a lot of detail in the news at risk of disappearing forever and began taping. In an interview, Metelits stated that she "channeled her natural hoarding tendencies" to the task of creating an archive. She housed her collection of VHS and Betamax tapes in her home, garage, and rented apartments. Her will instructed that the collection eventually be donated for charitable purposes, her taped legacy to be used for the benefit of the public good. When the collection was eventually donated to The Internet Archive in San Francisco, it was valued at several million dollars.

From a distance, I make Marion Stokes as a Giver and believe it would have been very easy for psychologists, psychiatrists, doctors, and family members to have misunderstood Marion fundamentally because of a lack of Gift Knowledge. I suspect that words like "triggers" and "hoarding" from the mouths of others probably floated around Marion's ears (and spirit) quite a bit.

I don't know about you, but I see a gulf between garbage and useless items being crammed into a hoarder's living space and Marion Stokes' important collection given for the greater cause of society. Imagine if the Gifts were a naturalized part of medicine, of psychology, and an integral part of treatments in those realms. Imagine if any counselor, youth or otherwise, began a discussion with an elaboration of and a look into the Seven Gifts. Imagine if someone had actually looked into Marion Stoke's eyes and said: "I see exactly what you are doing and I understand precisely why you are doing it. Thank you so much for your generous, selfless, and giving spirit…your seemingly endless capacity and desire to sacrifice your own comfort and resources for the greater good of all. Thank God, our world and society are blessed with people like you. You are rare. Priceless even."

What do you think Marion would say? I'll bet she may have started crying because finally someone saw who she was. If a counselor or therapist had said this to her, don't you think she may have become more open to adjusting for the sake of her family? Isn't it reasonable to think she may have felt she would not have to hold on so tight if someone could see her, affirm her, and lift up her efforts? What if her counselor could have understood more deeply the difference between an obsession versus a Gift stuck in an overdrive gear?

What if the therapist's office had a Gift Specialist? What if the Gift Specialist came in and suggested calling in some of the other Gifts to see what they had to say about this grand, masterful project Marion had engineered? What if I was a Gift Volunteer and they called me in? An Organizer might be a good place to start, I think, and I can tell you exactly what an Organizer would say: Centralize, Unify, and Delegate.

I would say, "Marion, let's really do this right. Let's make this even more effective and efficient so you can achieve this wonderful objective even better." How is she going to argue with that? "Let's start a small non-profit organization that can have a name, an identity, and a clear mission statement. You can pick up some tax advantages for your family because the expenses can become deductible charitable contributions. No reason for you or your family to suffer financially more than you have to in your cause, Marion. By the way, people can donate money to the organization so you don't have to pay for everything yourself."

"Marion, let's also enlist others to help. A Mercy could help us create a promotional flyer, one that has nice colors and scenes, one that telegraphs an emotional message. A Server could help with manning the recording machines, especially at ungodly hours. A Teacher could research more efficient ways of recording, better devices, longer lasting tapes, and ways to automate further. A Prophet, whom we will first have to convince that the project is the right thing to be doing, can help enforce the definitions, run the schedule, and make sure people are in line. An Exhorter could make sure the organization has fun along the way and arrange for competitions, outings, maybe even some Karaoke."

Additionally, the Exhorter could surprise Marion when it's her turn and put on *I've Got News For You* by Ray Charles or *Bad News* by Johnny Cash. That may help Marion put a couple of needed quarts of oil in her engine.

Maybe she would buy into all of it, knowing that she was getting input Gift-to-Gift. Maybe she could have some extra time and money to spend with and on her son Michael and her husband and herself. Maybe Marion could enjoy the status of a leader, a visionary, a form of a philanthropist, instead of a "hoarder who gets triggered."

I can see the lack of accurate psychological diagnosis in the case of my own Gift. I hear terms thrown about like OCD (Obsessive Compulsive Disorder) when someone describes a person's habit of keeping an absolutely flawless closet, who keeps articles of clothing immaculately folded and each shoe spotlessly wiped down. As an Organizer, one who is soothed by order, one who lives by and practices a philosophy that the order one can create in the outer world reflects the order of the inner world, I have different psychological terms that should be used to describe the person's behavior whose closet manifests the same mindset: *Normal*. Perfectly normal. Even preferable.

I am convinced that future Giftologists eventually will make this book look like the first radio waves that could only travel a few hundred yards. The applications are absolutely endless, mind-blowing even. I ask myself every day, with every person I encounter, what the individual's Gift might be…mechanics, managers, baristas, train conductors, waitresses, etc. Every single person has a Gift. There are no exceptions.

As such, couldn't we begin to notice what Gift an autistic child possesses? A person with terminal cancer? A rape survivor? A convicted inmate? A person with disabilities? A veteran with PTSD? Why couldn't the Seven Gifts be used in treatments of all kinds? Couldn't this information be applied to people with dementia as way of unlocking and healing the psyche? Couldn't a doctor use it to help encourage people to use their Gift Force to diet and exercise, to help people better understand their own perspectives and impulses? Couldn't researchers begin to unlock the Gift Genome to discover if there were Gift Patterns embedded in specific neuroses, maladies, obsessions, depressions, even physical ailments?

What if testing revealed that 90% of all hoarders were, in fact, Servers who were driven to not throw anything away out of fear it would not be available for use by another in the future? If something like that were revealed, wouldn't it then enable us to dive in the matter more effectively *inside* the subject, rather than hopelessly trying to wrestle with it from the *outside*? What if this hypothetical subject could be convinced from the Server's *own perspective* that one could serve even more effectively by employing better, healthier approaches? Isn't it possible the Server would jump at the chance to?

Couldn't Gifts be used in hiring processes in business? More formally in evaluations? As a means to understand business clients? Co-workers? Managers? In small business or corporate team-building? Why couldn't Gifts be used in child rearing, family counseling, and marital counseling?

In troubled youth programs? To help young gangbangers cross over into the civilized world?

Criminals, murderers, and drug dealers have Gifts too. Could the Gifts be a possible path to redemption? Couldn't there be educational curriculums in grade schools, middle schools, high schools, and universities dealing with Gifts? Why couldn't there be summer camps for a particular Gift or in chatrooms on the web?

My favorite school, my ultimate university, is life itself. I have taught myself quite a bit about the Gifts through trial and error and observation, but I am very aware I have just scratched the surface. Maybe even animals have Gifts.

Like deep space, knowledge and application of the Gifts may go on forever.

I might be crazy,
but it has kept me from going insane.

Waylon Jennings, Country Western singer

GRIEF AND LOSS

I DON'T *THINK* MY DAUGHTER LEFT THIS EARTH doing what she loved best; I *know* she did. Liza was a joyful Prophet with boundless energy, smart as a whip, a Dean's List student at Loyola University here in Chicago. She roomed with Tiffany, her dear friend, and worked as a shift manager and barista at a local university coffee shop, where she made her coffee art with glops and ribbons of carefully placed milks and creams that eventually achieved legendary status. Papa's coffee pot and my mother's clown plates had made their way through into her DNA.

I remember at her memorial service a young man, a fellow coffee worker, describing how after Liza had finished a long, late-night shift, had stayed to be with the next girl on duty, so that she would not be lonely and proceeded to knit her a pair of mittens to boot for the cold Chicago winter. Liza's Gift gave her endless motivation to act in the world, to engage it full-on, to do what is right, to protect, and to love.

That fateful morning, Liza roused her roommate early from bed. Tiffany had been struggling with mild college depression and Liza recognized the condition as a natural foe. She insisted Tiffany wake up so that they could enjoy a bike ride together in the morning sun on Chicago streets and try out a new coffee shop in an adjoining neighborhood. Tiffany resisted initially. Liza would have none of it. Her Gift would lead both of them into the light, towards a better, freer, and nobler place. *No way, José*, she probably thought. *You are getting up and we are going.*

Liza did not make it to the new coffee shop. Her life was cut short as she slipped and fell under the wheels of a delivery truck. Wheels I have longed to embrace on her behalf in my nocturnal dreams. Tears and wheels. *A wheel breaks the butterfly* ... a fateful line from Coldplay's song *Paradise.*

As her father, I am comforted in the midst of the most unimaginable torrent of sadness by the fact that I know her through and through, know the nature of her Gift, and know as certainly as the sun is in the sky that she passed on from us in a way that glorified her Gift, in a manner that was perfectly in union with who she was at her core. She would have had it no other way, to gently bow from the stage fighting for what is right, standing up strong and clear for growth and love and grace.

Knowing a departed loved one's Gift and being able to enjoy reflecting in light of the person's Gift helps with the grief of loss. My dear friend Lita, the very first friend I started to learn the Gifts with, who passed from this earth too young as well at the age of 56, was also a Prophet like Liza. I reflect on how hard Lita battled to raise her three boys with a sense of discipline, a strong work ethic, and an aspirational view of life. As I watch her and Big John's sons grow ever more successful, I am comforted to know that Lita is smiling, beaming, glowing amidst gentle rays of Prophet Sunlight wherever she is now. Knowing her Gift helps me to not cry when I miss her. It helps me to smile.

And Papa, an obvious Exhorter as there ever was. When I miss him, I sometimes pull his Gift down off the shelf to spend some time with the old man. I talk to a security guard, something I would normally avoid in the midst of my goals and objectives of efficiency. I tell a story to a man behind a deli counter, talk to a waitress about a neighborhood happening, or work a little harder at befriending a neighbor. I spend time with Papa that way, doing my own impression of an Exhorter, feeling his glass, his glide, his waggle, his saunter, his harmless conspiracy once again.

299

MUSING

COULD THE GIFTS ALSO BE SEEN AS A different, or perhaps better, interpretation of the notion of reincarnation, the idea that the essence of a person is regenerated in another life, in a different shape and size and color and gender?

Are the Gifts part of Nietzsche's *Eternal Recurrence*, the theory that the universe and all existence and energy has been recurring, and will continue to recur, in a self-similar form an infinite number of times across infinite time or space?

There is a flawless beauty in this thought…the idea that our essence, our Gifts, spring eternal and repeat in nature and in our universe.

That we are all a lot more alike than we would ever have guessed at and always have been through centuries of time.

That our Gift will live on and endure immortal.

That our Gift will always be.

Gift Dream

Rain.

Warm rain on my face.

In my dream, I am awake and aware I had just seen the remake of the movie *Blade Runner*. From the original version of the film locked in my memory, now released in my dream, I watch the scene in the dark rain when Roy, the replicant version of a human being, wraps his powerful hands around his creator's face, Tyrell, the manufacturer. Roy demands to know how long he has left in this life.

I see Tyrell calmly smile despite Roy's grip.

Tyrell delivers his one line sermon faithfully. I have heard it in my head so many times before. It echoes once again, just as it always does. The rain drops shatter on the pavement around them as he says it.

The shatters echo.

I hear Tyrell tell Roy that his rare candle has burned so brightly in this life, and therefore can only burn shorter.

The light that burns twice as bright burns half as long,
and you have burned so very, very brightly…

Bright.
Echo.
Short.
Echo.

I am in the scene with Roy and Tyrell. I can feel the warm rain on my face.

My eyes close and I stretch my face to the sky.

Bring all the rain. Bring all the rain on me. I want to scream but no sound arrives. I stretch my arms out wide, like an eagle, and then… unexpectedly…like a silent lightning strike…

Tears.

Tears in warm rain.

Rain of warm tears.

I spread my arms even wider. I reach as high as I can to hug the sky.

As my arms spread, I feel the softness of sheets, awake or asleep, I can't tell the difference anymore. I am still. And slowly, gently, like clouds floating overhead, as slowly as distance itself…

I hear Alma Deutscher's fragile piano playing. The young prodigy, the little girl whose music ascends and tries to carry us with it, with it to Heaven. To the sky. And then her voice singing.

I recognize the flow of joy and sadness and longing. *Cinderella: If I Believe in Love.* The image of Alma Deutscher as a little girl, dressed as a princess, the one that appears on my Spotify when that song comes through to my ears, echoes of pictures of Liza as a little girl, dressed as a fairy princess with fairy wings, the same sacred and mythic fairy wings affixed to her Ghost Bike at the corner of Hamlin Park where she ascended to Heaven, the same fairy wings my mother would conjure for my little sister out of metal clothes hangers and women's hose.

The young woman's light singing travels up into the echo. Up into the shatters.

I open my eyes, awake in my dream now, as I begin to hear the patter of feet downstairs on the hardwood floors. Giggling. Little voices. The beginnings of mischief.

I watch myself outside myself as I appear at the mission table, the same one I used to occupy with Liza and Lauren. They are sitting there too, seven and six years old, unaged, smiling and laughing, like a pair of matched unmatched Gifts, exact opposites and complements, hearts beating in time. Breathing together.

We. Alive. Vibrant. Electric. The day, the hour, the moment is ours to pounce on like cats on yarn balls. Furiously. Greedily.

I had my alligator clips on, clips hanging from a half-necklace, clips holding my napkin in place, feeling grateful that I had enough to eat and that Mom didn't have to sneak into the dumpsters at the City Market anymore. Happy that I did not have to hold the farmer's box for the vegetables, on the lookout for the imaginary City Market Police.

We had all gotten away somehow. Escaped all prisons of fear, of grief.

Liza and Lauren giggled and pointed at people walking by, as they told them to come to the table and play the Gift Game with us. I realized as I looked around that there were other people at other tables wearing napkins with alligator clips, imitating Harvey Keitel and mobsters, shirts and blouses and dresses immaculately covered by napkins.

Strangers sat together and asked questions, talked, laughed, told stories, and looked closely at one another, trying to see inside.

To discern. To love.

Darius, the young Black boy with the runny nose, sat right next to Wild Child. I found myself marveling at Wild Child's asking Darius questions, both smiling, finding things in common.

Sosland, the rich envelope man with shiny shoes, put his arm around Caleb, the janitor, as they discovered they were both Servers.

Aunt Dolly, an obvious Exhorter, kissed Jean Harlow, an obvious Exhorter, a little too hard, but then Jean kissed her back laughing and I saw the two little girls in them, determined to dance it all out after *The Game*.

Larry the mason sat with soulful eyes listening to the young athlete speak in both of their native Italian tongues, hearing that the athlete's family was from the same province that Larry's tribe came from, that the athlete was training for national competition, hoping that he could make his immigrant father proud, a father who had worked three jobs to put his son through school and give him a better life. His father was in Heaven now and the athlete found peace and solace in his laser focus for competition, knowing his father would be pleased. Larry saw that both of them were Organizers and that the intense young man had his own type of chisel.

C.B. Lueck, the prep school accountant, offered to glob fake Folger's coffee from Papa's kitchen table in the ensemble pimp's coffee cup, as Lueck played butler, repenting.

Next to them, Minnesota Fats was whispering something into Jackie Onassis's ear, probably something inappropriate, but she seemed to be enjoying it regardless. Minnesota's eyes danced in conspiracy, just like Papa's.

In this dream version, to play and win, every person at the table wrote down on a piece of paper what each thought another person's Gift was. When all were done, when everyone was ready to give it a best shot, the pieces of paper revealed insights.

I felt my own Gift Eclipse, release and take flight, my drive and intensity now freed. With the world in order now, all organized, I had been relieved of duties to enjoy the form and beauty of this moment. This absolutely perfect, flawless moment.

And this gathering, this Gift Ball of sorts, this Gift Painting, this frozen moment of space-time exploded into a poem, into a song, into beams of light that Liza and Papa and Lita could also see from up in the echo in the sky. The rain above me expanded from the impact and I fell backwards gently before and again, falling faster than the rain, smiling with joy.

Liza and Lauren screamed and laughed with delight once again, seeing all the world through little-girl-daughter eyes, just as some of the answers were right and some wrong and some still uncertain, happy to be at our table once more, with more little friends, and big ones as well, this table of gifts.

This table of the Seven Gifts.

Postscript
The Pandemic and the Seven Gifts

As the book made its way to press in the beginning of 2021, the pandemic acted to magnify many things around us in the world, including the Gifts.

The Teacher will prove to be the Gift Hero. Research, facts, analysis, statistics, testing, and vaccines rule the day. Dr. Anthony Fauci puts a face to all of this...calm, non-plussed, unwavering, and undistracted by emotions, politics, even death threats. I am convinced of the durability of the Gifts as it relates to the survival of our species. Different types of crises could imply different Gifts might be the ultimate heroes. This time around, the heroes are the Teachers. Teachers all day long.

Dark Prophets are showing up at capital buildings declaring the government has no right to tell them to wear masks. They won't be told what to do. Some carry guns. Light Prophets are confronting people not wearing masks and informing them of the real truth.

Servers are out in force. You see them leaving their own families and traveling across the country to help in hot spots as nurses, emergency technicians, and food workers. Servers are manning stations everywhere.

Givers are making an absolute fortune. Look at the examples provided of Jeff Bezos and Elon Musk. Their stock prices have soared as a result of positioning themselves in the right place for the future world to come, the world that has now arrived. Perhaps some sharp money manager will start a Giver Fund, investments in companies run by Givers who are blooming. It would seem the fund would do quite well.

Organizers want to take over and solve the issues in an orderly sequence. One of the most visible is Andrew Cuomo, the governor of New York. His strict, concise, visible, consistent structure stood out as he organized the virus's demise in one of the largest, concentrated populations in the country. It's too bad there are not more Organizers in politics. I think Organizers conclude politics and government are too messy. They prefer, for example, the purer form of absolute power enjoyed by a CEO.

Mercys, the most plentiful of the Gifts, are everywhere, helping lonely medical patients connect with their families on Zoom, assisting the homeless with food and masks, and checking in on isolated elderly neighbors. They are also feeling a little lost with all the boundaries and distances; on one hand, they want to extend and, on the other, they do not want to offend.

But the Gift that seems to be in the most existential pain is clearly the Exhorter. If you think about it, we are disconnected and separated in this pandemic, the direct mirror opposite of what inspires an Exhorter. To boot, the fracturing and discord brought about by the protests, rioting, and looting are more than the Exhorter can bear. The Exhorter is essentially trapped in a psychological and emotional cage, a prison of estrangement and open conflict. Exhorters want to look away, to escape, and they simply can't.

For me, I daydream how Gift Teams could be deployed for different purposes across cities everywhere. I think about what the world would be like if we all understood the Gifts and the value of their specific areas of expertise…

Acknowledgments

I WOULD LIKE TO ACKNOWLEDGE AND THANK a small group of friends with whom I have shared Gift discoveries, experiences, and revelations over the last several years. They include one of my dearest friends in life, Lita Delgado-McCollum, lost to cancer last year and her husband, my great friend, Big John McCollum, who wrote the foreword to this book. Without these people to validate and add to things, I may have concluded I was imagining it all. May we all learn more as we go further and deeper in our Gift Journey.

Much thanks to Edward Quigley, my high school English teacher, who helped reveal a direction of study for me. Clare Rosenfeld, my university English professor, took over for Mr. Quigley later and helped me in invaluable ways. After I write, I faithfully read out loud so my ear can hear the words and vacuum for me. Thank you both so much for helping to inspire a love of words so I could go on my literary walkabout.

I was told that a wealthy woman provided the scholarship funds for me to attend the Pembroke Hill School for Boys in Kansas City, so that I might do something meaningful with my life. Thank you so much, whoever you are, and for the opportunity you gave to me. I am forever touched by your kindness.

Thanks to Tammy and all my five children for learning the Gifts with me and putting up with me when I talk too much about the subject. Thanks to my college roommate, lifelong friend, and now esteemed Hollywood entertainment lawyer, Carlos Goodman, who had the audacity to suggest I write this book. Thanks to another roommate, Chris

Brancato, a creator and writer of *Narcos*, the famous Netflix series, who was kind enough to give me batting tips during the writing of it and not laugh at my naiveté. My deepest gratitude to my various beta readers, readers who also represented different Gifts and Gift views for me, including Tara Moore, Michael Haynes, Gregory Renz, Carol Blunk, Steven Nicol, Brian Schneider, and Dean Moya. Thanks as well to Maria Vlahos for her daily support.

Without the other three venerable and talented members of my Gift Team, this book would never have made it into your hands. My publisher, Kira Henschel, graciously agreed to waive the requirement of the initial "Book Proposal," a phenomenon I encountered everywhere, something I could never bow to because it offended my sensibilities so deeply. (How can you plan magic?) Kira proved throughout she is on a serious mission to preserve the opportunity for unknown writers to get a swing at bat, which only inspired me to try to go for the fence. My illustrator, Syed Muhammad Waqas, a.k.a. "Chashie Boy," a 19-year-old Pakistani, worked with us from the other side of the globe and developed fragile, emotional, and beautiful drawings to animate the tale. I hope I get to meet him face to face someday. My creative director, Michelle Lawrence, showed her versatility in areas too numerous to name, including cover design, graphics, imagery, psychology, and writing. She built and refined the "museum" of the book that could house my writing, Syed's drawings, and Kira's administration and acted as curator. The wonderful energy these three people from different generations brought to this effort pushed things to a higher altitude than I thought was possible.

I want to thank my parents for giving me the messiest, most exciting, unpredictable, changing, and awesome childhood a kid could ever hope for. I would not change one moment of it.

And finally to Papa, for expanding my vocabulary as I sat on his porch table.

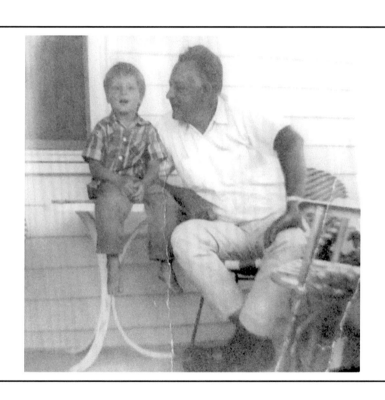

Gift Cliff Notes
Polar Gifts
Gift Glossary

Mercy

Special Abilities

- Very considerate of others' feelings
- Able to visualize emotional causes and effects on others
- Excellent memory for special dates and occasions in other people's lives, as well as other people's preferences
- Remains in the background in silence
- Avoids confrontation
- Superior short-term memory
- Attracted to misfits
- Possesses subtle palate and ability to detect precise smells
- Skilled visually and musically
- Can confidently play characters or roles in public settings
- Alert to areas of social injustice

Areas of Concern

- Struggles with self-esteem and victimization feelings
- Projects irrational fears
- Assumes negative motives in others
- Fear of rejection may cause violation of convictions
- Closes spirit to those they feel are insensitive
- Calculates vengeance when wounded

Polar Gift: Prophet

317

SERVER

SPECIAL ABILITIES

- Perceives and anticipates the needs of others
- Tireless worker
- Extremely loyal
- Excellent memory for details pertinent to others
- Conscious of thriftiness
- Willingness to use personal funds to prevent projects from being hindered
- Hates red tape

AREAS OF CONCERN

- Disapproves of others' inabilities
- Overlooks personal problem areas while too busy serving others
- Difficulty saying no to people
- Would benefit from developing leadership qualities and delegating skills
- Needs to become alert to areas he or she is not responsible for
- Can feel personally rejected when services are not needed
- Should learn to allow other people serve them
- Often has low self-esteem
- Frequent lower digestive tract issues due to excessive worrying

POLAR GIFT: ORGANIZER

EXHORTER

SPECIAL ABILITIES

- Anxious to please
- Sees the importance of the individual
- Natural networker
- Positive outlook
- Quick to grasp solutions
- Able to see chronological sequence when putting things into steps
- Encouraging speaker
- Superior communicator and storyteller
- Makes friends easily
- Concerned about personal application to avoid being a hypocrite

AREAS OF CONCERN

- Bends personal convictions to seek approval of others
- Can develop mechanical responses on subjects deemed unimportant
- Truth and facts can be gray
- Rules are for others to follow
- Reserved in personal commitment to people
- Spontaneity disrupts other people's schedules
- Closes spirit down and becomes retaliatory in confrontations
- Not detail-oriented

POLAR GIFT: TEACHER

319

ORGANIZER

SPECIAL ABILITIES

- Sees problem areas clearly in advance
- Extremely orderly and efficient
- Accomplishes duties and tasks quickly and efficiently
- Visualizes long-range accomplishments
- Coordinates manpower effectively
- Identifies and uses power and leverage quickly in situations
- Extremely creative
- Able to make decisions unemotionally

AREAS OF CONCERN

- Through pride can become power-hungry
- Insensitive to other people's desires when they conflict with his or hers
- Will work excessively to accomplish tasks and expect others to as well
- Causes others to feel regimented and unloved
- Accepts character flaws in others to get the job done
- Organizes the demise of others when angered

POLAR GIFT: SERVER

Prophet

Special Abilities

- Able to discern true commitment in others
- Aggressive with speech
- Able to grasp concepts quickly
- Strong long-term memory
- Willingness to be condemned for what is right
- Powerful desire to inform others
- Responsive to (spiritual) conviction

Areas of Concern

- Quick to judge
- Looks for negatives while being overly critical
- Should become alert to the reactions of others to learn sensitivity
- Intolerant of other people's pain
- Prideful in personal abilities and skills
- Needs to develop meekness

Polar Gift: Mercy

Teacher

Special Abilities

- Delights in detailed studies
- Serious nature
- Quick mind for deductions and reasoning
- Mellow and even temperament
- Interesting conversationalist (for those who are searching)
- Extremely self-disciplined

Areas of Concern

- Concentrates on facts and details to the detriment of personal application
- Thinks others will be better off when informed by the Teacher's learning
- More interested in research than people
- Determines who or what is qualified or is to be dismissed
- Feels above restriction

Polar Gift: Exhorter

GIVER

SPECIAL ABILITIES

- Keen desire to see humanity's causes advanced
- Financial keenness
- Personal needs are secondary to the needs of others

AREAS OF CONCERN

- Can become prideful as a result of the gift given
- Builds personal power through giving of things
- Evaluates others according to their wealth
- Presumes they can see larger need and solution
- Feels rejected personally when gift is not needed or rejected

POLAR GIFT: SPOUSE/PARTNER

GIFT GLOSSARY

Baskin Robbins: An ice cream store that sells 31 different flavors, so that people can make their own choices according to who they are, because they have free will

Clutch: A device on a car driven by centrifugal forces that, when engaged, allows the driver to shift gears manually, the loss of which would cause the car to be stuck in a specific gear, perhaps a high-speed one

Dark: A term used in this book to describe areas of concern in a Gift

Exhorter: The Gift that wants to party, be the life of the party as well, and rejoices in others' coming to fruition

Gift: A unique set of skills, abilities, characteristics, and weaknesses given to a unique individual for use in life *(capitalized Gift)*

gift: Something given, a present (noun); to give permanently (verb)

Gift Algebra: Using basic reasoning skills when applying Gift knowledge, sometimes to calculate probabilities

Gift Algorithm: A virtual understanding of the Seven Gifts, with abilities including calculating one's Gift, and then automating interactions based on that knowledge, including communication style, color choices, persuasion, and solicitation

Gift Club: A group of people who gather for the purposes of celebrating the Gifts, pursuing deeper understanding, feeling affirmed, and having Gift Fun

Gift Compass: A symbol for the aspirational goal of manifesting all Seven Gifts within oneself

Gift Dance: The most helpful Gift interaction between romantic partners

Gift Dictionary: A glossary of Gift language that can inform different ways of seeing and using Gift knowledge

Gift Eclipse: A moment of nirvana when one can strongly feel the fruition, the full realization of the urges and purposes embodied in his or her own Gift

Gift Engine: The natural, everlasting energy that drives a Gift to perform its higher functions, causing a person to experience a virtually inexhaustible drive

Gift Explorer: One who is excited and joyful to discover new facets and nuances of the Seven Gifts

Gift Force: The power that a Gift seems to produce on its own accord, seemingly outside of the will of its owner or inhabitant

Gift Freedom: A state of complete and unabashed freedom to fully embrace and animate one's Gift, without any fear or reserve

Gift Game: The process of turning the discovery of a person's Gift into an act of play

Gift Genome: A metaphor for the idea that there is infinite knowledge within the Gifts, as vast as human nature itself, waiting to be unlocked by collective study and research, for the purpose of constructive application

Gift Humor: Teasing the person's Gift, as opposed to the actual person

Gift Irony: A subtlety in a Gift that seems counterintuitive or nonsensical

Gift Journey: The process of discovering the universe of one's own Gift, the Gifts of others, and the Gifts that also can reside and grow in us that are not our own

Gift Language: Speaking in a manner that is sympathetic or sensitive to one's Gift for the purpose of greater mutual connection and understanding

Gift Legend: A story that contains truisms about qualities pertaining to the Seven Gifts, similar to a myth

Gift Mirror: A metaphor intended to remind us that before we go off making fun of the peculiarities of other folk's Gifts, we would be wise to remember our Gifts have peculiarities too

Gift Moment: An existential event where a Gift, through the exercise of its unique powers, reveals something plausible and distinct that only it could have

Gift Mystery: A fact about a particular Gift that you have to keep thinking about and watching closely to eventually figure out

Gift Poetry: Prose that speaks to one's Gift, or how the Gifts of a couple can become intertwined

Gift Pranks: A prank that is designed specifically to provoke a characteristic of the person's Gift, as opposed to the actual person

Gift Reflex: An automatic, programmed response of one's Gift

Gift Sense: Reasoning or syllogisms based on a Gift's logic, involving understanding the rationale of a Gift, or the rationale of a Gift's given set of characteristics, as opposed to a person's

Gift Shelf: A metaphoric place where one can draw from a body of Gift knowledge and characteristics for emotional, practical, or spiritual purposes

Gift Specialist: A hypothetical position that would apply Gift insights and call in other Gifts as needed for purposes of psychological, psychiatric, or medical counseling, healing, and treatment

Gift Team: When two or more people of differing Gifts come together and unify their Gifts to soar to a new height together

Gift Tell: A singular, sometimes subtle action, behavior, or expression that can immediately and decisively reveal one's Gift

Gift Test: A homemade test created for the purpose of identifying Gifts, the contents of which can be created when five people of the same Gift answer a proposed test question the same way

Gift Tip: Knowledge of the Gifts that result in an arbitrage opportunity

Gift Tribe: Members of the same Gift

Gift Unicorn: A person whose Gift appears to be in some stage of fuller bloom, where the person seems to have found a great combination of using the positive powers of the Gift and also telling the negative elements of the Gift to take a chair

Gift Wheel: The natural sequence or order of the Seven Gifts, determined by overlapping qualities

Giver: The Gift that is given to create or provide for larger causes for a larger group of people, or for society in general

Light: A term used in this book to describe special abilities of a Gift

Making Someone's Gift: Identifying one's Gift, just as a detective would "make" a perpetrator

Mercy: The Gift that is most emotionally intelligent of all and that basks in relationship

Motivational Gifts: A term used to describe the Seven Gifts and meant to signal that these Gifts are determined by why people are driven to do what they do, as opposed to what they are driven to do

Organizer: The Gift that naturally aspires to efficiency, precision, and order in nearly all things

Polar Gift: The Gift that is most likely the natural opposite and converse of another Gift, the inverse or flip side of a Gift

Primary Thinking: Using one's natural observational abilities, intuition, and independent reasoning skills as a source of knowledge and truth

Prophet: The Gift that is driven to determine right from wrong and that desires to inform others what is right and wrong

Server: The Gift that perseveres daily to put others before themselves, to notice other's needs and provide for them

Sideshow: A barely controlled digression; part of a personal collage

spirit: With a small s, referring to soul, heart, inner self

Splitter Question: A query that can distinguish between two or more Gifts

Teacher: The Gift that dismisses information at face value and researches beyond it to determine efficacy and accuracy

The Seven Gifts: The oldest and most accurate personality typing system in human history, found in the Bible, that describes more about a person's nature in the shortest amount of time than anything else

Toxic Gift: A person who has allowed the darker elements of a Gift to go unchecked and get the best of them

About the Author

DAVID B WHITACRE IS A PROFESSIONAL planner living in Chicago, the White City, and working in a skyscraper next to what most locals still call the Sears Tower. David was born in 1962 in Columbus, Ohio but grew up mainly in Kansas City. He graduated with Honors in English from Brown University in Providence, Rhode Island, and also studied Philosophy and Psychology there. David is father to Liza (Rest in Peace), Owa (Lauren), and Max, and is stepfather to Lolo (Lauren) and Evan. He lives in the West Loop, loves fast cars, and enjoys Recreational Organizing.

The Seven Gifts was written over four years as an act of love for the kids, friends, and eternity while riding the train to and from work and in neighborhood coffee shops.

David is still in pursuit of his Gift PhD.

www.sevengifts.com
www.davidbwhitacre.com

 DavidBWhitacre@TheSevenGifts

 The_Seven_Gifts